'Lemma has become one of the modern leaders in psychoanalysis. Her contribution to understanding this most fundamental of psychoanalytic concerns – our relationship to our bodies – has been immense and is growing. This book is an essential source of inspiration for clinicians to help them listen to and hear their patients' deepest concerns more clearly. An extraordinary achievement.'

Peter Fonagy, Freud Memorial Professor of Psychoanalysis and Head of the Research Department of Clinical, Educational and Health Psychology, University College London, UK.

'In this insightful and innovative book Alessandra Lemma revisits and explores further some of the subjects she considered in *Under the Skin*, her psychoanalytic study of body modification, whilst also addressing new subjects such as transsexuality, hair and the analyst's toilet. The author is at her fluent best as she examines how we ascribe meaning to experience through our bodies, and attempts to illustrate how the analyst can help patients re-integrate mind and body.

Lemma makes clever use of British object relations theory, lending a sound theoretical frame of reference to her discourse. Her book is brimming with clinical material of the most fascinating kind. To date there has perhaps been a denial of the significance of the body in psychoanalytic literature, and the author attempts to challenge this attitude through her highly original arguments. This is an innovative approach to a fascinating subject. I defy any book browser to peruse its tantalising chapter titles and not want to read the whole book. *Minding the Body* is a must read.'

Antonino Ferro, President of the Italian Psychoanalytic Society and Consultant Associate Editor of the *International Journal of Psychoanalysis*. He is a training and supervising analyst in the Italian Psychoanalytic Society, the American Psychoanalytic Association and the International Psychoanalytical Association.

Minding the Body

Minding the Body: The body in psychoanalysis and beyond outlines the value of a psychoanalytic approach to understanding the body and its vicissitudes and for addressing these in the context of psychoanalytic psychotherapy and psychoanalysis. The chapters cover a broad but esoteric range of subjects that are not often discussed within psychoanalysis such as the function of breast augmentation surgery, the psychic origins of hair, the use made of the analyst's toilet, transsexuality and the connection between dermatological conditions and necrophilic fantasies. The book also reaches 'beyond the couch' to consider the nature of reality television makeover shows.

The book is based on Alessandra Lemma's extensive clinical experience as a psychoanalyst and psychologist working in a range of public and private health care settings with patients for whom the body is the primary presenting problem or who have made unconscious use of the body to communicate their psychic pain. *Minding the Body* draws on detailed clinical examples that vividly illustrate how the author approaches these clinical presentations in the consulting room and, as such, provides insights for the practising clinician that will support their attempts at formulating patients' difficulties psychoanalytically and suggest how to help such patients. It will be essential reading for psychoanalysts, psychologists, psychiatrists, mental health workers, academics and literary readers interested in the body, sexuality and gender.

Alessandra Lemma is Director of the Psychological Therapies Development Unit at the Tavistock and Portman NHS Foundation Trust. She is a Consultant Adult Psychotherapist at the Portman Clinic. She is also a Fellow of the British Psychoanalytical Society, Visiting Professor in the Psychoanalysis Unit at University College London and Honorary Professor of Psychological Therapies in the School of Health and Human Sciences at Essex University. She is the Clinical Director of the Psychological Interventions Research Centre at UCL, Visiting Professor at Istituto Winnicott, Sapienza University of Rome and Centro Winnicot, Rome. Professor Lemma is Editor of the New Library of Psychoanalysis book series (Routledge) and one of the regional editors for the *International Journal of Psychoanalysis*. She has published extensively on psychoanalysis, the body and trauma.

The New Library of Psychoanalysis
General Editor: Alessandra Lemma

The New Library of Psychoanalysis was launched in 1987 in association with the Institute of Psychoanalysis, London. It took over from the International Psychoanalytical Library, which published many of the early translations of the works of Freud and the writings of most of the leading British and Continental psychoanalysts.

The purpose of the New Library of Psychoanalysis is to facilitate a greater and more widespread appreciation of psychoanalysis and to provide a forum for increasing mutual understanding between psychoanalysts and those working in other disciplines such as the social sciences, medicine, philosophy, history, linguistics, literature and the arts. It aims to represent different trends both in British psychoanalysis and in psychoanalysis generally. The New Library of Psychoanalysis is well placed to make available to the English-speaking world psychoanalytic writings from other European countries and to increase the interchange of ideas between British and American psychoanalysts. Through the *Teaching Series*, the New Library of Psychoanalysis now also publishes books that provide comprehensive, yet accessible, overviews of selected subject areas aimed at those studying psychoanalysis and related fields such as the social sciences, philosophy, literature and the arts.

The Institute, together with the British Psychoanalytical Society, runs a low-fee psychoanalytic clinic, organises lectures and scientific events concerned with psychoanalysis and publishes the *International Journal of Psychoanalysis*. It runs a training course in psychoanalysis which leads to membership of the International Psychoanalytical Association – the body which preserves internationally agreed standards of training, of professional entry, and of professional ethics and practice for psychoanalysis as initiated and developed by Sigmund Freud. Distinguished members of the Institute have included Michael Balint, Wilfred Bion, Ronald Fairbairn, Anna Freud, Ernest Jones, Melanie Klein, John Rickman and Donald Winnicott.

Previous general editors have included David Tuckett, who played a very active role in the establishment of the New Library. He was followed as general editor by Elizabeth Bott Spillius, who was in turn followed by Susan Budd and then by Dana Birksted-Breen.

Current members of the Advisory Board include Liz Allison, Giovanna di Ceglie, Rosemary Davies and Richard Rusbridger.

Previous members of the Advisory Board include Christopher Bollas, Ronald Britton, Catalina Bronstein, Donald Campbell, Sara Flanders, Stephen Grosz, John Keene, Eglé Laufer, Alessandra Lemma, Juliet Mitchell, Michael Parsons, Rosine Jozef Perelberg, Mary Target and David Taylor.

Titles in this series

Impasse and Interpretation Herbert Rosenfeld

Psychoanalysis and Discourse Patrick Mahony

The Suppressed Madness of Sane Men Marion Milner

The Riddle of Freud Estelle Roith

Thinking, Feeling, and Being Ignacio Matte Blanco

The Theatre of the Dream Salomon Resnik

Melanie Klein Today: Volume 1, Mainly Theory Edited by Elizabeth Bott Spillius

Melanie Klein Today: Volume 2, Mainly Practice Edited by Elizabeth Bott Spillius

Psychic Equilibrium and Psychic Change: Selected Papers of Betty Joseph Edited by Michael Feldman and Elizabeth Bott Spillius

About Children and Children-No-Longer: Collected Papers 1942–80 Paula Heimann. Edited by Margret Tonnesmann

The Freud–Klein Controversies 1941–45 Edited by Pearl King and Riccardo Steiner

Dream, Phantasy and Art Hanna Segal

Psychic Experience and Problems of Technique Harold Stewart

Clinical Lectures on Klein & Bion Edited by Robin Anderson

From Fetus to Child Alessandra Piontelli

A Psychoanalytic Theory of Infantile Experience: Conceptual and Clinical Reflections E Gaddini. Edited by Adam Limentani

The Dream Discourse Today Edited and introduced by Sara Flanders

The Gender Conundrum: Contemporary Psychoanalytic Perspectives on Femininity and Masculinity Edited and introduced by Dana Breen

Psychic Retreats John Steiner

The Taming of Solitude: Separation Anxiety in Psychoanalysis Jean-Michel Quinodoz

Unconscious Logic: An Introduction to Matte Blanco's Bi-logic and its Uses Eric Rayner

Understanding Mental Objects Meir Perlow

Life, Sex and Death: Selected Writings of William Gillespie Edited and introduced by Michael Sinason

What Do Psychoanalysts Want?: The Problem of Aims in Psychoanalytic Therapy Joseph Sandler and Anna Ursula Dreher

Michael Balint: Object Relations, Pure and Applied Harold Stewart

Hope: A Shield in the Economy of Borderline States Anna Potamianou
Psychoanalysis, Literature & War: Papers 1972–1995 Hanna Segal
Emotional Vertigo: Between Anxiety and Pleasure Danielle Quinodoz
Early Freud and Late Freud Ilse Grubrich-Simitis
A History of Child Psychoanalysis Claudine and Pierre Geissmann
Belief and Imagination: Explorations in Psychoanalysis Ronald Britton
A Mind of One's Own: A Psychoanalytic View of Self and Object Robert A Caper
Psychoanalytic Understanding of Violence and Suicide Edited by Rosine Jozef Perelberg
On Bearing Unbearable States of Mind Ruth Riesenberg-Malcolm
Psychoanalysis on the Move: The Work of Joseph Sandler Edited by Peter Fonagy, Arnold M. Cooper and Robert S. Wallerstein
The Dead Mother: The Work of André Green Edited by Gregorio Kohon
The Fabric of Affect in the Psychoanalytic Discourse André Green
The Bi-Personal Field: Experiences of Child Analysis Antonino Ferro
The Dove that Returns, the Dove that Vanishes: Paradox and Creativity in Psychoanalysis Michael Parsons
Ordinary People, Extra-ordinary Protections: A Post Kleinian Approach to the Treatment of Primitive Mental States Judith Mitrani
The Violence of Interpretation: From Pictogram to Statement Piera Aulagnier
The Importance of Fathers: A Psychoanalytic Re-Evaluation Judith Trowell and Alicia Etchegoyen
Dreams That Turn Over a Page: Paradoxical Dreams in Psychoanalysis Jean-Michel Quinodoz
The Couch and the Silver Screen: Psychoanalytic Reflections on European Cinema Andrea Sabbadini
In Pursuit of Psychic Change: The Betty Joseph Workshop Edited by Edith Hargreaves and Arturo Varchevker
The Quiet Revolution in American Psychoanalysis: Selected Papers of Arnold M. Cooper Arnold M. Cooper, Edited and Introduced by Elizabeth L. Auchincloss
Seeds of Illness and Seeds of Recovery: The genesis of suffering and the role of psychoanalysis Antonino Ferro
The Work of Psychic Figurability: Mental States Without Representation César Botella and Sára Botella
Key Ideas for a Contemporary Psychoanalysis: Misrecognition and Recognition of the Unconscious André Green
The Telescoping of Generations: Listening to the Narcissistic Links Between Generations Haydée Faimberg

Glacial Times: A Journey through the World of Madness Salomon Resnik

This Art of Psychoanalysis: Dreaming Undreamt Dreams and Interrupted Cries Thomas H. Ogden

Psychoanalysis and Religion in the 21st Century: Competitors or Collaborators? David M. Black

Recovery of the Lost Good Object Eric Brenman

The Many Voices of Psychoanalysis Roger Kennedy

Feeling the Words: Neuropsychoanalytic Understanding of Memory and the Unconscious Mauro Mancia

Constructions and the Analytic Field: History, Scenes and Destiny Domenico Chianese

Projected Shadows: Psychoanalytic Reflections on the Representation of Loss in European Cinema Edited by Andrea Sabbadini

Encounters with Melanie Klein: Selected Papers of Elizabeth Spillius Elizabeth Spillius

Yesterday, Today and Tomorrow Hanna Segal

Psychoanalysis Comparable and Incomparable: The Evolution of a Method to Describe and Compare Psychoanalytic Approaches David Tuckett, Roberto Basile, Dana Birksted-Breen, Tomas Böhm, Paul Denis, Antonino Ferro, Helmut Hinz, Arne Jemstedt, Paola Mariotti and Johan Schubert

Time, Space and Phantasy Rosine Jozef Perelberg

Rediscovering Psychoanalysis: Thinking and Dreaming, Learning and Forgetting Thomas H. Ogden

Mind Works: Techniques and Creativity in Psychoanalysis Antonino Ferro

Doubt Conviction and the Analytic Process: Selected Papers of Michael Feldman Michael Feldman

Melanie Klein in Berlin: Her First Psychoanalyses of Children Claudia Frank

The Psychotic Wavelength: A Psychoanalytic Perspective for Psychiatry Richard Lucas

Betweenity: A Discussion of the Concept of Borderline Judy Gammelgaard

The Intimate Room: Theory and Technique of the Analytic Field Giuseppe Civitarese

Bion Today Edited by Chris Mawson

Secret Passages: The Theory and Technique of Interpsychic Relations Stefano Bolognini

Intersubjective Processes and the Unconscious: An Integration of Freudian, Kleinian and Bionian Perspectives Lawrence J. Brown

Seeing and Being Seen: Emerging from a Psychic Retreat John Steiner

Avoiding Emotions, Living Emotions Antonino Ferro

Projective Identification: The Fate of a Concept Edited by Elizabeth Spillius and Edna O'Shaughnessy

Creative Readings: Essays on Seminal Analytic Works Thomas Ogden

The Maternal Lineage Edited by Paola Mariotti

Donald Winnicott Today Edited by Jan Abram

Symbiosis and Ambiguity: A Psychoanalytic Study Edited by John Churcher, José Bleger and Leopoldo Bleger

Psychotic Temptation Liliane Abensour

Supervision in Psychoanalysis: The Sao Paulo Seminars Antonino Ferro

Transference and Countertransference Today Robert Oelsner

Living Psychoanalysis: From Theory to Practice Michael Parsons

Imaginary Existences: A psychoanalytic exploration of phantasy, fiction, dreams and daydreams Ignês Sodré, edited and with an Introduction by Priscilla Roth

Minding the Body: The Body in Psychoanalysis and Beyond Alessandra Lemma

TITLES IN THE NEW LIBRARY OF PSYCHOANALYSIS TEACHING SERIES

Reading Freud: A Chronological Exploration of Freud's Writings Jean-Michel Quinodoz

Listening to Hanna Segal: Her Contribution to Psychoanalysis Jean-Michel Quinodoz

Reading French Psychoanalysis Edited by Dana Birksted-Breen, Sara Flanders and Alain Gibeault

Reading Winnicott Lesley Caldwell and Angela Joyce

Initiating Psychoanalysis: Perspectives Bernard Reith, Sven Lagerlöf, Penelope Crick, Mette Møller and Elisabeth Skale

Infant Observation Frances Salo

Reading Anna Freud Nick Midgley

TITLES IN THE NEW LIBRARY OF PSYCHOANALYSIS 'BEYOND THE COUCH' SERIES

Under the Skin: A Psychoanalytic Study of Body Modification Alessandra Lemma

Engaging with Climate Change: Psychoanalytic and Interdisciplinary Perspectives Edited by Sally Weintrobe

Research on the Couch: Single Case Studies, Subjectivity, and Psychoanalytic Knowledge R. D. Hinshelwood

Psychoanalysis in the Technoculture Era Edited by Alessandra Lemma and Luigi Caparrotta

Moving Images: Psychoanalytic Reflections on Film Andrea Sabbadini

Minding the Body

The body in psychoanalysis and beyond

Alessandra Lemma

LONDON AND NEW YORK

First published 2015
by Routledge
27 Church Road, Hove, East Sussex BN3 2FA

and by Routledge
711 Third Avenue, New York, NY 10017

Routledge is an imprint of the Taylor & Francis Group, an informa business

© 2015 Alessandra Lemma

The right of Alessandra Lemma to be identified as author of this work has been asserted by her in accordance with sections 77 and 78 of the Copyright, Designs and Patents Act 1988.

All rights reserved. No part of this book may be reprinted or reproduced or utilised in any form or by any electronic, mechanical, or other means, now known or hereafter invented, including photocopying and recording, or in any information storage or retrieval system, without permission in writing from the publishers.

Trademark notice: Product or corporate names may be trademarks or registered trademarks, and are used only for identification and explanation without intent to infringe.

British Library Cataloguing in Publication Data
A catalogue record for this book is available from the British Library

Library of Congress Cataloging in Publication Data
A catalog record for this book has been requested

ISBN: 978-0-415-71859-2 (hbk)
ISBN: 978-0-415-71860-8 (pbk)
ISBN: 978-1-315-75882-4 (ebk)

Typeset in Times
by Saxon Graphics Ltd, Derby

To Matteo

Contents

	Foreword by Donald Campbell	xv
	Acknowledgements	xxvii
	Introduction: when the body speaks	1
1	Envy and the maternal body: the psychodynamics of cosmetic surgery	23
2	Whose skin is it anyway? Some reflections on the psychic function of necrophilic fantasies	41
3	An order of pure decision: growing up in a virtual world and the adolescent's experience of being-in-a-body	57
4	Present without past: the disruption of temporal integration in a case of adolescent transsexuality	74
5	The body one has and the body one is: the transsexual's need to be seen	88
6	Trauma and the body: a psychoanalytic reading of Almodóvar's *The Skin I Live In*	102
7	The body of the analyst and the analytic setting: reflections on the embodied setting and the symbiotic transference	111
8	Rapunzel revisited: untangling the unconscious meaning of hair	128

9 Off the couch, into the toilet: exploring the psychic
   uses of the analyst's toilet   143

10 Entrepreneurs of the self: some psychoanalytic
   reflections on the psychic and social functions of
   reality TV makeover shows   160

   References   169
   Index   182

Foreword

Donald Campbell

Introduction

Minding the Body is not only about what Alessandra Lemma discovers about the relationship between the mind and the body, but how she discovers it. This intellectually stimulating book will appeal to the professional, the academic and the lay-person who is interested in the nature and function of the body and its various and often puzzling manifestations. Lemma's research is broad and thorough. She has referenced papers from across the psychoanalytic spectrum, has studied biology, philosophy, film and fairy tales, and cited neuro-scientific research. *Minding the Body* deepens and broadens Lemma's understanding of the territory she explored in her previous book *Under the Skin: A Psychoanalytic Study of Body Modification* (2010).

At the outset Lemma informs us that the evidence that supports her findings comes mainly from her three- to five-times-weekly psychoanalytic work with adolescents and adults. Mental health professionals will be helped enormously by Lemma's honest, open and detailed clinical accounts of her sessions with patients who present with physical symptoms, and especially her understanding of the way these patients affect her. Lemma's experience of the transference, countertransference, and particularly her own bodily countertransference is her primary resource for understanding her patient's state of mind and determining how and when to intervene.

Lemma's basic assumption is that embodiment shapes the mind. As she points out, following Freud, the most primitive form of self-representation is a body representation. The body anchors the ego in physical reality. The ego emerges in relation to the body. Lemma's view is that the 'body is a basic fact of life that supports all other psychic functions' (Freud, 1927).

Bisexuality

An early link between psychoanalysis and biology was based on Freud's view of a constitutionally inherent bisexuality, which was derived from the anatomy and embryology of his day. As he said at the end of his life:

> Psychoanalysis has a common basis with biology, in that it presupposes an original bisexuality in human beings (as in animals). But psychoanalysis cannot elucidate the intrinsic nature of what in conventional or in biological phraseology is termed 'masculine' and 'feminine': it simply takes over the two concepts and makes them the foundation of its work. When we attempt to reduce them further, we find masculinity vanishing into activity and femininity into passivity, and that does not tell us enough.
>
> (Freud, 1920: 171)

Today, psychoanalysts recognize that masculinity cannot be reduced to activity any more than femininity can be considered only in terms of passivity, and we have broadened our understanding of the complexity of gender. However, retaining the concept of bisexuality can guard against a reductionist view of sexuality.

Although Freud's psychoanalytic perspective was focused on an *intra-psychic* bisexuality, he clearly viewed bisexuality as embedded in the body. In *Minding the Body* Alessandra Lemma returns again and again to explore the relationship between the biological and the psychological. For Freud, bisexuality was always secondary to infantile sexuality, which he considered the chief motive force in the formation of symptoms, and the Oedipus complex as the nuclear complex of neurosis. Nevertheless, the inherent and idiosyncratic nature of our bisexuality will inform Oedipal conflicts and the way they are resolved. The individual's idiosyncratic bisexuality will also inform their phantasies about their body, phantasies that feature so prominently in Alessandra Lemma's patients.

I am not considering the practice of bisexuality, but will focus on intra-psychic bisexuality and the way it manifests itself developmentally and clinically. Smith (2002) summarized three aspects of bisexuality, which are relevant to our understanding of the patients Lemma describes in her book: (1) Unconscious bisexual identifications can be observed in all of us, whether we define those identifications as male and female, masculine and feminine, or maternal and paternal; like Freud's (1920) female adolescent patient, we are all mixtures of all of the above, and, in that sense, bisexual. (2) As a consequence, we can observe in the *behaviour* of all individuals a mixture of masculine and feminine traits. (3) Every sexual object choice is bisexual; that is, again like Freud's patient, we seek objects that unconsciously remind us of both male and female figures from our past (Freud 1920: 552). As Freud (1985) wrote to Fleiss, 'Every sexual act is a process in which four individuals are involved.'

The tragedy of bisexuality is that it is an incomplete state: neither all one nor all the other. As we develop, we use our inherent bisexuality to identify our body as more or less masculine or feminine to the extent that our self-image becomes fixed in the usual course of development by the end of adolescence. In the adolescent and adult patients described by Lemma there has been a breakdown in the usual developmental trajectory. However, given the complexity of our bisexual disposition, it is not surprising that arriving at congruence between our body and our self-image is often a turbulent process.

Although we would expect our active and passive impulses to be informed by our bisexuality, they are also stimulated by internal physical states, such as illness, fantasies and mental states, such as mania or depression, external factors, such as traumatic experiences and object relationships. Our bisexual make-up is an instinctual resource that we use to respond to any stimulus. Our bisexuality is more visible in our active and passive personality traits, especially as expressed in our aggressive and sexual behaviour.

During the oral phase of development the child's skin and mouth are the first organs of sexual/erotic satisfaction and mediums for a *psychosensual* intercourse between mother and child. From birth the build-up of a sense of me and not-me occurs in a bisexual domain; the experience of a hard nipple and a soft breast, psychic intrusion via projection into the mother of instinctual needs, incorporation via reception of mother's milk, and active exploration and containment. The baby's first object of identification, its first object 'choice', as it were, is the mother, particularly her breast and body. During its first year the child identifies with mother's bisexuality, her masculine and feminine characteristics, before recognizing her gender.

The psychic experience of bisexuality is often an uncanny one. Freud (1919) describes the uncanny as frightening, that is not homely, *unheimlich*, and, at the same time, familiar, like a vague sense of 'home'. Freud reminds us that the original home (*heim*) 'of all human beings, a place where each one of us lived once upon a time and in the beginning was the female genital organs' (1919: 245). The original home of all of us was an intra-uterine existence, the core of the mother's femininity. Freud describes two classes of uncanny experiences; one arising from the revival of previously surmounted primitive beliefs, and the other, which is germane to my point, arising from the lifting of the repression of infantile complexes as the result of 'some impression' (249), like the boy's (re)discovery of the female genital.

I have the impression that the uncanny dynamic of the co-existence of the familiar and the strange is embedded in the bodies of some transsexual patients that I have seen. As Kohon (2014) reminds us, 'The uncanny may also emerge when something is present but it has not yet become explicit' (24). The transsexual feels estranged from their body. The uncertainty and terror of the bisexual tension, that is, not being exclusively masculine or all feminine, is unbearable. Complementarity is impossible. The aim of a surgical intervention (SRS) is to obliterate external evidence of the uncanny, that which feels incomplete and foreign.

The comfort, nurturance and safety that the baby boy derives from its contact with the mother's body may reinforce feminine aspects of its bisexuality. This feminine component of the male's original bisexual template may be forgotten but is revived later, much like the experience of the uncanny.

The opportunities afforded by our bisexuality also include the capacity to identify, express and appreciate masculine and feminine characteristics in others and ourselves. The boy's experience of the primary feminine and masculine objects will influence either a negative or positive identification with the revival of its uncanny feminine 'home'. The boy's observation of the genitals of the other sex as different from his own, generates an uncanny sense that there is something familiar in the otherness of the other based on his earliest identification with the feminine, which leaves an unconscious residue that someone else has something he almost had, but not quite. This may lead to a feeling of inferiority, or a devastating lack. In other individuals a feeling of the uncanny as their sexual home may leave them feeling deprived or stolen from.

Our psychic bisexuality plays an unconscious role in the individual's dialogue with its primary internal objects. Freud considered that the masculine component of the woman's bisexuality contributed to the girl's wish for a penis and envy of the boy's penis. The feminine aspect of her bisexuality converted the envy of the penis into a wish for a baby. The 'appeased wish for a penis is destined to be converted into a wish for a baby and for a husband, who possesses a penis' (Freud 1937: 251).

A common denominator of the patients that Lemma worked with was their aversion to reflection and their reliance upon action to resolve internal conflicts. Each patient found it very difficult to use a reflective part of their mind to think about their body. Their development did not proceed toward an integration of their bisexuality in an Oedipal structure and symbolization of conflict, but continued in a two-dimensional sexual identity with no place for the structuring function of a father's penis. The consequent fragmentation could only be contained physically.

Ferraro (2001) notes that Birksted-Breen's (1996) concept of the penis as link joins the mother and the father and, thereby, consolidates bisexuality in the Oedipal couple (Freud's intercourse of four people). The patients that Lemma describes have not been able to integrate a penis with a linking function. For her patients the body is still experienced as a pre-symbolic, concrete object. Ferraro reminds us that this way of thinking 'turns the body into a phallus, hallucinatorily enslaved to a fantasy of self-sufficiency and invulnerability, thereby blocking the disposition to internalize the father's penis in its structuring function' (Ferraro, 2001: 497). The consolidation of the bisexual in an enduring Oedipal constellation creates the possibility of symbolic dialogue with a three-dimensional reality.

But what if the experience of the uncanny, which is often reported by transsexual patients, is of a 'home' that is an absence or a threat to survival? For these individuals the mother is an alien and uncertain presence, which is projected onto their body. The transsexual seeks to utilize SRS to consciously and concretely get rid of a threatening object, now identified with their body, and create a known and better body as Lemma's patients illustrate in Chapters 4 and 5.

Self-mutilation by proxy

Lemma emphasizes throughout this book that the compelling need to modify the body, in actuality or in imagination, that distinguishes these patients, is driven by conscious or unconscious phantasy, which motivates its enactment. The phantasy itself is the psychic solution to anxiety, fear, psychic pain, despair, violent states of mind, and, particularly, anxieties about mother's failure to cathect or over cathect the child's body. Understanding these phenomena is essential if the patient is to be helped.

One unconscious phantasy that featured in some of the patients I saw who requested Sexual Reassignment Surgery (SRS) was a phantasy of self-mutilation by proxy. At the Portman Clinic, where I worked for 30 years, I treated a number of patients who mutilated themselves by cutting their bodies with razors, knives or scalpels, or by burning, typically with a cigarette. I also saw individuals who sought SRS, which I think is a misnomer based on the assumption that one's gender can be assigned, and were referred to the Portman to think with someone about their wish for SRS prior to a decision to be operated upon. As Alessandra Lemma points out, a decision to undergo SRS is driven by the wish to fulfil a phantasy, which, in turn, is a solution to deep-seated psychic pain. I found that many of the patients seeking SRS had displaced impulses to mutilate themselves onto surgeons, so that one component of their phantasy was self-mutilation by proxy.

There are important differences and similarities between self-mutilation and self-mutilation by proxy that, in my experience, feature in the phantasies of some patients who search for surgeons to perform SRS. The obvious descriptive difference is that acts of self-mutilation tend to function in an acute and temporary way, and can and often are repeated. Whereas SRS is most likely to be a singular irreversible event. In both acts the body is an object of projections. But in SRS, as Lemma illustrates so clearly in Chapters 1, 3 and 4, the surface of the body is more likely to be the focus of cathexis.

An individual who mutilates him or herself (like Sharon in Chapter 3) has a complicated and ambivalent relation to the surface of their body. Kafka (1969) emphasized the importance of the skin as a transitional object in his analysis of a young girl who cut herself. The skin, which is the child's first medium of sensual contact, comfort and communication, may also register the failure of mother's containment and the child's unmitigated physical pain, discomfort and rage. When the projection of rage at the uncertaining mother is turned against the self, the child's skin may become a bad object and a target for revenge. In this respect, the surface of the body is an object of projection for the self-mutilator and the person seeking SRS.

However, I have found that the self-mutilator is usually primarily preoccupied with the interior of their body, namely the blood. Caroline Kettlewell vividly describes this phenomenon in her memoir *Skin Game* (2000) thusly:

> In the razor's wake, the skin melted away, parted to show briefly the milky white subcutaneous layers before a thin beaded line of rich crimson blood seeped through the inch-long divide. The blood welled up and began to distort the pure, stark edges of my delicately wrought wound.
>
> The chaos in my head spun itself into a silk of silence. I had distilled myself to the immediacy of hand, blade, blood, and flesh.
>
> (Kettlewell, 2000)

My patients had different associations to the appearance of their blood. For some, the erotic gratification derived from the act of releasing the blood from the confines of the skin was palpable. These patients often felt trapped in their bodies, just as they felt suffocated by their mothers, not unlike some of the patients Lemma worked with. The cutting was a sexually charged release. Kafka's patient described the blood as defining and caressing the body 'being like a voluptuous bath which, as it spread over the hills and valleys of her body, moulded its contour and sculpted its form' (1969).

For others, the blood had a more toxic quality and represented disgusting aspects of themselves that they got rid of as the blood flowed out. A patient of Rob Hale (Campbell and Hale, 2014) put it this way: 'The pain becomes unbearable and you cut to see blood. I was always convinced that inside me was green mucus. So, instead of blood, I would have filth and snot in my veins. And sometimes you would hear this voice saying, "You're dirty, you're muck". And you just slash … anything to prove its blood.'

While SRS can become an *idée fixe* for some individuals, self-mutilation can become addictive. Coid et al. (1983) observed that the act of cutting was accompanied by raised plasma endorphin levels, the body's naturally occurring opiates. Rob Hale (Campbell & Hale, 2014) reported patients saying that they experienced an endorphin high before cutting or burning themselves. There were two results: first, there was no feeling of physical pain, and, second, the psychological experience was of elation, sexual excitement and relaxation of superego control.

The male who pursues SRS has two aims in mind. First, the aim is to cut out or mutilate that part of their body that they experience as alien and uncertain, such as their penis. In the patients whom I have treated this wish to attack their body is motivated, in part, by identification with a mother who was experienced as absent, destructive and negating of their masculinity. Second, there is a wish to create another body through the hands of a surgeon, again someone identified with mother. One source of the excitement generated by this wish is the belief that the surgeon, on their behalf, will surgically sculpt from the gender of their given body the depiction of another gender. The surface of the body is the medium, which the surgeon cuts for them.

Unfortunately, psychic bisexuality, represented by the uncanny, has been negated by the transsexual and, therefore, does not foster a three-dimensional internal structure to build upon and the individual is left with a two-dimensional surface. Consequently, the transsexual unconsciously constructs a surface that imposes upon and contradicts its interior. There is a discontinuity between the interior and exterior, and the viewer is left with the feeling of incongruity that the patient grew up with what Lemma describes in Chapter 5.

Although the transvestite is also preoccupied with the surface of their body and it visual presentation, it is worth noting that the transvestite who dresses in the clothes of the opposite sex, and even tries to pass as a member of the other sex, is not interested in modifying their sexual body, but in hiding it. One aim of the cross-dressing is to disguise themselves in the clothes of the opposite sex in order to deceive and mislead the other about the existence of a transvestite's hidden genitals. Another aim is to vicariously feel they are inside mother's body, and, thereby, overcome anxieties associated with being lost, rejected or abandoned by the mother. A modern development of cross-dressing is female masking in which a man may order a silicone mask or body suit of a woman's head and/or body made to the measurements of his own body. These body suits mimic the appearance of a doll that is a replica of a replica of a woman. A crucial part of any cross-dressing is the ability to get out of the woman's apparel, to be able to escape from the mother's body that threatens to engulf them and annihilate their sense of self (Glasser, 1979; Campbell, in press).

The aftermath of SRS and self-mutilation plays an important but different role. Lemma draws our attention to the role that the post-operative SRS body plays in representing incongruity to the outside world. However, the wounds and scars of a body that has been self-mutilated are often presented to sadistically shock or disgust others, or to insure that medical and nursing staff tend to them. Sometimes the masochistic component is more prominent and the wounds are kept secret, often to fester and prolong the process of suffering. The self-mutilator may also actively interfere with the healing process, inserting foreign objects into the wound. Masochism is also mobilized in the service of sadism. Rob Hale and I have known patients who have encouraged the attending doctor to suture without an anaesthetic, drawing the doctor into collusion to inflict further pain. In the longer term the wounds may be a source of shame, guilt and embarrassment to be kept covered from the view of others (Campbell & Hale, 2014). However, I also met with post-operative SRS individuals who realized they had made a mistake – that was irreversible. They were enraged at the surgeons, hated their mothers, and were suicidal with despair and guilt.

Lemma's thoughts about the body

In Chapter 1 Alessandra Lemma shows how three phantasies that arise in response to the child's experience of the mother motivate wishes for cosmetic surgery. In one group of patients Lemma notices a particular envy of a mother who possesses what the child needs but withholds it. The child's phantasy is that this envy can be overcome by getting the surgeon to give him/her the body that the mother refused to give. Lemma identifies this as the *self-made phantasy* in which the individual acts on their omnipotent phantasy of giving birth to the self by designing and constructing a perfect body. In this way, the individual triumphs over the withholding (m)other, and circumvents any experience of dependency on the 'object of desire' (Britton, 1998). Lemma makes clear that the self-made phantasy is distinguished from other phantasies by the underlying envious attack on the depriving mother and the generative parental couple.

Some of Lemma's patients felt trapped in their mother's body. A phantasy of reclaiming their body from the mother emerged as a solution to an annihilating anxiety about engulfment. Lemma found that in a *reclaiming phantasy* the claustrophobic space inside the mother had been projected on to the self's body, which is then experienced as an alien malevolent presence.

The subject's body, not the mother's body, is experienced as threatening to engulf and destroy the self. The action solution to this terrifying fantasy about survival is to surgically remove that aspect of the body that represents the alien presence. Unlike the self-made phantasy, one can see the life and death struggle that motivates the violence and pain required to expel the life-threatening object.

Several of Lemma's patients experienced their mothers as failing to cathect the child's body or actively rejecting it. Lemma identified in these patients a phantasy of creating a new body that is a *perfect match* for their mother, which will be a body that is desired by her. Cosmetic surgery would overcome forever the pain of disappointment or rejection by insuring the mother would always love and desire the self. The mother's narcissism plays an important role in the development of these phantasies, but in the perfect match phantasy the mother's over-cathexis of the child's body seems to support the belief that surgery can create a fusion with the longed for and idealized object. The three phantasies of the self-made body, the reclaimed body and the perfect match may, in some cases, overlap as, for instance, the reclaiming phantasy may play an important role in achieving the perfect match.

Just as Alessandra Lemma draws from many sources to develop her theories, each chapter includes detailed clinical material, which conveys the subtlety and complexity of Lemma's psychoanalytic work. The reader will have an opportunity to see in detail Lemma's interaction with patients who are mainly borderline personality disordered, are difficult to understand, and often difficult to treat analytically. In Chapter 1 Lemma's slow and detailed work with Ms A. follows the shift from Ms A.'s unbearable psychic pain to the psychical pain of the implant operation to enhance her breasts. The reader will learn how Lemma came to understand that the implant represented for Ms A. the theft of an artificial object, implicitly from her mother's body, that is reified as an idealized breast.

In Chapter 2 Alessandra Lemma examines the psychic function of necrophilia fantasies that aimed to reverse a narcissistic injury, which arose from being looked at with disgust by the mother. Lemma's analytic work with Mr B. illustrates the maxim that 'If patience is a virtue, waiting is an art'. Time and again she feels uneasy and stops to listen to Mr B. and her own associations. More than once waiting and listening protected Lemma from being drawn into premature interpretations that would have actualized the patient's fear of being groomed to be in perfect synchrony with the analyst/mother, being in the same skin, the eroticization of Mr B.'s necrophilia fantasy. Behind Mr B.'s necrophilia fantasy was the image of his mother dead, her corpse rendering her safe, thereby protecting him from the annihilation he fears on entering a woman. Lemma emphasized that an important dynamic in these cases is the experience of humiliation, which creates a hypersensitivity to being looked at. For Mr B. the eyes were felt to be castrating. Hence, the creation of a necrophilic fantasy in which the object has no eyes.

In Chapter 3 Lemma explores how the virtual world of the Internet may become compelling to some adolescents because it bypasses the need to link distinctively different inner and outer realities, and enables the creation of the illusion that internal and external reality are isomorphic. In virtual reality the Internet becomes attractive because there are no limits, and no boundaries. What can be imagined can be actualized. Helplessness is replaced by omnipotence. Estrangement is replaced by omniscience. Avatars replace real people.

Puberty propels the body onto the centre of the psychic stage. It is not unusual for the adolescent who is confused and frightened by the hormonal and physiological changes in his or her body to experience their body as a threatening monster or alien, an altogether other object that is not part of the self (Campbell, 2003). Virtual reality may stimulate sexual fantasies and masturbation, but it bypasses touch through which the sensual body comes into being (Anzieu, 1989). Through the Internet the body may become a source of sexual gratification for individuals who feel helpless with and estranged from their body, but it is not the basis for a connectedness with others.

Lemma presents two adolescent patients to illustrate how cyberspace can provide a means of escaping from the body and the mind. Through Lemma's sensitive analytic work we learn how immersion in virtual reality enabled two adolescent patients to control a frightening otherness that resided in their bodies.

The reader of this book will be introduced to patients who have rarely been written about. In Chapter 4 Lemma considers how the extensive modification of the body of a male to female transsexual adolescent, referred to as Paula, affects her experience of her body in time. Lemma uses this case to consider the way one's body serves as a reminder of the parental couple that excluded us and created us. The body's origins concretely represent a 'before-me' time dimension, a 'before-me-ness'.

Chapter 5 explores the importance for the transsexual of creating a state of ambiguity in others through the visual presentation of their body. Lemma extends her study of the subjective experience of embodiment through her interviews of eight transsexual individuals and a five-year-long, once-weekly psychoanalytic psychotherapy with a male to female transsexual Ms C., who underwent SRS. The first theme that emerged in these contacts was the incongruity between the given body and the body these individuals identified as their true physical home. The second theme was the importance of being seen as a visual object, which Lemma sees as the core experience of the transsexual. What was strikingly absent was a receptive mind that could have provided a home for the ambiguity, confusion and uncertainty that was lodged in the body. Lemma believes that the absence of an early mirroring of this incongruity exposed the child to an intolerable experience of feeling dissociated from its given body, which led to a search for the 'right' body to relieve the pain of incongruity. Lemma makes the fundamental point that the internal incongruity of the transsexual is manifest externally, that is, visually, and draws the observer's attention to the subject's sense of incongruity.

In Chapter 6 Lemma uses her study of Almodóvar's film *The Skin I Live In* to reflect on the impact of the mother's internal image of her son's masculine gender identity. Lemma vividly describes how the main character, Dr Ledgard, who is unable to grieve the loss of his daughter Norma to her breakdown and withdrawal, kidnaps Vincente, a young boy, holds him captive and treats him like an animal. During Vincente's captivity Norma, like her mother, commits suicide. Ledgard regresses to a paranoid-schizoid state of mind and surgically castrates Vincent by performing a vaginoplasty, thereby enacting his own impotence and revengeful rage in the face of loss. *The Skin I Live In* confirms what we see in Ms A. (in Chapter 1), namely, in spite of hope and illusion and powerful projections of the bodily surface onto observers, external change to the body does not affect internal identity. Almodóvar presents Vera, before we know she is really Vincente, as having a secure internal identity as a man. Lemma observes that what keeps Vincente alive in Vera's body is his belief that his mother will be searching for him. Unlike Ms A. (in Chapter 1) and Ms C. (in Chapter 5), whose mothers gave up looking for their child's internal gender identity, Vincente always believed that there was a maternal mind that holds onto his masculinity.

When working with patients whose body is the primary medium for unconscious communication, it is inevitable that the analyst's body will feature in the treatment as an invariant, embodied part of the setting. This is the subject of Chapter 7. For Alessandra Lemma the analyst's physical appearance and presence provides an embodied containment of the patient's anxieties and phantasies. Lemma also refers to the way the analyst listens to his or her body's free associations, a kind of somatic countertransference. The embodied setting is particularly useful in identifying and working with a nucleus of a symbiotic core of primary undifferentiation, which Bleger (2012[1967]) believes exists in patients who present with a split between neurotic and psychotic parts of the personality. With these patients the body of the analyst becomes the depository for unconscious pre-symbolic elements that cannot be integrated. This leads Lemma to an understanding of the way core primitive anxieties about non-differentiation from the object impact on the analyst's body 'in a mutual symbiosis between patient and analyst as "embodied phantasies"' (Bronstein, 2013).

In conceptualizing the analyst's body as an embodied form of the setting Lemma uses Bleger's formulations to reflect on her analysis of Ms D., for whom the patient's inhalations, her hair and Lemma's hair were embodiments of a symbiotic setting. As a consequence, there was no 'as if' space, which could have given meaning to a transference interpretation. Lemma's lengthy and intricate analysis of Ms D. shows the reader how Lemma was able to meet Ms D. in her own setting, which lacked differentiation, and help her understand the terrifying psychotic anxieties that emerged from a separateness that was represented by changes in Lemma's body, namely when Lemma cut her hair. Lemma continues to explore the meaning of hair in Chapter 8 by revisiting the fairy tale of Rapunzel.

In Chapter 9 Lemma explores the psychic uses of the analyst's toilet by distinguishing between two uses. The first involves a perverse use of the toilet to enact sexualized, hostile, intrusive dynamics in relation to the analyst. In the second use of the toilet that Lemma identifies, the patient is anxious about phantasized damage done to the object if the patient exposes unacceptable, messy parts of the self. Lemma notes that these patients are unable to use the analyst as the toilet-breast, which preserves a more idealized relationship with the analyst (Meltzer, 1967).

Alessandra Lemma has studied disturbing *public* representations of the relationship between the self and the body, not only from her consulting room, but also from the television studio. For 13 years Lemma screened participants to ensure that they were psychologically 'fit' to take part in reality TV (RTV) makeover shows. In Chapter 10 Lemma uses her clinical and theoretical understanding of psychoanalysis to identify some of the functions of RTV makeover shows. As the result of her experience of assessing potential participants for makeover TV programmes, Lemma found that the creation of a part-object universe takes place within the normalizing framework of the popular reality TV genre that masks the individual's actual distress, which all too often lies behind the conscious wish to participate in these shows. Lemma describes the makeover show as existing in a paranoid-schizoid universe where depression, anxiety and injustice can be eliminated by the manipulation of the body's surface in conformity to socially determined norms.

At the close of this final chapter, Lemma returns to one of the abiding themes of her book. RTV not only uses the surface of the body to gratify the gaze, but to perpetuate in the public arena the private phantasy of the patients described in this book, namely that changing the external can, indeed, gratify a specious omnipotent phantasy that can undo internal anxieties about our unavoidable lack and dependency.

Conclusion

In a fitting end to her book, Alessandra Lemma reminds us that the voyeur, which is in all of us, always participates, though the gaze, in someone's trauma: 'We can never be innocent bystanders.' I think that the same can be said of the reader of *Minding the Body*. This book will sharpen your understanding of some of the more extreme representations of the body and the human being that inhabits it. Once we have seen something, we cannot unsee it. The gaze can never be innocent, and, I would add, it can never be neutral, because, as Lemma emphasizes, we are never entirely free from the influence of our unconscious, an aspect of being human that we share with the victim and the perpetrator. However, if we 'commit ourselves to an ongoing analytic process' (Lemma, p. 167, this book) we can remain open to recognizing the way each of us unconsciously defends against our anxieties, about our inevitable lack and dependency.

References

Almodóvar, P. (2011). *The Skin I Live In* [film]. Warners España, Spain.
Anzieu, D. (1989). *The Skin Ego*. New Haven, CT: Yale University Press.
Birksted-Breen, D. (1996). Phallus, penis and mental space. *International Journal of Psychoanalysis*, 77: 649–59.

Bleger, J. (2012[1967]). Psychoanalysis of the psychoanalytic setting. In J. Churcher and L. Bleger (eds), *Symbiosis and Ambiguity: A Psychoanalytic Study*. London: Routledge.

Britton, R. (1998). *Belief and Imagination*. London: Routledge.

Bronstein, C. (2013). Finding unconscious phantasy in the session: Recognising form. *Bull. Brit. Psychoanal. Soc.*, 49(3): 16–21.

Campbell, D. (2003). Dario Argento's phenomena (1985): A psychoanalytic perspective on the 'horror film' genre and adolescent development. In A. Sabbadini (ed.), *The Couch and the Silver Screen: Psychoanalytic Reflections on European Cinema*. Hove and New York: Brunner and Routledge, pp. 128–138.

Campbell, D. (in press). *The Core Complex, Violence and Perverse Solutions: Mervin Glasser's Contributions to Psychoanalysis*. London: Routledge.

Campbell, D. and Hale, R. (2014). *Understanding the Pre-Suicide State of Mind*. London: Routledge.

Coid, J., Allolko, B. and Rees, L. H. (1983). Raised plasma metenkephalin in patients who habitually mutilate themselves. *The Lancet*, 3 December.

Ferraro, F. (2001). Vicissitudes of bisexuality: Crucial point and clinical implication. *Int. J. Psychoanal.*, 82: 485–499.

Freud, S. (1919). A child is being beaten. *Standard Edition*, 17: 177–243.

Freud, S. (1920). The psychogenesis of a case of homosexuality in a woman. *Standard Edition*, 18: 145–172.

Freud, S. (1927). Fetishism. *Standard Edition*, 21: 149–157.

Freud, S. (1937). Analysis terminable and interminable. *Standard Edition*, 23: 209–253.

Freud, S. (1985). *The Complete Letters of Sigmund Freud to Wilhelm Fliess 1887–1904* (trans. and ed. J. M. Masson). Cambridge, MA: Harvard University Press.

Glasser, M (1979). From the analysis of a transvestite. *International Review of Psycho-Analysis*, 6: 163–173.

Kafka, J. (1969). The body as transitional object: A psychoanalytic study of a self-mutilating patient. *British Journal of Medical Psychology*, 42: 207–212.

Kettlewell, C. (2000). *Skin Game: A Memoir*. New York: St Martin's Griffin.

Kohon, G. (2014). *Reflections on the Aesthetic Experience – Psychoanalysis and the Uncanny*. London: Routledge.

Lemma, A (2010). *Under the Skin: A Psychoanalytic Study of Body Modification*. London: Routledge.

Meltzer, D. (1967). *The Psychoanalytic Process*. London: Heinemann.

Smith, H. F. (2002). On Psychic Bisexuality. *Psychoanalytic Quarterly*, 71: 549–558.

Acknowledgements

All of the chapters in this book, with the exception of the Introduction and Chapter 8, are modified versions of previously published papers in academic journals over a three-year period, during which time I have focused my attention specifically on thinking and writing about the body – a strong interest of mine that has spanned two decades.

I would like to thank the following journals for their kind permission to reprint parts of the papers that they originally published: *International Journal of Psychoanalysis* (Chapters 5, 6, 7); *Journal of the American Psychoanalytic Association* (Chapters 3, 9); *Psychoanalytic Quarterly* (Chapter 1); *Psychoanalytic Inquiry* (Chapter 4); *Rivista Italiana di Psicoanalisi* (Chapter 2); *Organisational & Social Dynamics* (Chapter 10). In particular I would like to thank the journal editors and peer reviewers who helped me to articulate my ideas more clearly through their generous feedback as part of the peer review process. Special thanks are due to Dana Birksted-Breen who has taught me a lot about how to write through the way she approaches the peer review process of the *International Journal of Psychoanalysis* and whose own ideas about sexuality and the body have been influential in my thinking.

Although the process of writing can at times feel like an isolating experience, and for me at least this is a necessary part of the process, it is also always a process that relies for its completion on the love, good humour and feedback of those closest to me. I would like to thank in particular my son Matteo for putting up with my preoccupation with this book. I would also like to thank Nicholas Kemp, Susan Levy, Linda Young and Heather Wood for their invaluable feedback and friendship throughout the gestation of this book and beyond. Finally, I would like to acknowledge the inspiring supervision I have had the good fortune to receive over many years from Dr Robin Anderson.

Introduction
When the body speaks

The body always speaks. The task of the analyst is to listen to what it expresses or conceals in its relative noisiness or quietness. In some cases the patient's body is 'loud' and is the presenting complaint: it is a hated body or a body felt to be in physical pain. In others the body is 'quiet', neglected or denied in the patient's experience, and yet powerfully present in the analytic relationship echoing in the analyst's somatic countertransference where its as yet unarticulated story is received and gradually put into words.

How we listen to the body and its narrative is filtered through the analyst's own subjectivity (which comprises bodily and psychic components) and her guiding theoretical and technical principles or assumptions. As analysts we all implicitly and/or explicitly orientate ourselves in our encounters with patients according to theories and assumptions that ideally function as flexible 'guides' in our work allowing us to meet the needs of the patient at any given point.

In this book the reader will notice at least four such assumptions, which I will briefly outline and which function as a constant background to my attempts to understand the patients I describe here. I hope that these assumptions have not acquired in my thinking the status of 'overvalued ideas' (Britton and Steiner, 1994) – the danger that they can function as such, and can be thus used defensively by the analyst, is always present and needs to be closely monitored.

The book draws on my applied psychoanalytic work with adolescents and adults in forensic and psychiatric settings within the public health service as well as my work as an analyst seeing patients on the couch 3–5 times weekly. In my view psychoanalytic work is defined as such first and foremost by the analyst's internal setting (Parsons, 2007) and not by the external setting in which one practises or the frequency of sessions offered to the patient. The distinctiveness of psychoanalytic work lies in the analyst's *systematic use* of the transference, which involves maintaining an analytic stance rooted in the analyst's experience of the transference in order to inform her understanding of the patient's state of mind and how to intervene most productively.

As analysts we probably all 'use' the transference in this sense, but it is also important to be open to the different ways we can engage and support the patient's curiosity about his own mind, not least, but not only, through the verbal interpretation of the transference. From this perspective, representational work or supportive work is no less 'analytic' than transference-focused work (e.g. Lecours, 2007; Ogden, 1982; Lemma, 2013) and may be essential in the early stages of an analysis or psychoanalytic psychotherapy with the kinds of patients I shall be describing, who typically challenge the analyst with their marked difficulties in representing their experience in their minds.

There are, of course, differences in the depth of analysis that can be achieved in a once-weekly psychotherapy compared to a more intensive analysis, but it would be a mistake to dismiss the less intensive work as irrelevant or marginal to the development of our discipline. On the contrary, such work, which typically allows us to engage with patients who would never, or seldom, come into analysis, provides invaluable insights into pathologies that, in turn, enrich our understanding of the mind. For example, in this book I present work with transsexual individuals and those who compulsively pursue cosmetic surgery. Such individuals rarely come into analysis or manage to sustain it even when they do. And yet my understanding of the mind–body relationship and of how the modification of the body may be used to 'cure' the psyche has been enriched by my work with these patients. Whilst not psychoanalysis, this work is nevertheless psychoanalytic in so far as it is rooted in an analytic model of an unconscious mind and makes use of the analytic relationship to bring to life in the here-and-now of the encounter relational constellations, and the associated unconscious phantasies, that are felt to be necessary to the patient's psychic equilibrium.

As will become apparent in the pages that follow, in order to understand the body and the analyst's somatic countertransference I do not restrict myself solely to psychoanalytic contributions; rather, I also draw on neuroscientific research. In my view psychoanalysis is enriched by engagement with other disciplines not because the phenomena that interest us as analysts can be reduced to brain sites or mechanisms, but because together these disciplines advance a more sophisticated understanding and knowledge of what it means to be embodied beings.

The embodied self

The first assumption that informs my work is that *embodiment shapes the mind.* As such it is essential for the analyst to always keep the body in mind even when the patient does not bring the body explicitly as the problem with which he wants help. Mind and body are inseparable. The mind is indeed inconceivable without some sort of embodiment, a notion now espoused by many (e.g. Lakoff, 1987; Rosch, 1992; Edelman, 1992; Damasio, 2006).

The body is a basic fact of life that supports all other psychic functions; hence, when it is denied emotional, social and cognitive functioning, it can be severely impaired. Escaping the reality of the body invariably entails an escape from a place in the mind where thinking and feeling are possible and hence where relating to the other as 'other' is also possible. This is readily apparent in those individuals who defensively retreat into virtual reality as a means of bypassing the psychic implications of being-in-a-body – a need that may be particularly acute during adolescence when the body presents itself forcefully to the mind (see Chapter 3). Indeed, 'virtual technologies', writes Hillis, 'encourage belief that they constitute a 'transcendence machine' within which the imaginative self might escape its privatized physical anchor and live in an iconography of pleasure' (Hillis, 1999: 172).

As I discuss in Chapters 1, 3 and 4, the body ideally provides an anchor in reality, not least the reality of the parental couple who gives us birth and hence acts as a reminder imprinted on the 'given' body of the reality of difference and insufficiency that have to be borne rather than omnipotently denied. Being-in-a-body entails acknowledgement of the time of the couple – a time 'before' the body and hence before the self was given life. The body is integral to the establishment of the *temporal link* that provides a sense of continuity in our experience of who we are over time and links us to the objects on whom we have depended and may continue to depend.

Extensive modification of the body, such as that undertaken by transsexual individuals, can impair their orientation in time as the new modified body, and hence the self, is unanchored in the 'given' body that provides the crucial link between past and present. The disruption of the temporal link is strikingly apparent in the case of the adolescent transsexual discussed in Chapter 4, where the suspension of puberty through hormones led to a highly disruptive psychic and physical hibernation.

Physically edited bodies are always bodies with a history: the given bodily configuration and appearance, even when at odds with subjective experience and the wished-for body image, informs the representation of the body in the mind and needs to be integrated into the self's experience. For the patients described here this typically involves painstaking work in order to enable them to 'personalize' the body (Winnicott, 1945).

The mind–body conundrum has taxed some of the greatest minds in science, philosophy and psychoanalysis. It is not the aim of this introduction or this book to provide a comprehensive overview of the various arguments that have been put forward; rather I will restrict the focus here to some key psychoanalytic contributions. This selection is inevitably subjective and represents those views that I have found helpful, some because they have challenged my assumptions, and others, perhaps inevitably, because they resonated with my preconceptions.

The key notion that informs my work above all else roots us firmly in Freudian territory, namely as Freud (1923) famously put it that the ego is 'first and foremost a body ego; it is not merely a surface entity but it is itself the projection of a surface' (1923: 26); that is, the most primitive form of self-representation is a body representation. In a footnote dated 1927, Freud added:

> The ego is ultimately derived from bodily sensations, chiefly from those springing from the surface of the body. It may thus be regarded as a mental projection of the surface of the body, besides ... representing the superficies of the mental apparatus.

For Freud the ego was thus represented as a psychical map, a projection of the surface of the body. More specifically, the ego was seen to be a mental representation of the individual's perceived *libidinized* relationship to his body.

One important implication of this, which has been richly elaborated since Freud, is that the ego derives its functioning from body models (Lichtenberg, 1978). This is perhaps most evident in Klein's writings where the mind is described as a kind of 'alimentary tract' (Caper, 1999) taking in (introjecting) and expelling (projecting) psychic states. In a similar vein, Fenichel (1945) emphasized that the baby's first reality is what can be swallowed: the acts of taking into the mouth and spitting out formed, according to him, the foundation of all experience.

Freud (1923) and later Schilder (1950) in his landmark study of the body image, propose that proprioception has a decisive place in the development of the body-related sense of self. They both essentially underline how at the beginning of life internal perceptions are more fundamental than external ones in shaping the ego. In other words, throughout life ego structure and identity are founded to a significant degree on the sensations and awareness of the body (Hägglund and Piha, 1980). Freud thus cemented the view, later developed by others, that the body-self is the container and foundation for the sense of self (Winnicott, 1966, 1972; Mahler and Furer, 1968; Haag, 1985; Krueger, 1989; Sandler, 1994).

For Freud the drives always had their source in the most inner part of the body. He defines the drive as 'the psychical representative of the stimuli originating from within the organism and reaching the mind' (Freud, 1915: 122). He adds that the drive is a 'measure of the demand made upon the mind for work in consequence of its connection with the body'. If we think of his definition of the drive, it is this reference to 'work' that explains the transformations that take place, changing the contents of its initial expression. Green underlines that this highlights

> a double process: the first one is the transformation of the stimuli born in the body and reaching the mind, changing themselves from somatic excitations to psychic representatives; the second is the work imposed on the mind in aiming to change *the situation of frustration in communicating his represent-ations to the other*.
>
> (Green, 1998: 655; my italics)

Although Freud emphasized the importance of both the drive and of the object, the importance of the object was more explicitly and richly elaborated by his successors. As far as the drive is concerned, however, his rigorous description helpfully brings together the notions of anchorage in the soma, excitation reaching the psyche, and the measure of the demand for work imposed on the psyche due to its link with the body.

Freud's emphasis on the body is well placed and ties in with current neuroscientific perspectives, and indeed anticipates them. Physical movement and the registration of that movement in a developing proprioceptive system, that is a system that registers its own self-movement, contributes to the self-organizing development of neuronal structures responsible not only for motor action, but also for the way we become conscious of ourselves, for how we communicate with others, for *how we live*. Physical movement (and, of course, how others respond to that movement) prefigures the lines of intentionality, gesture shapes the contours of social cognition. It is in this most general *and* most fundamental sense that embodiment shapes the mind.

Drawing on psychoanalysis Merleau-Ponty (1962) suggested that the body 'operates according to a latent knowledge it has of the world – a knowledge anterior to cognitive experience' (233). 'To have a body,' he adds, 'is to possess a universal setting, a schema of all types of perceptual unfolding' (Merleau-Ponty, 1962: 326). His model of embodied intentionality includes a space for the *body schema* – an anterior condition of the possibility for perception. The body schema needs to be differentiated from the notion of the body *image*, which will be more familiar to analysts. It refers to the system of sensory-motor processes that constantly regulate posture and movement and is a 'set of laws' rather than images (Gallagher, 2005).

As analysts we tend to be concerned with the *body image*, that is, the representation we have of our body in our mind with the attendant affect and phantasies associated with it. It is the psychic/libidinal map of the body organized not just by the laws of biology, but also by the meanings and phantasies we bring to our experience of the body. It is in fact more apt to say that we are dealing with an imaginary anatomy.

Although the felt experience of the body is to varying degrees always in flux, it is also the case that out of the early experiences of body states and bodily exchanges with others we develop a representation of our body that is more or less enduring and that contains both perceptual and evaluative components. Damasio (1999) likens the representation of the body-self to a map in the brain which provides continuity across different states. Although Damasio does not elaborate this, we should add that it also provides the essential continuity in the quality and range of the affective core (Bucci, 2008).

Whereas the body schema is constitutionally based, the body image therefore rejoins us to the importance of the intersubjective context in which the given body develops. The body image is not innate, and here psychoanalysis can make a valuable contribution in understanding the developmental factors and phantasies that play a part in shaping and affectively colouring the representation of the body in the mind. In my work I approach the perception the patient has of his body as reflecting certain dispositions that he has towards it (beliefs and phantasies) as well as certain dispositions that his body has towards the world (a particular posture, a sense of balance and other visceral, autonomic aspects of embodiment). The body schema, we might therefore say, constrains intentionality (Gallagher, 2005), but object relations lend to it its affective resonance as reflected in the patient's body image.

In order to underline what I consider to be the essential *dynamically unconscious* dimension of the representation we have of our bodies at any point in time, I prefer to use the term *body imagining(s)*. This term more accurately denotes the potential fluidity in our body image whilst also underscoring that the representation of the body in the mind is an unconscious psychic organization powered by particular phantasies of the self and of the other, which can be elaborated in the transference relationship. Body imaginings grow out of the earliest internal bodily experiences, for example, of pain and pleasure, in relation to others and colour the individual's experience of his body-self. The body imagining is therefore the image we have of our bodies in our minds, as Schilder noted, resulting from the idiosyncratic meanings which the body has been endowed with through these earliest exchanges. It is built on projective and introjective mechanisms. Importantly, the body representation is fundamentally a function of libidinal cathexes.

The way we represent our body in our mind is always object-related, even if its original source lies in the body's potential and limitations. Indeed representation always requires the object's involvement, as Green put it:

> The figuration of the object combines with a mode of representation arising from the body's exigencies. The unconscious emerges from this conjunction, and it is the hazards of this encounter that shed light on its failures.
> (Green, 2000: 31)

This theme is elaborated on in a later paper:

> From that first union between the psychic representative emanating from the body and the memory traces of the image of the object, a new entity is created: the object representation. In this new mixture, the subject has worked out all inherent subjectivity, not only because of the projection, but also because of something stemming from the inner sense of the subject's body feeling, to which he or she has given a conceivable and meaningful form.
> (Green, 2004: 120)

The way we experience our body is shaped by the meanings and phantasies of others, hence our body recounts the story of several generations. Our body representation results from the internalization of the (m)others' body imaginings through the unconscious transmission of gestures, posture, mannerisms, rhythms – all of which contain affectively laden representations of self-in-interaction-with-the-other:

> A pre-verbal infant absorbs not the words but the implicit intentions of communication ... This register is conveyed through physical contacts, facial expressions, gesture, vocal tone.
> (Raphael-Leff, in press)

The early physical experiences with primary objects core to the establishment of an appropriately libidinally cathected body-self are stored as procedural memories.

In order to understand how body imaginings can be transmitted intergenerationally we need to take a brief detour into the functioning of memory.

Memory research has delineated two kinds of memory systems: declarative and implicit (Schacter, 1995). Declarative memories can be recalled and verbalized and give us the narrative of our lives. Implicit memories, by contrast, are pre-verbal (typically relating to the first two to three years of life) and therefore cannot be directly accessed and cannot be repressed on account of the slower maturation of the brain structures necessary for explicit memory – in other words, they are descriptively unconscious, not dynamically unconscious (Clyman, 1991).

The implicit memory system includes procedural, emotional and affective memories. This is of central importance to how we represent the body because the earliest sensorimotor experiences, which stimulate emotions and carry affects, are most likely encoded as procedural memories of my-body-with-an-other. They are thus most likely stored in the non-repressed unconscious. These memories – also referred to as 'emotion schemas' (Bucci, 2008) – incorporate representations of other people validating or repudiating the child's body-self. An emotion schema can be activated directly by sensory features in perception or from memory. This is clinically relevant because it suggests that the analyst needs to be attuned to sub-symbolic communication that is embodied (Bucci, 2008), that is, we are talking about somatic and sensory processes that can neither be verbalized nor symbolized and that may operate outside of intentional control or organized thought and may be registered by the analyst through their somatic counter-transference (see below and Chapter 7).

Procedural memories of physical experiences are then rooted in physical experience with an 'other' that will stamp how the baby will experience his body and so view himself. Experiences of feeling merged with the mother's welcoming body or of feeling unheld by her will be accompanied by intense affects that most likely do impact on memory, wish and phantasy (Pine, 2000):

> The tactile sensations that a baby has while being nourished at the breast (especially in the oral and perioral zones in the hands, which are ready to grasp the breast and anything within reach of the palms, such as garments near the breast) become in this way some of the first fragmentary (focalized) experiences formed by the primitive mind.
>
> (Gaddini, 1987: 321)

The importance of early relationships in giving shape and meaning to the bodily given was well grasped by Winnicott, who aptly refers to 'corporization' to denote the fact that we each have a body in which we live and which we have to make our own:

> Equally important with integration is the development of the feeling that one's person is in one's body. Again it is instinctual experience and repeated

quiet experiences of body-care that gradually build up what may be called satisfactory personalization.

(Winnicott, 1945: 139)

Just like her baby, the mother will also have internalized (and stored as a procedural memory) an experience of her body-with-an-other. The mother's experience of her own body will influence how she relates to the baby's physicality. Infants who are classified as anxiously attached frequently have mothers who demonstrate an aversion to close body contact (Ainsworth et al., 1978). Main (1990) underlines that the amount of touching has no observable consequences, but the manner in which the baby is held (e.g. affectionately versus awkwardly) does. She found a significant relationship between the parent's own reported experience of rejection by the mother during childhood and subsequent observed aversion to physical contact with the baby. The immediacy of the physical contact with her baby will most likely activate the mother's own latent, primitive sensations, phantasies, wishes and anxieties that will reflect her own early experience. In other words, what the mother sees as she looks at her baby (and this of course also applies to the father), whether she is able to avail herself to him both physically and mentally, will be shaped by the quality of the relationships felt to reside inside her, not least the quality of the relationship between, and with, her own internal parents.

The baby's experience of his own body is thus mediated by what he experiences as the (m)other's relationship to his body (Laufer, 1981). And what she feels about his body will be mediated by what she feels about her own body. Where the mother (or father) have experienced difficulties in this respect the baby's body may become the receptacle for their own projections. Unresolved trauma may indeed manifest in *body modification by proxy*, as it were, leading to intrusions into the other's body as I illustrate in Chapter 6 through a psychoanalytic reading of Almodóvar's film *The Skin I Live In*.

Given all of the above considerations we can see why reductionist neurological accounts of the body can never capture adequately the schematic operations in which the body acquires a specific organization or style in its relationships with others, that is, within a particular emotional and social context. And yet by rejoining psychoanalysis with neuroscientific perspectives we are helpfully reminded of the importance of both the body schema that leads to habitual dispositions *and* how this always develops in a dynamic relationship to emotional environments. Understanding the body thus requires explanatory accounts that fall short of intentionality and transcend neurophysiology.

So far I have outlined an object relational perspective on the development of the body image that denotes my personal position on this question. However, in order to approach the body we need to sensitively straddle between a one-person, intrapsychic model and an object relational model. Too much emphasis on the latter and we run the risk of eclipsing the importance of the given body. An emphasis on constitutional factors was of course central to both Freud's and Klein's thinking. So-called 'conflict theories' that accord importance to constitutional 'givens' or forces generating conflicts is sometimes contrasted to 'deficit theories' that accord central importance to environmental influences. In my view this is a false dichotomy and my own approach is rooted in a belief that for many patients (and certainly for the ones discussed in this book) both conflicts and deficits need to be taken into account in order to understand psychic structure and what they are able to tolerate within an analytic treatment.

Ferrari (2004), in his penetrating account of the ontogenesis of thought, applies himself to the question of the relative weighting of constitutional factors (i.e. the body) and object relations in shaping the mind. He links the beginning of mental functioning with the first registering of sensory perceptions foregrounding the relationship between the ego and the body over the contemporary focus on the relationship between the ego and external object. He proposes that the earliest ego has to relate from the outset to the sensuous experience of its own body and that the ego thus first relates to the body. Ferrari refers to the body as the 'concrete original object' (COO), suggesting that this is the beginning of the psychic self:

> The COO represents each individual person in its original aspects and not in relation to the world ... it can be described as the original specific nucleus, differentiating since birth each individual person from all other human beings. It is an Object because it is there ... it isn't the result of a development (of a process, for instance, of introjection-projection) but it is the child himself ... the object is concrete because its primary quality is its physicality. Physicality consists of being a man or a woman, and even more, of being that man or that woman with that specific instinctual cathexis and endowment of a bodily apparatus.
>
> (Ferrari, 2004: 48)

At this early developmental stage Ferrari appears to be describing a primitive body that lacks a thinker (Green, 1998). If all proceeds well in development, the COO is 'eclipsed' (rather than replaced) by thought, that is, the individual moves from sensual apprehension of the body to the symbolic awareness of another mind, which coincides with the transition to distance perception facilitated by the visual and auditory senses. Healthy development charts the ascendance of relationships with others over the more immediate relationship with the body, (i.e. a development from what I have referred to elsewhere as from a monadic body to a dyadic body) (Lemma, 2010).

Sensory bodily experience needs to be contained in order for it to be represented in the mind and here Ferrari underlines the importance of the role of the mother. In other words, Ferrari charts the emergence from corporeality – from the 'biological stage' to a 'psychical stage' (Resnik, 2005: 53) of the body (the represented body) – through the process of what some call mentalization (Fonagy et al., 2004). As Green put it:

> We have to distinguish between psychic events, which have to be understood as rooted in the body, thoughts without a thinker, which are very close to this

> primitive psychic activity and thinking, which has to be thought by a thinker and therefore can be communicated to another thinker.
>
> (Green, 1998: 652)

Ferrari's account does not neglect the importance of object relations. He proposes two relational vertices: the 'vertical relation' denotes the relationship between the COO and its representation in the mind, whereas the 'horizontal relation' denotes the relationship between the baby and the mother. Here Ferrari stresses the important maternal function of containing and organizing the baby's earliest sensations.[1]

In many respects Ferrari's ideas find a receptive home in Kleinian territory where corporeity was central to Klein's account of early development through her emphasis on the structuring impact of the relationship to the maternal breast, and to her body more broadly (see Chapter 1). Like Klein he draws attention to constitutional factors, closely linking somatic experience with the first psychic experiences, and hence as the basis for early unconscious phantasies and somatic memories (see also Segal, 1964; Bronstein, 2013). Indeed Bion (1967) too regarded sense data as the starting point for the development of thought and considered that psychic pain is stored in what he called a 'proto-mental' state.

However, it is important to note that Ferrari's conception of the COO is a complex of somatic functions (sensory, metabolic), but it is not an introjected object, that is, he proposes that the COO precedes any kind of introjective processes. Corporeality is thus the 'raw' material for the development of the mind. Although the baby is clearly physically dependent at birth and therefore in relationship, from the outset, with those around him, Ferrari underlines the fact of the baby's biological independence, thereby drawing attention to how we conceptualize the bodily endowment.

Part of the problem one encounters on reading Ferrari is his emphasis on the primacy of the bodily 'given' over the impact of the intersubjective environment coincident with birth. What can be considered primary in this respect remains a matter of debate. It is a moot point indeed as to whether one can ever meaningfully separate the physical 'given' from the responses such a given will invite from the environment, which will, in turn, shape the baby's own experience of this bodily given. Moreover, as Mancia (1994) points out, Ferrari does not concern himself with the impact of defensive processes such as splitting and projective identification, which presumably impact on the relationship with the COO. Ferrari does nevertheless refer to the use that the individual may make of the COO by treating it as a substitute for the external object.

I am not persuaded that we have much to gain clinically if we uphold Ferrari's notion of the COO exactly as he proposes it. Yet I have dwelled on his ideas because his evocative image of the 'eclipse of the body' charts the hazardous journey we all have to make as we move away from the concreteness of our bodily self to a representation of our bodily self in the mind. Lombardi (2002) helpfully draws on Ferrari's work, but manages to strike a clearer balance between the intrapsychic and the interpersonal poles of experience. Driven by a concern with the patient's difficulty in integrating sensory and bodily experience, where the body either imposes itself, as in the *pensée opératoire*[2] (Marty and de M'Uzan, 1963), or where the body is altogether excluded, Lombardi emphasizes the importance of keeping in mind, when interpreting, both the intrapsychic and relational aspects of the transference.

A focus on the body raises important questions about pre-symbolic experience and how this is encoded, as discussed earlier, but also how it is then communicated to others. From a clinical point of view this, in turn, alerts us to the arduous work of helping patients who have deficits in their capacity to mentalize experience. An interesting contribution to this complex area can be found in the work of Fonagy and Target (2007) on the 'embedded mind'. They engagingly link attachment theory, cognitive science and psychoanalysis to suggest that the mind is organized around a series of core representations that arise from early sensorimotor, emotional and environmental experience with the primary object. They propose that language, symbolic thought and defences are built on prototypical pre-verbal, 'embodied' experiences of gestures with the primary object. The capacity for abstraction that develops over time allows us to infuse these basic representations with meaning by drawing metaphorical comparisons between abstractions (e.g. the idea of a mother) and sets of mental images embedded in physical experience with the primary object. They draw on the work of George Lakoff, especially the key idea that thought is rooted in the body (and indeed Freud too argued that thought was 'trial action'), and on the linguistic theory of gestural language proposed by Ivan Fonagy.

Ivan Fonagy suggests that gestural language, which is isomorphic with the bodily gestures characteristic of the earliest form of pre-verbal exchange, is stored in procedural memory and gives shape to an individual's pattern of speech and language. This is a very important and helpful observation because it adds a subtle, but rich dimension to the notion of 'levels of communication': while we communicate through our culture's grammar and lexicon, the derivatives of gestural language, which express themselves as the prosodic elements of speech (such as rhythm or tonality), are like a 'primordial grammar' (Fonagy and Target, 2007) that provides a secondary channel for communication conveying what is non-conscious (in a descriptive sense) and that might only subsequently be dynamically excluded from consciousness for defensive purposes.

Considerations about gestural language and what is implicitly communicated through the body rejoins us again with other disciplines that are relevant to approaching the body both conceptually and clinically. Neuroscientific research in particular has clarified how the infant is equipped with a body schema and with the proprioception, intermodal transducers and mirror neurons, genetically coded for the expressive intersubjective movement that is human interaction. Crucially the body image originates in the intermodal and intersubjective interaction between proprioception and the vision of the other's face.

The intentions of the other person, and the embodied possibilities of the interacting infant, can be directly read in the face and physical actions of the other. This provides another angle on the importance of the quality of the *embodied* experience with the caregiver and, we might add, between patient and analyst. During such non-verbal exchanges, in which both parents and infants express their minds and respond to the other's mind, mainly without awareness and often through the body, the parent's ability to make sense of the infant's *non-verbally expressed internal world* is key to laying the foundations for developing the capacity to mentalize experience. Indeed it has been proposed that Parental Embodied Mentalizing (PEM), which can now be measured, is a key feature of the development of mentalizing (Shai and Fonagy, 2013). PEM refers to the parental capacity to:

> implicitly, and not necessarily consciously, conceive, comprehend, and extrapolate the infant's mental states (such as wishes, desires, or preferences) from the infant's whole body kinaesthetic expressions, namely changes in body movement and posture and (2) adjust their own kinaesthetic patterns accordingly.
> (Shai and Fonagy, 2013)

The notion of embodied mentalizing provides a helpful perspective in relation to the tensions that can be discerned in the literature between one- and two-person psychoanalytic models with respect to the body because it reconciles the *fact* of the body and its individuality and predispositions (i.e. constitutional endowment) and how the experience of being-in-a-body requires the body and mind of an other to encourage the capacity to mentalize one's bodily experience and hence to regulate affective experience. Indeed in Chapter 5 I share some speculations about a deficit in an intersubjective mirroring process in relation to body states that might help us to understand the plight of some transsexual individuals. I also propose that marked and contingent mirroring of the self's bodily experience is most likely, for us all, a vitally important feature of the development of a coherent sense of self firmly rooted in the body.

Focusing on our embedded nature reminds us that our first perceptions and phantasies are sensory in quality and content (Isaacs, 1983; Bronstein, 2013). Our first feelings are connected with experiences such as hot/cold, soft/hard, wet/dry. Rooted in Tustin's (1981) notion of an 'autosensual phase', Ogden (1989) proposes an autistic-contiguous position, which is similarly grounded in an appreciation of a pre-symbolic sensory level of experience. This 'position', that is, a psychic organization, is said to both precede Klein's paranoid-schizoid and depressive positions and yet also to co-exist dialectically with them. Ogden's description of the autistic-contiguous position focuses on the nature of what he terms 'sensation dominated experience', out of which meaning emerges. He suggests that the most rudimentary experience of self grows out of relationships characterized by sensory contiguity, such as stroking, and out of continuity of bodily experience, which protect the baby from the experience of physical and hence psychic disintegration. Contiguity and continuity contribute to the development of a 'bounded sensory surface' on which the baby's experience unfolds.

Finally, it is worth noting the important contribution of Julia Kristeva's ideas to our understanding of pre-symbolic experience. Much of her work has concerned itself with the mind/body dichotomy, showing how bodily energies permeate our signifying practices, and hence how body and mind can never be separated. She outlines an important difference between what she calls the *semiotic* and Lacan's *symbolic*:

> the semiotic [which] consists of drive-related and affective meaning organized according to primary processes whose sensory aspects are often non-verbal (sound and melody, rhythm, colour, odours and so forth), on the one hand, and linguistic signification that is manifested in linguistic signs and their logico-syntactic organization, on the other.
>
> (Kristeva, 1995: 104)

The semiotic (i.e. the study of signs) is thus the pre-verbal way in which bodily energy and affects make their way into language. In other words she suggests that Lacan's imaginary realm, rather than being transcended and hence beyond the ken of analysis, is instead discernible (and needs attending to) thanks to its traces in the semiotic. The semiotic could thus be seen as the modes of expression that originate in the unconscious, whereas the symbolic could be seen as the conscious way a person tries to express himself using a stable sign system (e.g. written or spoken). In this way her framework sidesteps unhelpful dichotomies, arguing instead that the semiotic pole (nature/body/unconscious) always makes itself felt, that is it is discharged into the symbolic realm (culture/mind/consciousness).The pre-symbolic dimension, with its affect-driven modes of signification, is therefore never out of range and remains a constant companion in the process of signification.

Nowadays, as we have seen in this brief and selective review of the literature, analysts, philosophers and neuroscientific researchers regard the body as far more than a neutral shell, allowing for a view of the self that encompasses a far more subtle and complex blend of body and mind. This view is not incompatible with the emphasis on meaning – especially unconscious meaning – that is the hallmark of psychoanalytic approaches. It merely underlines that body and mind are an inseparable unit and it is this view that informs my approach in this book. As Gaddini aptly put it:

> For psychoanalysis the body and mind form a functional continuum, the main element of which is a process of differentiation going from body to mind, but through which psychoanalysis, going by way of the mind can ultimately arrive at the body.
>
> (Gaddini, 1987: 315)

Keeping the two bodies in mind: making use of the analyst's somatic countertransference

The second assumption that informs my work and that flows from the notion of an embodied self concerns the *clinical implication* of Freud's theoretical insights about the importance of the body ego. This is well-captured by Henry Rey, who reminds us that 'in every analysis one has to arrive at the body-self if one wants to achieve deep and enduring change' (1994: 267).

Understanding the patient's experience of the body-self is fundamental to understanding his psychic structure. This is important with all patients but it is even more prescient with patients whose psychopathology is expressed through the body. This focus is well developed in the work of many analysts past and present (e.g. Hoffer, 1949, 1950; Marty and De M'Uzan, 1963; Gaddini, 1987; Lombardi, 2002; Ferrari, 2004; Aisenstein, 2006; Bucci, 2008; Bronstein, 2013).

As analysts we always work on the frontier of the soma and the psyche. Because our experience of the world is inevitably mediated from the unique perspective of our body, to understand the relationship between the body and the mind we have to think on the boundary of the real and of the imagined body, on the boundary of one body and of two or more bodies. Indeed the *analyst's body* acts as a powerful catalyst for the patient's associations and phantasies, not least when the body is altered somehow, for example, through illness or in more mundane ways such as through surface changes in appearance (e.g. a haircut). In Chapter 7, I give consideration to the analyst's body and whether it may be useful to conceptualize it as a feature of the analytic setting. The body behind the couch that is visible to the patient at the start and end of sessions needs to be considered alongside the consciously and unconsciously fantasized body of the analyst outside of the actual consulting room itself. In Chapter 9, for example, I discuss the use made by the patient of the consulting room's toilet and how it may be related to as a place where 'dirty' secrets may be excitedly deposited and where perverse sexual fantasies involving the analyst's body can be fuelled and acted out.

Those patients who have difficulty in establishing and maintaining a stable differentiation from the object typically present with marked difficulties in symbolization and may powerfully project into the analyst's body, as analysts working with psychotic patients and autistic children also often note. The analyst's consequent somatic countertransferential reactions may be understood to result from projective processes that bypass verbal articulation and that are deposited in the body. By *somatic countertransference* I have in mind a plethora of sensory and motoric experiences such as the analyst feeling discomfort in the body, alterations in breathing, feeling tired, sleepy or restless, feeling itchy or nauseous and so on.

Again, in order to understand the underlying mechanisms of somatic countertransference, I have found it helpful to turn to neuroscientific research. Nowadays the motor system is no longer relegated to a merely executive role; rather it is thought to be far more complex, formed by a mosaic of frontal and parietal areas that are closely interconnected with the visual, auditory and tactile areas. One implication of this is that perception appears to be directly immersed in the dynamics of action. Mirror neurons exemplify this as they show how recognition of other people's actions, and even of their intentions, depends in the first instance on our motor resources. To put it simply, the discovery of mirror neurons reveals that thought originates in the body-in-movement.

The work of Vittorio Gallese and colleagues is especially pertinent to our understanding of the somatic countertransference. Gallese (2006) proposes that

> Social cognition is not only 'social metacognition', that is, *explicitly* thinking about the contents of someone else's mind by means of abstract representations. There is also an experiential dimension of interpersonal relationships, which enables a direct grasping of the *sense* of the actions performed by others, and of the emotions, and sensations they experience. This dimension of social cognition is *embodied* in that it mediates between the multimodal experiential knowledge we hold of our lived body and the experience we make of others.
> (Gallese, 2006: 16, italics added)

Gallese has suggested that the mirroring mechanism for action and other mirroring mechanisms in our brain represent instantiations of embodied simulation. Embodied simulation provides a new empirically based notion of intersubjectivity, viewed first and foremost as what he refers to as 'intercorporeity'. Internal non-linguistic representations of the body states associated with actions, emotions, and sensations are evoked in the observer, as if he or she were performing a similar action or experiencing a similar emotion or sensation to the person that is being observed.

By means of an isomorphic format we can map others' actions onto our own motor representations, as well as others' emotions and sensations onto our own visceromotor and somatosensory representations. Our brains, and those of other primates, Gallese suggests, appear to have developed embodied simulation as a basic functional mechanism that gives us a direct insight into other minds, thus enabling our capacity to empathize with others and, we might add, the capacity to mentalize.

If we return to the analytic situation, we recognize as analysts that the patient's 'bodily states of mind' (Wyre, 1997) inevitably impact on, and are impacted on, by our bodily states of mind: the patient communicates through his body and the analyst receives such communications in her body. This cannot, however, be considered to be an identical reflection of what the patient experiences because in the process of being received by the analyst what is projected is also modified by the analyst's own internal world (Arizmendi, 2008).[3]

Nowadays the inevitability of the analyst's own subjectivity is recognized by analysts across many different schools (even if the technical implications of this 'fact' are approached very differently across schools). This subjectivity involves a bodily dimension and is expressed through the analyst's physical presence and the accompanying emotional atmosphere that the analyst's physicality contributes to. It is therefore incumbent on the analyst to be connected to what being-in-a-body means to her. Our embodied nature poses challenges to us all as well as providing a vital register of what transpires between analyst and patient through the somatic countertransference. Analytic work requires that we keep in mind not just the patient's body, but also our own, so as to monitor our body-based 'blind spots'.

Throughout life the body is the arena of a potentially terrifying lack of control. The body is disturbing because it always bears the trace of the other. This fundamental psychic truth must somehow be integrated into our image of ourselves. Facing the reality of the body thus involves a paradox: it means simultaneously taking ownership of the body, including its desires and limitations, and integrating the fact that the body is the site where we meet the other, where we negotiate the meaning of sameness and difference, dependency and separation. The extent to which the body may then be felt to be a hospitable or inhospitable home for the self will reflect the quality of the earliest identifications in both analyst and patient.

When we consider pre-symbolic forms of communication that bypass verbal articulation we are immediately alerted to the fact that in the clinical situation the scope for enactments is always wide since we are here in the realm of pre-symbolic functioning in the patient *and* potentially also in the analyst, whose capacity for symbolic elaboration of their own bodily experience may be temporarily disrupted. Such bodily experiences need to become 'thoughts with a thinker', to play on Bion's (1967) turn of phrase, and eventually shared with the patient in order to support the development of a capacity to symbolize.

However, with these patients the analyst's 'sensory acceptance' (Lombardi and Pola, 2010) of the patient's projections may be an essential prerequisite before interpretations can be helpful. This way of working requires that the analyst contains the patient's 'proto-emotions' (Ferro, 2003), that is, the analyst needs to focus on the patient's sensoriality before analysis can proceed along more standard lines and the sensoriality can then can be transformed into thoughts. This requires that what is projected into the body of the analyst is represented first in the mind of the analyst, where it may need to be contained for some time before it can be presented to the patient.

The body in the consulting room: face-to-face and on the couch

My third assumption is that seeing and being seen are central dynamics in early life that shape the development of the self and specifically of the self's experience of embodiment. These dynamics are played out in modified form in the transference and need to be worked through in the analytic relationship such that we always need to consider *the reciprocal observation in the consulting room,* that is, the way in which both analyst and patient function as visual objects for the other.

In normal development we recognize that in order for us to see ourselves we must be seen. From the moment of birth we see our own possibilities in the faces of others (Gallagher, 2005): what we don't see shapes our internal experience as much as what we do see. The self as visual object for the other is a challenge we are thus all faced with.

Sartre (1943) captured very well the interpersonal tension we all have to manage in his discussion of 'the look'. He described two different kinds of looking: there is the me-who-looks (the voyeur), but this me-who-looks gives way to the me-who-is-on-view (the spectacle). The tables turn round – always. The realization that the world assumes its coherence in relation to the other's perspective is deeply threatening, not least because this other perspective is inaccessible to us in so far as we cannot control in any absolute way the other's thoughts, feelings or perceptions. Being cognizant of our own specularity leads to the discovery that our foundations lie outside of ourself or, as Sartre put it, that we 'exist for the other'. This 'existing for the other' implies a state of dependency that is experienced first and foremost in the body.

Lacan's field of vision adds to this by introducing the central role of desire.[4] He proposes that the other's gaze, through which the voyeur becomes the spectacle for the other, strips him of his sense of illusory mastery. Lacan helpfully points out that at the core of human being is an exhibitionistic impulse: in order for us to see ourselves we must be seen. He compares this visual mediation to photography:

> in the scopic field, the gaze is outside, I am looked at, that is to say, I am a picture ... what determines me, at the most profound level, in the visible, is the gaze that is outside. It is though the gaze that I enter life and it is from the gaze that I receive its effects ... the gaze is the instrument through which light is embodied and through which ... I am *photographed*.
>
> (Lacan, 1977: 106)

The problem with being a photograph for the other is that it can feel as if we become a still, imprisoned in someone else's moment over which we have no control. No matter how we present ourselves, we cannot ultimately control what the other sees. This is so because the other's perception of us is embedded in a shifting matrix of their own unconscious feelings, memories and phantasies, and it is filtered through projective mechanisms that either make us libidinally resonant, 'bad' or invisible to the other.

Both Sartre and Lacan are approaching 'looking' from very different conceptual frameworks but their ideas converge over the way that one's body for the other is also a potential site for alienation. This understanding has clinical implications for the use of the couch or the chair with patients whose psychic pain is primarily expressed through the body and who, in my view, require particular consideration of the experience of the visual relationship between patient and analyst.

The widening scope of the pathologies now worked with by analysts challenges us to continually think about how we work and to consider whether changes to the analytic setting are enactments or necessary adaptations that will enable some very disturbed patients to manage an analysis. I am only concerned here with the use of the couch.

I can think of several patients who experienced the couch as intolerable and others who took to it easily but not for the 'right' reasons. For some the couch was resisted because it deprived them of visual contact with me that was felt to be important; others preferred it *because* it protected them from my gaze that was felt to be threatening.

Freud's original justification for using the couch was informed as much by his belief that suppressing motoric action enhanced reflection as his personal discomfort at being stared at for long stretches of time:

> Before I wind up these remarks on beginning analytic treatment, I must say a word about a certain ceremonial which concerns the position in which the treatment is carried out. I hold to the plan of getting the patient to lie on a sofa while I sit behind him out of his sight. This arrangement has a historical basis; it is the remnant of the hypnotic method out of which psycho-analysis was evolved. But it deserves to be maintained for many reasons. The first is a personal motive, but one which others may share with me. I cannot put up with being stared at by other people for eight hours a day (or more).
>
> (Freud, 1913: 133–134)

I am not presenting a case 'for' or 'against' the couch: this is not the issue. I am of the view that for most patients the use of the couch is a very important part of the analytic process and facilitates it. It is nevertheless important to engage in thinking about why we use the couch and whether it is *always* helpful to our patients. It is worth asking ourselves whether the use of the couch fits in better with who we are and how we function optimally as analysts and how we think the patient will best be helped, or whether sometimes *we* need to 'hide' behind it.

Research in this domain is relatively sparse and unlikely to settle the question in either direction. No empirical study has investigated the effect of the couch on the psychoanalytic process or outcome. Lingiardi and De Bei (2011) question the utility of the couch in terms of therapeutic action, bolstered by recent contributions from affective neuroscience, infant research and other psychotherapy research. Schacter and Kächele (2010) observe that there is no empirical foundation for putting all analytic patients on the couch or to suggest that the couch encourages greater free-association.

Moreover, many analysts now recognize that non-verbal experiences and phantasies may be initially available only through motor-based enactments (Celenza, 2005). These manifestations of the unconscious mind may be facilitated when sitting face-to-face and the patient can see the analyst's face and reacts to it as well as being more accessible to the analyst's own field vision, allowing her to discern more readily those conflicts, for example, that are enacted in changes in posture or gaze (Goldberger, 1995). Indeed, as Celenza notes:

> because lying down is also facing away, there are two variables to consider (from the analyst's perspective) in comparing the couch and the chair: one is the experience and meaning of the placement of the body, i.e. lying down or sitting up; and the other is the experience and meaning of having visual access to the analyst's face.
>
> (Celenza, 2005: 1648)

Notwithstanding the absence of empirical evidence in this domain we nevertheless all probably recognize from our daily practice that when the patient uses the couch we feel freer to restrain from responding to the patient from moment to moment and we are better able to maintain free-floating attentiveness (Ross, 1999). The use of the couch thus acts as a kind of corrective against enactments that are more likely to occur when we are face-to-face and feel under pressure to respond rather than to reflect and engage with our reveries, which can provide rich insights into what is transpiring unconsciously between analyst and patient. It is also the case that from the patient's point of view not having access to the analyst's facial expressions provides fewer clues to the analyst's feeling state and thereby encourages the elaboration of unconscious phantasy.

However, I want to suggest that, with some patients, the analyst, to avoid the impact of the patient's gaze that is felt to be too disturbing or somehow intrusive, may use the couch defensively. I suspect that Freud did not relish being stared at all day because sustained visual relating exposes the analyst to a host of experiences that are all the more viscerally powerful when the analyst and patient are face-to-face.

My work with some of the patients described in this book was carried out face-to-face, and as such represents a departure from a more standard analytic setting. Whilst face-to-face work imposes a range of restrictions and demands on both patient and analyst, it may also nevertheless afford important insights because it engages us in considering the reciprocal visual impact of patient and analyst on one another (e.g. Wright, 1991; Steiner, 2004, 2011; Peringer, 2006) in a sustained manner and not only at the beginning and end of sessions.

As analysts we may be seduced by the containing function of words. Yet, for some patients, the visual relationship matters more – at least until some inroads have been made in understanding their use of the body and their experience of the gazing relationship. In my experience, for some of these patients, the use of the couch is unhelpful (at least to begin with), not because it provokes a malignant regression (though it may do that too), but primarily because it bypasses the visual field and the conflicts that are encapsulated through the meeting of the two gazes. The invitation to lie on the couch may indeed be welcomed by some of these patients because they want to avert the mutual gaze of analyst and patient, out of fear of what it might do to them (for example, they may feel shamed as the therapist looks at them), or out of fear of what their gaze might expose to the therapist about their hatred. Conversely, some patients seek out the visual relationship to intimidate or humiliate the analyst. But here, too, I have wondered whether the use of the couch is primarily protective for the analyst rather than necessarily helpful for this kind of patient.

In my work with both transsexual individuals and those who modify their bodies extensively through cosmetic surgery (see Chapter 1), piercings and tattoos (see Lemma, 2010), I have been repeatedly struck by the impact of their visual presentation on me. In the work I describe with Ms C. in Chapter 5 – a male-to-female transsexual – I was aware, for example, of how her detailed descriptions of sex reassignment surgery (SRS) affected me as I processed them in my mind *whilst she looked at me*. Not infrequently as Ms C. inched closer to the day of her sex reassignment surgery, I felt as if I was being forcefully made to look, there and then, at a body part that needed to be edited out as if she really needed me to conjure up this disturbing image in my mind, to really 'look' at it, whilst I was still looking at her, so that she could quite literally look at my face. I thought she needed to see not only that I could understand how trapped she felt in her male body but also to help her to see that what she was doing was indeed deeply disturbing, as reflected no doubt in my own facial responses. In other words, whilst mirroring of her subjective experience was important, it was also vital that she could see literally and metaphorically that I also had my own perspective on this and that it was different to hers – a perspective that eventually, albeit only after the SRS, helped her to connect with the loss that ravaged her life.

Lastly, I have been interested not only in the visual relationship between patient and analyst but also in the *olfactory relationship* between them. We all carry within us a deep-seated sense that what emanates from our body reveals not only our physical interior but also our psychic interior. The perverse use of the analyst's toilet by the patient I describe in Chapter 9 is contrasted in that same chapter with the case of Ms C., whose anxieties about the destructiveness of her aggression at first led to a phobic avoidance of my toilet and then evolved towards the use of the toilet as the container for the felt-to-be-bad and unacceptable parts of herself, protecting the relationship with me when I could not yet be trusted to receive and survive her 'smelly' projections. In these cases the toilet becomes quite concretely the location of the 'toilet breast' (Meltzer, 1967b) so as to preserve a more idealized relationship with the analyst. Underpinning this patient's difficulties was a deficit at the level of the olfactory container. My work with her helped me to understand the developmental necessity early on for the baby to feel that the object is prepared to enter, without intrusion, the intimate physical space between them, and is able to breathe and smell the baby and so receive its bodily projections and transform them into alpha elements.

Work with all the individuals I describe in this book, and to whom I am indebted for all that they have helped me to understand about the mind, analytic work and myself, required a particular attunement to the body-self and to the bodily countertransference. The aim of the work, to borrow Lombardi's apt turn of phrase, is to construct 'a language to enable corporeity to speak' (Lombardi, 2002: 370).

The maternal body

My fourth and final assumption, which is elaborated in detail in several chapters and hence I only want to mention it very briefly here, is that in order to understand the patient's experience of the body-self we need to understand the primordial relationship we all have with the maternal body. This relationship may be one primarily characterized by envy (see Chapter 1) or by the dread of falling back into the mother's body (see Chapter 2). Being trapped inside the maternal body may be dreaded because it is engulfing, but it may also be sought after through violent projective identification because 'inside' the individual is spared the narcissistic injury associated with being 'outside' and separate.

Separation from the maternal body always entails a degree of trauma and hence how this separation is experienced leaves emotional residues in us all. Analytic work with the patients discussed here has helped me to appreciate that the patient's deficits and conflicts often relate to the vicissitudes of separation from the mother's body that may manifest in a variety of ways, for example, as dermatological conditions (see Chapter 2) or somatization disorders (see Chapter 9) or in the patient's relationship to the analyst's hair and to her own hair, for example (see Chapters 7 and 8 respectively for an exploration of the meaning and use made of hair in the analytic relationship).

Indeed a recurrent theme throughout many of the chapters in this book is the way several of the patients described appeared to have deficits in relation to the development of a solid sense of their body as a boundaried physical space and the painful difficulty of living in their own skin (see Chapter 2 in particular but also Chapters 4, 5 and 9). Instead they sought to recreate a state of fusion with the maternal body that was then subjected to perverse and or violent assaults in their own mind.

Concluding thoughts

The individual body does not exist in a vacuum: it develops and reacts to external forces as well as the internal ones that are the primary focus of this book. However, one final personal stance comes into play here: as an analyst I have found it not only stimulating but also integral to my relationship to psychoanalysis to extend its application beyond the consulting room.

Over the past 13 years I have consulted to television production companies involved in making reality TV shows. This has typically involved screening participants to ensure they are psychologically 'fit' to take part. During this time I have developed a particular interest in 'makeover' shows that provided me with invaluable insights into the way individual dynamics interact with social processes in relation specifically to the body. Beyond this it also stimulated thoughts about the quality of the gaze itself that is promoted by such programmes, that is how we, the viewers, are invited to look at the participants in these shows. My personal reflections on what I refer to as the 'ethics of the gaze' and its corruption form the concluding chapter to the book illustrating, I hope, the relevance and reach of psychoanalytic ideas beyond the confines of our consulting room.

Notes

1   He speaks of the unity of self and body as a 'onefold dimension' (i.e. the baby/child perceives himself as a concrete object – he has to face what arises from his body) and the relationship with objects and their mental representations as the 'twofold dimension'. Whatever else one might think about Ferrari's hypothesis concerning the COO, the onefold/twofold dimensions provide a helpful way of keeping in mind the self's relationship with the body and the inextricable synchronism of the vertical and horizontal dimensions without privileging one over the other. It also alerts us to how regression to a onefold, sensory dimension can be used defensively, as we can observe in primarily somatic clinical presentations. The onefold dimension allows us to think about the

'sedimentation' (Ferrari, 2004) of an experience that originates in the body (e.g. due to birth complications) rather than through the introjection of an external object.

2   This is characterized by a strong cathexis of the physical senses, eclipsing the representation of experience.

3   The highly complex relationship between unconscious motor, affective, memory and phantasy processes is beyond the scope of this introduction.

4   For Lacan, however, desire is a linguistic process, detached from any taint of bodily excitation. Indeed, Lacan's notion of lack is a recent avatar of the metaphysical tradition that set up a dualism of body/mind and of nature/culture. In this respect I find Julia Kristeva's views more attuned to the importance of the body. She helpfully elaborates Lacan's views of the subject as an effect of its linguistic practice, retaining what I consider to be an essential connection with the body, through her emphasis on the pre-symbolic dimension of experience, namely the 'semiotic chora'. She is referring here to the space in which meaning is semiotic, that is, below the surface of the speaking being (e.g. bodily energies, rhythm). She therefore distinguishes between:

> the semiotic, which consists of drive-related and affective meanings organised according to primary processes whose sensory aspects are often non-verbal ... and linguistic signification that is manifested in linguistic signs. (Kristeva, 1995: 104)

Chapter 1

Envy and the maternal body
The psychodynamics of cosmetic surgery

Across all ages and cultures we can find examples of body modification. The first recorded plastic surgery technique was performed as early as 1000 BC, in India, to replace noses that had been amputated as a form of punishment or had literally been bitten off adulterous Hindu wives by their enraged husbands (Favazza, 1996). The Italian surgeon Gaspare Tagliacozzi is often credited as the father of modern plastic surgery. During the sixteenth century, inspired by the need for plastic reconstructive surgery due to frequent duels and street brawls, Tagliacozzi pioneered the Italian method of nasal reconstruction (Gilman, 1999). The origins of cosmetic surgery are therefore to be found in the 'covering up' or repair of violent interactions – a dynamic that I will be suggesting is central for understanding *some* individuals who seek cosmetic surgery. I wish to emphasize 'some' because we must beware generalizations: there are no single psychodynamics that can account for the decision to pursue cosmetic surgery in all cases.

In this chapter I will firstly consider cosmetic surgery broadly, but I will focus the clinical example on a patient who sought breast augmentation specifically, because it is not only the most common surgery, but also because it illustrates very clearly some of the dynamics around envy and grievance that, I am suggesting, fuel the pursuit of surgery in some patients, especially those seeking breast augmentation.

My approach here is psychoanalytic and focuses on intrapsychic variables but, of course, the subjective experience of one's body develops in a given family, in a given culture, and at a particular point in time, that is, the individual body is always also a social body and, importantly, it is a *gendered* body. The experience of being in a female body will differ from the experience of being in a male body, and this, in turn, will be coloured not only by internal world dynamics, but also by the prevailing cultural projections into the respective female or male body. This is a vitally important dimension of an individual's experience of being-in-a-body, and one that has been eloquently articulated by many authors (see, for example, Cixous, 1976; Grosz, 1990; Frosh, 1994; Orbach, 2009). It is indeed impossible to think about the body outside of the cultural, social and political discourses that frame all of our lives, and that exert more or less pressure on us, in particular on our pursuit of a desirable appearance. But in this chapter I am primarily concerned with the internalized object relationships that drive the pursuit of cosmetic surgery in some patients and consequently I will not be addressing the contribution of sociocultural factors.[1]

A cross-cultural overview makes it clear nevertheless that a variety of body modification practices have now entered the mainstream in both Western and non-Western cultures: not only cosmetic surgery and procedures, but also tattooing, piercing and scarification (Pitts-Taylor, 2003, 2007; Lemma, 2010). Their widespread use, at the very least, suggests a degree of caution in assuming pathology too readily in those individuals who avail themselves of such practices. After all, we all modify our bodies if only through clothes, make up, hair dye, orthodontics or contact lenses. Body modification per se is thus not the province of a group of people who are very different to the rest of 'us'. But body modification can acquire a more compelling quality and its pursuit may then function as a way of holding the self together.

Cosmetic surgery today: some facts and research findings

As analysts we should be concerned by the staggering increase in people availing themselves of cosmetic procedures. All over the world (i.e. not just in Western cultures) cosmetic surgeons now yield their scalpels to reveal so-called 'new' bodies. The trend to relate to the body as a 'project' (Giddens, 1991) has fuelled the global beauty business that is growing rapidly and continues to thrive even in times of economic recession. In 2012 board certified doctors in the United States performed over ten million cosmetic surgical and nonsurgical procedures.[2] Such procedures increased more than 3 per cent in 2012. Surgery accounted for 17 per cent of all procedures performed, representing 61 per cent of total patient expenditures. In the UK a total of 43,172 surgical procedures were carried out in 2012 according to the British Association of Aesthetic Plastic Surgeons (BAAPS), an increase of 0.2 per cent on the previous year.[3] In both countries the most frequently performed surgical procedure was breast augmentation, followed by liposuction, abdominoplasty, eyelid surgery and rhinoplasty. Recent market research suggests that the proportion of young people in particular who would consider having cosmetic surgery has risen sharply, reporting that young people are now less accepting of bodily 'faults' and that 35 per cent of young women would have breast implants if they could afford to do so (Mintel, 2010).

On the whole the research literature in this area is somewhat ambiguous. Most interview-based studies report evidence of psychopathology in patients undergoing cosmetic surgery, though this is not reliably the case when using standardized psychometric measures (Sarwer et al., 1998). Studies looking at the prevalence rate of mental health problems in those requesting surgery nevertheless suggest a higher percentage (19%) than that found in other surgery patients (4%) (Sarwer et al., 2004). The rate of patients with Body Dysmorphic Disorder (BDD), which one might expect to be high in this population, has been reported as varying between 9 and 53 per cent – this variability most likely resulting from the use of different measures (Ercolani et al., 1999; Phillips et al., 2000; Aouizerate et al., 2003). What is clear, however, is that there is a greater representation of patients with BDD amongst cosmetic surgery patients than in the general population, where the rate of BDD is 1–2 per cent. Requests for unusual facial cosmetic changes, for example, involving bone contouring, bone grafting or cheek and chin implants (when the face is felt to be too wide or too thin), are typically associated with a significant impairment in psychological functioning (Edgerton et al., 1990). Significantly, and in keeping with what we would predict psychoanalytically, relationship difficulties are associated with the contemplation of, and the decision to pursue, cosmetic surgery. Swami and Mammadova (2012) identified in their study that those women in more unhappy relationships were more likely to consider it.

The maternal landscape

Psychological research findings are relevant in so far as they confirm from a more systematic perspective based on large samples that the pursuit of cosmetic surgery cannot be reduced to a primarily sociocultural phenomenon but speaks instead of relational difficulties. As such it calls forth a fine-tuned understanding of internalized object relationships and how these impact on the individual's capacity to relate to others. More specifically it requires an understanding of the baby's relationship to the first body he interacts with – that of the mother.

Our sense of who we are is founded on the loss of the mother. A fundamental component of 'who I am' is inevitably 'a person whose mother is gone' since at birth the self is exposed to its first loss – the loss of residence inside the mother's body. The fact of separateness, and loss, is an important dimension of subjectivity, and it is intimately linked to the experience of envy: when dependency and loss cannot be borne envy can dominate the psychic landscape. In some of the individuals who turn to the modification of the body for a solution to psychic pain, we can observe how this serves the function of bypassing the experience of being given to, of being dependent in any way on the other.

I have come to understand that the more compulsive and extreme forms of body modification reflect a difficulty in integrating this most basic fact of life: we cannot give birth to ourselves. This 'truth' is felt nowhere more acutely than in our bodies. The body is testament to our interrelatedness. The shared corporeality of the mother and baby, from which we all have to emerge, is the embodied version of psychic dependency. The emergence out of this shared physical space is never absolute, however, because the body is indelibly inscribed with the imprint of the (m)other. When the fact of our dependency on others cannot be integrated into our sense of who we are, the subjective experience of the body is compromised.

Both mother and baby have to manage their way through the anxieties generated by dependence and separation. This is difficult enough when all is progressing relatively smoothly in the mother–baby dyad, but when there are complications in this relationship, psychic processes may be perverted. Instead of an experience of dependent receptivity to the object, there may be envy of, and triumph over, the object.

Placing envy at the epicentre of our emotional life, Klein's understanding of the baby's early experience also placed the maternal body centre stage as the first site of the baby's most intense psychical activity. Several of her papers underline the baby's primordial relationship to the maternal body. The baby then appears to structure a world of meaning around it, especially through experiences of gratification and frustration, not only at the breast, but through the sensory exchanges that characterize the earliest exchanges. The experiences of the mother's body and of the baby's own body are, in Klein's view, thus inextricably linked.

Klein proposed that the mother's body houses her gratifying possessions, signified by the internal contents of faeces, babies and an incorporated penis. She suggested that the most primitive prototype of envy is envy of the physical possibilities of the other's body felt to be denied to the self: envy of the breast's ability to nourish is followed by envy of the maternal capacity to derive sexual pleasure from the father's penis and the ability to procreate.

The baby's relationship to the mother's body could therefore be said to be acquisitive. This is intensified by the epistemophilic instinct – the baby's urge to discover and conquer the internal territory of the mother's body. The early Kleinian baby is thus presented as driven by its bodily needs and oral impulses to obtain from the mother the sustenance and prized goods that she, the mother, is seen to possess, quite concretely, in her body.

Although both boys and girls envy and covet the mother's body, and its possessions, there is an experiential difference between the sexes: the girl can take comfort in her knowledge that, one day, she will attain the mother's female attributes, but the boy has to accept that his wish to procreate like his mother is doomed to fail. The girl's narcissistic mortification appears, at first glance, to be less harsh than the boy's, and yet both boys and girls are faced with the physical impossibility of giving life. In this sense they both have to bear their relative impotence, and must share the realization that they cannot give birth to themselves. The body is 'given' to the child. We will return to this point shortly.

One way to manage the painful gap between self and other is through identification – a process that has been invariably disturbed in the patients I am describing. In his paper, *On Narcissism*, Freud (1914) reminded us that: 'What man projects before him as his ideal is the substitute for the lost narcissism of his childhood' (Freud, 1914: 94). The vicissitudes of identification are such that the fate of the idealized other can be uncertain depending on the self's capacity to grant the other its separateness and autonomy. A healthy identification is inspired, as it were, by the perceived ideal form of the other, but it is not equated with it. Rather it involves 'forming an imaginary alignment' (Silverman, 1996: 71) in our minds, acknowledging its source (the object of identification), and then making it our own. For example, a young woman with profound anxiety about her appearance came for her session with me one day dressed in exactly the same dress I had worn the previous week. Some years later, when the therapy ended and she had made considerable progress, she reflected on this phase of the therapy and observed: 'Now I would never do that and yet I feel that I do dress a bit like you.' It was her capacity to draw a clear distinction between 'a bit like you' and her early projection of herself into my body such that she had to 'be me', that evidenced the change that had taken place.

This brings us to the important question of identification – a process that has been invariably disturbed in the patients I am describing. The problem is well illustrated in the ever-popular TV 'makeover' shows. Here, we can observe how these shows support the aim *to become the ideal*, and not simply to strive to *be like it*, as we would expect if a more ordinary identificatory process were at work. The unconscious psychological mechanism deployed by this programme format is what Resnik (2005) refers to as 'physical transvestism': the self acquires another person's bodily shape and character, dressing in someone else's clothing, imitating their gestures and looks (as in the shows that invite participants to select their surgery according to the look of a particular 'star'). Imitative identifications of this kind may conceal deep feelings of envy because they are an appropriation of the other through imitation. As Gaddini (1969) observed, imitation precedes identification and takes place primarily through vision. Such imitations are phantasies of being or becoming the object through modification of one's own body. But there is an important difference between the object one would like to be and the object one would like to possess. The latter, according to Gaddini, bears the hallmark of envy.

Those who yearn to be the ideal apprehend the futility of their efforts through the dystopia of the fragmented body, not infrequent in the dreams of body dysmorphic patients, for example, attesting to their struggle to integrate the body into their image of themselves. Dream images of distorted, attacked, cut up bodies lay bare the envy that is felt towards those whose imagined bodily integrity and beauty is but a sore reminder of their felt insufficiency. Analysis reveals how these attacks are unconsciously aimed at a bountiful, but unyielding maternal body and what it stands for in the unconscious. For these patients the object is perceived to possess the wholeness or unity of which the self feels deprived. This has been a striking feature in my work with several women who underwent cosmetic surgery and who, through the surgery, appropriated something 'better' (e.g. the bigger breasts) that did not belong to the self, and that the internal (m)other was felt to possess and to withhold.

In normal development, the mother's capacity to enjoy the baby's body allows him, in turn, to enjoy it as separate from hers. For his part, the baby has to 'accept' that his mother – who originally gave her body to him (what Guignard, 2008, refers to as the 'maternal mother') – is capable of making him feel loved and admired, but she cannot *always* make him feel this way since she is separate and has her own sexual partner. The child has now to contend with the 'sexual mother' (Guignard, 2008), a reality that imposes painful distance between the self and the maternal object.

The maternal 'sexual' body arouses envy because it is perceived to be the object of desire and, as such, it can both 'stand as the cause of desire', as Lacan put it, that is, it exposes the self to its need for the object, as well as to its inability to exclusively satisfy the object's desire – an impossibility for the child. We are then faced with a central paradox: we cannot fulfil the mother's desire, yet we bear the imprint of her desire (or lack of) on our body.

This predicament is particularly difficult to manage internally where there has been an actual undercathexis of the bodily self by the mother. In these cases it is possible to discern envy of the maternal body – envy that is more or less virulently destructive in any given individual depending on their particular developmental trajectories. Whatever the cause of the mother's lack of interest or rejection, or even in some cases the active projection into the baby's body, the self may experience this as a refusal to give what is needed in order to feel desirable. The maternal object is felt to indulge in the withheld goods and the self may hold a grudge against the felt-to-be depriving object. In some individuals this state of deprivation fuels the omnipotent phantasy of 'becoming mother' that is enacted through the pursuit of cosmetic surgery.

Of course, it is neither helpful nor possible to generalize about the meaning and functions of any kind of body modification because the motivations underpinning the decision to modify the body are complex and diverse: superficially similar methods of body modification may have diverse ends. But one thing binds them together: given that the body develops within and through our early relationships with other people – most notably with key attachment figures – its modification invariably expresses something about the quality of internalized relationships, and impacts on both internal and external relationships.

Understanding the dominant unconscious phantasy underpinning the pursuit of cosmetic surgery and/or procedures is central to helping these patients. I will now describe three unconscious phantasies – there are probably others – that I have observed in the patients I have seen. I am suggesting that these phantasies may be felt to be necessary to the psychic equilibrium of individuals for whom the modification of the body has acquired a more compelling quality, namely the *self-made* phantasy, the *reclaiming* phantasy and the *perfect match* phantasy. These phantasies are not mutually exclusive: at any given point in time in an individual's experience the function of cosmetic surgery, for example, may shift and will be underpinned by different phantasies.

The self-made phantasy

'I like my beauty hardcore,' writes one individual,

> I want to see results, not just hope for them ... I have had fat syringes of Restylane slowly released into the tender flesh around my mouth. I have had my breasts augmented and my brows transplanted ... I have cried with pain in taxis on the way home from so-called 'lunch hour treatments'.
> (Avril Mair in the March 2009 issue of *Elle* (UK edn), p. 309)

She also adds that for her this is 'not an exercise in self-hatred'. Rather, she views it as a manifestation of the fact that she 'loves beauty'. Like Mair, many cosmetic surgery patients would see this as being their justification for altering the given body. But what does 'loving beauty' mean? I cannot presume to know what it means for this particular person, but I have a clearer sense about what 'loving beauty' has meant to some of my patients for whom the pursuit of beauty was a 'psychic retreat' (Steiner, 1993), that is, a place of 'relative peace' (ibid: 1) in the mind that allowed them to avoid reality.

For some of the patients I have in mind 'loving beauty', and hence its pursuit through cosmetic procedures/surgery, was a way of enacting the omnipotent phantasy of giving birth to the self by redesigning the body, thereby circumventing the (m)other, and hence any experience of dependency on the 'object of desire'[4] (Britton, 1998). The use made of the body by these patients bears witness to the need to remould the body according to one's own specifications without interference from the (m)other: it is an enactment of what I call the *self-made phantasy*.

The attempts to circumvent the (m)other are often supported by a state of mind in which the body becomes obsolete, the self is omnipotent and the (m)other is triumphed over.[5] The outcome of the modified bodily self makes it unclear 'who' the person is, and at a more concrete level, who s/he looks like. This brings to mind what Jean Baudrillard (1988) has called 'copies without originals': an ideal image of the self that is aspired to, and that cosmetic surgery in particular promises to deliver, but this image itself cannot be referenced back to an 'original', that is, I am suggesting, to the individual's given body by the (m)other.

The implicit attack on the object that I am proposing may provide a way of understanding the results of four large epidemiological studies, carried out in America and Europe, which have found a relationship between breast implants and suicide. Across these studies the suicide rate was two to three times greater amongst patients with breast implants compared to patients who underwent other cosmetic procedures (Sarwer, 2006). It is unclear as to what accounts for this finding. There has been a suggestion that the post-operative complications, which are not uncommon following breast augmentation, lead to depression and then suicide. It might also be the case that patients who seek breast augmentations have more unrealistic expectations and/or that they have greater pre-existing psychological problems. This view is supported by a study that found an increased prevalence of pre-operative psychiatric hospitalization in women who had sought breast implants relative to women who had undergone other kinds of cosmetic surgery (Jacobsen et al., 2004). I would like to suggest that in these patients the concreteness of the appropriation of the maternal breast fuels more acute paranoid anxieties of vengeance and retaliation, which may provide yet another explanation for the increased risk of suicide in some of these patients. In other words, the self-made phantasy distinguishes itself from the other phantasies I will be discussing due to the underlying envious attack on the phantasized maternal body/object that is its hallmark.

Of course, circumventing the reality of one's origins inevitably also entails a denial of the reality of the parental couple – not only of the reality of the shared corporeality of mother and baby. The attack on the parental couple is implicit in the self-made phantasy. In many of these cases it is indeed possible to discern the absence of what Birksted-Breen (1996) refers to as the 'penis-as-link', that is, the absence of the linking and structuring role of the knowledge that mother and father are linked and form a creative couple. Acceptance of this reality allows the individual to come to terms with both the fact of difference and of complementarity, and hence to accept his own insufficiency as well as his need for the other. The solution to this psychic dilemma is found in the enactment, through the manipulation of the body, of a phantasy that reassures the self of its omnipotence and self-sufficiency. This psychic position might well be termed 'phallic' in the sense that being the phallus represents a psychic state of complete self-sufficiency, and hence is an attack on otherness, and functions as a defence against dependency.[6]

The reclaiming phantasy

It is through the body that we experience most concretely the tensions that will arise in any kind of intimacy: between the desire to fuse with the other and the fear of being taken over by the other. In some individuals this may arouse profound claustrophobic anxieties that cannot be reflected upon, and the modification of the body may be understood as an attempt to manage this kind of anxiety.

Rey (1994) described a primitive universal position of claustrophobia and agoraphobia, which he rooted in the body:

> One of the various manifestations of the body self is its relationship with claustrophobia and agoraphobia. Claustrophobic space is the result of projective identification of the body and its inner space into the outside world ... It is therefore the child inside the mother's body who becomes claustrophobic inside the inner space of his mother projected into the outside world.
> (Rey, 1994: 267)

Glasser (1979) identified an internal scenario – the core complex – characterized by the wish to fuse with the object, but this fusion is felt to present a danger of total engulfment, and hence has to be violently resisted. This kind of tension is present in some of the patients for whom the modification of the body then provides the means through which they can reassure themselves that they are indeed separate from the other. It defends against the wish to fuse with the other, which would otherwise expose them to the terror of undifferentiation. I would like to suggest that for some individuals the removal or remodelling of a body part thus serves the function of reclaiming or rescuing the self from an alien presence felt to now reside within the body, that is, the modification of the body is driven by what I am calling the *reclaiming phantasy*.

The body may also be experienced as a container of the other's hostile projections, and consequently it may feel like an occupied territory. If this is the case the body may then have to be visibly modified – physically 'marked' as separate in some way – in order to create an experience of ownership of the body, and hence of the self, and so reclaim it from the perceived invasion. In other cases a body part(s) felt to be 'ugly' may literally need to be cut off or remodelled in some way so as to kill off the hated object that has become concretely identified with the felt-to-be ugly body part(s).

The reclaiming phantasy thus concerns the *expulsion* from the body of an object felt to be alien or polluting. The patient's subjective experience is of feeling possessed by the object, concretely felt to reside in the body, from which the self must free itself. The violence that underlines this phantasy is directed at expelling the object, but it is not aimed at triumphing over the object – a quality that is more characteristic of the self-made phantasy.

The perfect match phantasy

The early physical exchanges between mother and baby are vitally important for the establishment of attachment, but they are also central to shaping our experience of ourselves as desirable. This experience is, first and foremost, a bodily experience. For the rest of our lives, our bodies mediate desire. The experience of being-in-a-body, in turn, is profoundly shaped by the desires (or lack of) that are projected into it by others (Schilder, 1950; Lacan, 1977; Krueger, 1989, 2002; Grosz, 1990). In this respect the importance of the early gazing relationship, and of the skin-to-skin contact, between mother and baby cannot be emphasized enough. Touch and vision are inseparable, a single axis underpinning the earliest physical and psychical experiences. At their best, looking and touching can confer the gift of love. But when these are absent, or in short supply, or when looking and touching are laced with hatred, possessiveness or envy, then the body-self may feel neglected, shamed or intruded upon. In these cases the body that is felt to be the cause of the internal unease or turmoil becomes the canvas on which the psychic distress is externalized and worked on.

Desire lies at the heart of the earliest relationship between mother[7] and baby. In order to approach the experiential realm of being-in-a-body it is essential to think about desire. In order to feel desirable we are dependent on the other's libidinal cathexis of our body-self, most crucially in early development. Too much desire and the child will recoil, feeling his body to be colonized by the mother's 'demand'. But the absence of a mother's desire can be just as problematic. A mother's inhibitions as she handles the baby's body will also be indelibly inscribed in the body. The legacy of not being desired is as insidious as the pressure to meet the mother's demand (Olivier, 1989). This may lead to a need to alter the given body in search for a bodily form that will elicit desire.

In the *perfect match* phantasy, I am suggesting that the body modification serves the function of creating a perfect, ideal body that will guarantee the other's love and desire. In proposing this phantasy I have in mind two groups of patients. In the first group the patient appears to be primarily preoccupied with an internal object felt to be inaccessible or unavailable – one that is 'opaque' (Sodré, 2002), hard to read. Repeated exchanges with an actual mother felt to be inaccessible, for whatever reason, may contribute to the establishment of an internal tormenting experience of uncertainty about her feelings towards the self.[8] The search for absolute certainty in relation to what the other 'sees' when looking at the self may subsequently lead to desperate attempts to create the ideal body that will guarantee the other's loving, desiring gaze (Lemma, 2009). 'Being beautiful' can then become a dominant, unyielding organizing feature in the internal world, fuelled by the phantasy that through 'beautifying' the surface of the body, the self and the object will be tied together in a mutually admiring gaze. For these patients, I am therefore suggesting, cosmetic surgery is a means of averting the pain of the loss of an object that would *always* love and desire the self.

The patient's subjective experience is typically of a painful, humiliating insufficiency. This narcissistic wound is 'cured' by a manic flight into changing the body's surface. The perfect match phantasy therefore concerns the *fusion* of an idealized self (very concretely felt to be an idealized body) with an idealized object/body.[9]

Where there has been an undercathexis of the body-self by the mother, however, there may be not just the yearning for an idealized mother who will look at the self with admiring, loving eyes, but also an accompanying sense of grievance about the felt deprivation and hence a need to attack the object. Hostility towards the object may therefore be an integral part of the relationship towards the wished for, idealized, desiring and desired object.

Hypercathexis of the body-self can also lead to significant complications. Some of the patients I have worked with report in their histories and reveal through the quality of the transference that ensues an experience of relating to a mother who was very narcissistically invested in the patient's body and appearance (sometimes with clear sexual overtones), undermining attempts at separation. Here, instead of an undercathexis of the body-self, the mother's over-stimulation of the baby's body leads to a hypercathexis of the body-self (Lemma, 2009). The surface of the body is over-invested with concern, attention and projection of the mother's need for admiration. It is, to use Joyce McDougall's (1989) term, a case of 'one body for two'.

Although the individual may derive gratification from this excess of interest in his body, the body is often also felt to be the site for intrusive inspection and improvement and this, in turn, can mobilize hatred for the felt-to-be intruder. Where there has been a hypercathexis of the body-self, the individual may then oscillate between a wish to maintain the narcissistic fusion with the idealized object and attempts to separate from the felt-to-be possessive object through the redesign of a body part that has become unconsciously identified with the hated object. In other words, in this group, the psychic function of the fantasized surgery, or of the actual surgery, may fluctuate within the same individual, at times giving expression to the perfect match phantasy, while at other times it may represent an enactment of the reclaiming phantasy.

Making over reality: the case of Ms A.

So far I have been suggesting that in some individuals, the pursuit of cosmetic surgery/procedures serves the primary function of managing anxieties and conflicts that cannot be reflected upon.[10] It is the *compelling* nature of the pull towards modifying the body, whether in actuality, or as a comforting phantasy in one's mind, that distinguishes these patients.[11] The more compelling pursuit of cosmetic surgery/procedures is often underpinned by a despairing and/or violent state of mind towards the self and the object, which represents a more enduring, central, organizing function in the person's psychic economy[12] as I will now illustrate through my work with Ms A., who over time increased to a four-times-weekly analysis over a four-year period.

Ms A., an only child, was born prematurely. Due to birth complications, her mother had been seriously at risk as she gave birth to her. She recalled growing up in the shadow of these early events. She knew from her father that her mother had become very depressed following her birth and she had taken 'time out', as the family referred to it, leaving Ms A. for many months in the care of her father (who was often away on business) and her elderly paternal grandparents. Ms A. had therefore spent the best part of the first year of her life without a mother able to be responsive to her needs or to take pleasure in her. She made a point early on of telling me, reproachfully, that her mother had been unable to breastfeed her. Ms A. was clear that she had never felt close to her mother and that her mother had never taken much of an interest in her. Although her father was described as a more sympathetic figure, he was felt to have been largely absent.

As an adolescent Ms A. had become very preoccupied with what she perceived to be her small breasts. She felt deeply unattractive and she told me that she could barely think about anything else, counting the days till she could have surgery to enlarge her breasts. She hated swimming and the summer months because this exposed her 'disadvantage', as she put it. She vividly conveyed the way in which in her mind the world was full of people with large, plentiful breasts who had access to men, and all good things in life, that were instead denied to her.

Aged twenty-two, not long after she had left university and secured her first job, she underwent surgery to augment her breasts. She recalled this being the best time in her life: she felt confident, had her first sexual relationship and she appeared to have been less consciously burdened by her entrenched grievance towards her mother.

I met Ms A. when she was in her early thirties and she had just become a mother herself. It was this transition to motherhood that provoked a pronounced depressive breakdown. She found it hard to adjust to her baby's dependency on her and she did not breastfeed her daughter, who was said to have feeding difficulties. Her husband was described as very similar to her father: a reliable man whom she felt, however, was not very attuned to the difficulties she was experiencing. Nevertheless, he had supported her coming into treatment and she found it very difficult to credit him with this.

From the outset, even though Ms A. attended regularly, I was confronted by her difficulty in receiving any help from me as if the only tenable psychic position was to feel she could give herself all that she needed. Alongside this omnipotent stance, I felt very closely scrutinized by her. More specifically, as she arrived and left the sessions, I felt she closely surveyed my body. At times she explicitly made reference to what I wore, for example, speculating about the designers I liked, which she would then 'rubbish' with statements like: 'They are a bit passé but fashion recycles itself, I guess.' Several weeks after this statement Ms A. arrived wearing a very similar dress to mine (only the colour was different), but made no reference to this. Her interest in my bodily self felt controlling and intrusive.

The following brief excerpt is from a session that occurred towards the end of the first year of our work. In the preceding session Ms A. had become very preoccupied with a friend's decision to have a breast augmentation, depicting this friend as in 'desperate need' of the surgery because she was in such torment about her small breasts. Ms A. said her own breast augmentation had been a 'positive step' even though she was sure that I did not see it this way. In the same session Ms A. had also alluded to difficulties with her husband: she swayed between casually playing with the idea that she could leave him and the thought that *he* might leave her. In this session I had felt that she was the one in 'desperate need' given how difficult things had become in her marriage, and yet she was not connected to this in any real way.

[A = Analyst, P = Patient]

P: My friend has finally set a date for the surgery. I will accompany her – I keep telling her there is nothing to worry about, that she will be fine and will feel better once it's over ... had a weird dream last night that I found you walking in the street and you were wounded. ... I don't know why but I woke up this morning thinking that you've been looking very tired lately – you look like you have shrunk – and that ... maybe ... something's up in your life ...

[Her perception of me was interesting as I had in fact only returned a few weeks earlier from an evident break in the sun.]

A: What's on your mind in relation to that?
P: I saw a removal van outside in your street a few days ago. A man was loading a lot of things in it ... antiques ... I have seen him before ... I think it's your husband ... so I thought that this might be him moving out ... I was thinking that if x [the husband] and I ever split up it will be painful to divide our possessions – there are some things that I feel are mine and I would be determined to fight for them ... I guess that if it was your husband, you will not want to talk about it with me! Anyway, I know that therapists have their own therapy, lots of supervision, lots of money [laughs] ... so you're probably alright! [Her tone felt rather dismissive.]

A: In your dream you see me wounded, shrunken, with nothing left and yet there is another me who has it all: support, money, holidays …

Silence.

P: My friend will feel better – I have told her that the pain and discomfort she will feel post-op is NOTHING [her emphasis on this word was marked] compared to how much better she will feel eventually – anyway she can take pain relief … These days if you get the right anaesthetist and the right pain control you don't have to feel any pain [she then gives details of the breast augmentation operation she underwent. It all feels very removed from the difficult reality of our exchange as if she is now in a place in her mind where she is completely in control and can give herself the breasts she needs].

A: It's very hard to think with me about how *you* are actually feeling. Instead you retreat into a NOTHING part of your mind where you don't have to feel anything and you can provide for yourself.

P: [As she resumes speaking she sounds irritated with me] I feel fine … OK in as much as things are OK these days … as I said the other day [sighs in an emphatic manner], x [the husband] is becoming impossible – he needs so much from me that I simply can't give him … but I'm fine … It will all come out in the wash, but … sometimes it just feels like he demands too much of me … everyone wants a piece of me right now and I just want to say to them 'Keep out.'

A: That's what you are saying to me right now: 'Leave me alone, you are asking too much of me.'

Long silence.

P: My daughter is still fussing over food … she must be hungry but she seems determined not to eat … she refuses to eat, that's how it feels … purposeful … I will need to take her to the doctor again … [goes into long detail about her various consultations with doctors whom she invariably concludes cannot help. Although this has a distancing effect on me, I am struck that I remain very connected with, and moved by, the picture of the hungry daughter who refuses to eat].

A: You are also hungry and need help, but you come here determined to prove that what I have to offer will be useless to you. It's as if you have to deny what you need from me and refuse what I offer so as to hold yourself together.

A long silence followed during which the patient starts to cry.

P: My husband told me last night that he could not stand it any longer. He's thinking that he should move out for a while … [then details the row the night before and her anxiety is now more present in the room].

I will not go further into this session but suffice to say that I took up eventually the way in which she recognized at some level that she was rejecting of my attempts to help her and that she then feared that I would not 'stand it' any longer, that I would pack up and go, leaving her behind in a shrunken state.

Two weeks later Ms A. arrived for the first session of the week in a state of heightened anxiety. Her friend had the breast augmentation surgery and had suffered complications. She was now in a lot of pain. Ms A. told me that she had felt badly about this because she had been so sure that it would all be fine; it had all been fine for her, after all, she added. She spoke rapidly and it was clear that beyond the concern she felt about her friend's well-being, more was psychically at play here.

I said she was evidently feeling very responsible and guilty as if she had damaged her friend.

Ms A. paused. She then said that she did feel very badly about it all. She had been barely sleeping since it all happened. She then recounted a nightmare she had the previous night when she had taken a sleeping tablet and had managed to sleep for a few hours:

> *She is asleep and some aliens come through the window that she left open by accident. The aliens look very odd: they are all very small women – like dwarfs – and they gather around her bed. She feels terrified as they get out small carving knifes and start to make incisions all over her body. She shouts: 'What do you want from me!' but no one replies. They then cut into her breasts and dig out the implant and she feels the most acute pain.*

Ms A. said that this had been a terrible dream. She had struggled to shake it off: it 'got under my skin', she added.

I said that in the dream itself the small aliens had got under her skin, exposing her own breast surgery and removing her implants.

Ms A. said the dream must be connected to her friend's surgery but she was really struck by how 'nasty' the small aliens were.

I said it was interesting that they were all women …

'Yes,' said Ms A., 'but they were strange looking women because they had no breasts!'

I remained quiet as I hoped that Ms A. might elaborate on this interesting detail but in fact she went quiet.

I eventually said that something appeared to have made her go quiet.

Ms A. said she had no idea why. She had just suddenly run out of thoughts about the dream.

I said it was curious that she dried up just as she had revealed what seemed to be an important feature of the women aliens: they had no breasts and were violently ripping hers out in the dream.

Ms A. folded her arms as I spoke as if to protect her breasts. She looked very uneasy as she lay on the couch.

I said that she seemed to be feeling quite anxious again.

Ms A. said that it was a horrible image. She wondered if her friend might wish she had never undergone the surgery given how it had all gone wrong.

I said that her dream perhaps connected her to a part of her mind that recognized that even if the operation had been successful in her own case, the dream exposed her to another more 'horrible', violent perspective on the surgery and what it represented. She felt that she had 'stolen' the breasts and they were now being repossessed.

Ms A. was silent for a long time. She then said that one of the alien women reminded her of a dwarf woman she had seen in the street some months previously. She had found it impossible not to stare at her even though her mother had always told her not to stare at people less fortunate than herself.

I said that today she was very afraid that I was looking down on her shrunken self and she was the one without breasts.

Ms A. nodded, saying she thought I was lucky, that I had what I needed.

These two brief excerpts capture the quality of the transference that characterized the early phase of our work. At the start of the first session Ms A.'s vulnerability and felt-to-be humiliating smallness was projected into the friend and myself in the dream. Her own sense of feeling small and frightened and in need of help is apparent and yet she cannot allow herself to connect with it. She retreats instead into an anaesthetized state of mind where she feels no pain and in which she can give herself what she needs without recourse to another person/me.

In her first dream I am wounded and emptied out – a reflection, I thought, of her own attacks on me and of her wish to take from me what she feels should rightfully belong to her. Her associations to the dream suggest that I am also perceived by her to have more than enough already: the supervision, therapy and money she is sure I am getting and, I would add to this, her knowledge that I had just been away on holiday. The removal man/husband can be understood as reflecting the part of her that wants to remove the good things she perceives me to have and reduce me to a 'shrunken' shadow of my former self.

Towards the end of the first session I felt that Ms A. allowed herself temporarily to connect with what I had said. But the exposure of her vulnerability was felt to be deeply threatening to her delicate equilibrium. Indeed, in the next session, she elaborated further on the fantasy associated with the sight of a removal van outside my consulting room: she became explicitly triumphant and created a scenario in her mind where it was her supporting me by paying my fees. In this conscious fantasy my husband had left me, and I needed patients to keep going with my mortgage repayments. In other words, *I* was the one with the small breasts and I was stuck with them.

Where there has been an undercathexis of the bodily self by the mother, envy of the phantasized maternal body may be discerned. Whatever the cause of the mother's lack of desire, the self may experience this as a refusal to give what is needed in order to feel desirable. Instead, the maternal object is felt to indulge in the withheld 'desirable' goods. Deprived of sufficient gratification, the self then feels hard done by and may hold a grudge against the felt-to-be depriving object.

For Ms A., her grievance took the very concrete form of trying to acquire for herself the maternal breast through breast augmentation, that is, I understood this as an actualization of the self-made phantasy. The felt-to-be flawed birth by the biological mother is corrected omnipotently by the operative birth, but in my experience the 'surgical father' (Hurst, 2012:) is but a 'small' player, never credited with his separateness. In other words, in this phantasy the parental couple is killed off, not just the mother.

I understood Ms A.'s imperative as a young woman to modify the bodily *given* according to her own design as a concrete enactment of the imperative that dominated the transference: for some time she had to persistently deny her dependence on me and so she owed me nothing. The symbolic breast that Ms A. had internalized was one that was resentfully present and intimated the existence of something better and more exciting than her baby-self trying to feed from it. For example, Ms A. felt that her mother had always invested her energies in the pursuit of her own activities and friends to Ms A.'s detriment. She told me, too, that her mother would frequently talk about the fact that she had almost died giving birth to her. Ms A. felt that her mother 'used' this fact to extract guilt from her. The sessions were often dominated by Ms A.'s rage at her mother's demands on her time. I thought that Ms A. thus felt both obligated *and* devalued. In turn, obligation replaced gratitude. Gratitude can only flourish in a relationship where what is received has been freely given. In sharp contrast, the object one feels obligated to is experienced as owning the self: the object and self are thus tied together destructively.

One of the most recurrent themes in my work with women who have undergone breast augmentation is the paranoid quality of the anxiety that is evident in their dreams as well as in the transference, as the case of Ms A. illustrates. This is not surprising given that a core feature of the self-made phantasy is indeed the appropriation of something that belongs to another, or to put it another way, it belies the inability to receive and accept what the object has given. The given body is felt to not be good enough while the phantasized (m)other is felt to possess the goodness, which can now be literally incorporated through surgery (as I suggested earlier had been the case for Ms A.).

Women's (and men's) magazines are replete with striking illustrations of the kind of theft implicit in the appropriation of the (m)other's body – it appeared, for example, in a women's magazine, *In Style*, which regularly published a column aptly titled 'Steal This Look'. This is something for us to bear in mind since when working with some patients who undergo cosmetic procedures we can often observe heightened paranoid anxieties that speak to the unconscious recognition of the envious attack that belies the pursuit of the surgery ostensibly in order to improve appearance. This, in turn, gives rise to a fear of retaliation and hence paranoid anxiety is stirred. The only way to assuage this kind of anxiety is through the surgery, which, temporarily at least, covers up the 'ugly' feelings that belie its pursuit, through the surface beautification of the body – an oasis of calm after the storm – that also serves the function of reassuring the self and the object that no real damage has been done.

Conclusion

The decision to pursue cosmetic surgery/procedures is not always an indicator of pathology. Rather, in this chapter, I have emphasized that what requires understanding when such surgery is requested is the state of mind of the patient in relation to the surgery and the unconscious meaning this holds for him/her. More specifically, I have suggested that a more enslaved relationship to the pursuit of body modification can become a psychic retreat that belies a violent state of mind towards the object. Indeed cosmetic surgeons, too, recognize that some individuals who seek cosmetic surgery – the so-called 'insatiable' patient (Goldwyn, 2006) – will never be satisfied with the outcome because what they need cannot be delivered by the surgeon.

Both internal and external, societal processes operate in synchrony and conspire to create a world in which the appropriation of the other's physical attributes is commonplace, bypassing any experience of the differences between oneself and the object that we all need to bear.

In an external climate of seemingly infinite possibilities for self-creation, the potential for perverse solutions to psychic conflicts and anxieties is heightened. In the internal world, psychoanalysis allows us to understand that the real challenge is how to stand up to the seductions of identification with a narcissistic, omnipotent object.

Notes

1 A fuller discussion of these factors can be found in Orbach (2009) and Lemma (2010).
2 *Press centre American Society for Aesthetic Plastic Surgery* available at http://www.surgery.org/media/news-releases/ (accessed 25/03/13).
3 Source: British Association of Aesthetic Plastic Surgeons.
4 I am choosing the term *object of desire* as opposed to primary object or significant other to underline the sensory, sensual, bodily components of this earliest relationship and how critical it is to the establishment of a desiring and desirable body-self as the foundation for the expectation that the self will be loved and that it can love.
5 The self-made phantasy is graphically represented in the work of the French body artist, Orlan, and of the Australian cyberpunk artist, Stelarc. Their work powerfully and provocatively illustrates the way in which the body can become the site for the self's re-invention (see, for example, Goodall, 1990 and Lemma, 2010 for a discussion of their work).
6 Birksted-Breen (1996) has suggested that it is the failure to internalize the penis-as-link that underpins a number of pathologies, such as anorexia and suicide, where the body is the site for unconscious enactments.
7 I am using the term 'mother' because often the mother is the primary caregiver, but of course key attachment figures besides the mother also play a crucial part.
8 I am suggesting it is a *contributing* factor because I consider that the baby's innate dispositions also invariably interact with the mother's responses.
9 I understand the underlying dynamic in this latter group of individuals as similar to the unconscious phantasy, which I have described elsewhere, driving 'self-preservative lying' (Lemma, 2005). Like those lies used to serve up a fantasized, more attractive version of the self, so as to manage the anxiety generated by the object's inscrutability

or unavailability, the pursued 'new' nose is a kind of lie that is felt to guarantee an admiring, loving gaze. In these cases cosmetic surgery is an enactment of the perfect match phantasy.

10 Of course, cosmetic surgery also provides solutions to the difficulty in coming to terms with ageing and so with death. In this respect it is important to underline that the greater ease with which such procedures can now be accessed to stave off the signs of ageing can undermine the capacity to work through the difficulty we all have in accepting our inescapable transience (Bell, 2006).

11 I am not referring here to individuals who modify their bodies during an acute psychotic episode. The patients I will be describing were not floridly psychotic, but from an analytic point of view we would understand their decision to alter their bodies as being guided by the ascendance of a psychotic process in the mind.

12 The phantasies I am proposing reveal how the body may provide both the content of phantasy (Bronstein, 2009) and also become the canvass on which these phantasies are then enacted. These phantasies are attempts to describe, and to formulate, my own current understanding of the psychic function of body modification, hence they are provisional hypotheses, not 'facts' – though I am aware that hypotheses can all too readily lead to reification of processes that are, in reality, far more fluid and nuanced.

Chapter 2

Whose skin is it anyway?
Some reflections on the psychic function of necrophilic fantasies

In the last chapter I focused on envy of the maternal body and the importance of understanding this dynamic when working with individuals who pursue breast augmentation surgery. I now want to turn to another dynamic, namely the *dread* of the maternal body and its relevance in understanding necrophilic fantasies. Unlike Klein (1957), who stresses the envy provoked by the maternal body and its prized possessions, I am drawing here on Kristeva's (1984) evocative depiction of the dread of the maternal body, and hence the fear of falling back into the mother's body, specifying how it can be experienced as 'horrific'.

Necrophilia is a perversion that is quite remote from the daily practice of analysts. Only those working in forensic settings typically encounter it. Necrophilic fantasies, however, are more common even if patients quite understandably struggle to admit to them. Such fantasies have been considered as the 'neurotic equivalent of necrophilia' (Calef and Weinshel, 1972), involving sexual excitement about women who look dead or immobilized in some way, such as a woman who is asleep. Whilst it is important to draw some distinctions between necrophilia per se and its fantasy derivatives, it is nevertheless important to keep in mind that the fantasy itself *is* perverse in so far as it negates the object's separateness and is an expression of hostility towards it.

The connection between such fantasies and body image disturbances and other somatic presentations such as dermatological conditions has not been written about, but I have now observed it in three male patients with whom I have worked. Notwithstanding their different presenting complaints, these patients had in common disturbances experienced and/or enacted on the body and an early experience of a *hypercathexis* of the body-self by the mother whose investment in their bodies was felt to be excessive, resulting in a toxic mixture of idealization and denigration. In all three cases the patients manifested a dread of the female body. In the course of our work these patients disclosed necrophilic fantasies that appeared to function to reverse a narcissistic injury involving being looked at in disgust by the mother.

In the necrophilic fantasy the object, by virtue of being like a corpse, is captive and unable to reject the self. Several authors have observed this dynamic too (see, for example, Bonaparte, 1949; Segal, 1953; Baker, 1984). Significantly it is also a non-retaliatory container for a range of projections, not least for evacuating a sense of inner deadness. Here, however, I want to draw attention to another important feature, namely that one crucial aspect of the fantasy of sex with a corpse or with a woman who is asleep is that the object cannot *look at* the self – it is a non-seeing object/body. This visual dimension, I want to suggest, may be particularly relevant to understanding individuals who experience shame about their body and who turn to the necrophilic fantasy to reverse embodied shame.

In this chapter I therefore want to illustrate how the 'corpse' or corpse look-alike functions at several levels: (a) it is a safe object that will not engulf the self, (b) it is a non-retaliatory container into which the self can evacuate the sense of fragmentation and/or deadness and (c) it is a non-seeing body/object that cannot humiliate. I shall focus in particular on the latter because it proved to be an important dimension in work with patients whose psychic pain is located in the body.

Through the case of Mr B., with whom I worked for seven years in a five-times-weekly analysis, I will explore a possible way of understanding the function of his necrophilic fantasies, which were part of a dynamic relational constellation that encompassed his skin problem (eczema) and his dread of the maternal body. Mr B. did not consciously seek help with anxieties associated with his body or his sexual fantasies. Yet, his primary difficulties with feeling intruded upon and with separation could not be explored and worked through without detailed attention to how he related to his body, what it unconsciously represented and what he enacted through it. In particular I sensed that he felt quite literally trapped – claustrophobic – in his skin.

Mr B. was a highly intelligent, professionally successful, personable man in his late twenties. Yet beneath this surface presentation it was clear that in some fundamental respects Mr B. had struggled to take the necessary steps forward into adult functioning. This was especially apparent in his relationships with women, which were typically intense to begin with but always short lived. Sex was satisfying on the whole, but posed the threat of engulfment, which he then defended against by interposing emotional and/or physical distance between himself and the other.

On first meeting Mr B. his physical appearance struck me immediately: he was an attractive man and yet he appeared uncomfortable in his own body. The skin on his face, neck and arms was red and flaking in places. Its rawness alerted me to the urgency that belied Mr B.'s surface laid-back attitude to seeking help and his ostensible reasons for doing so.

Mr B. explained to me that many aspects of his life were progressing well, but he was seeking help because he was nevertheless worried by his escalating use of recreational drugs when he went to clubs, and his excessive smoking. He described considerable success in his career and yet he continued to live in what he tellingly referred to as 'my mother's house', sleeping in his childhood room. 'My mother's house' was, in fact, where both his mother *and* father lived.

Mr B. was the middle of three children. He presented his parents' marriage as a very unhappy one, which he thought was tolerated by the father for 'an easy life'. Mr B. described his father as a basically kind but ineffectual man who did reasonably well in his professional life, but was emotionally remote. His mother was depicted as an unstable woman, prone to 'hysterical outbursts'. Mr B. experienced her as controlling, intrusive and shaming. He felt she needed him to be by her side and nurse what he referred to as her 'insatiable need for attention'.

The body on the couch

In the early months of the analysis Mr B. refused to lie on the couch. He could not explain why but he simply said he felt uncomfortable. I was aware, however, that he was also uncomfortable being looked at by me. He scrunched himself up into a ball, in the chair opposite mine, often covering his face with his hands.

During this time he spoke a lot about his experience of his mother. As I listened to Mr B.'s descriptions, I was struck by their invariably visceral quality: for example, her voice was said to be 'cutting', her embrace 'crushing', her breath 'foul'. Kristeva's (1984) notion of the 'abject' mother – the mother that is felt to be repellent and has to be ejected – captured well Mr B.'s initial reluctance to use the couch, which I thought presented him with the prospect of being sucked back into the maternal body/me. This anxiety was present in his relationships with women generally: for example, he described how no sooner he reached orgasm, he needed to quickly withdraw his penis as if he feared disappearing inside the woman's body.

From a young age Mr B. appeared to have managed his bodily anxieties by retreating into the mind. In the analysis, all too often, his intellect and humour were attempts to seduce us both away from the more disturbing and painful reality of a primitive realm of his experience that was split off into his body. I felt powerfully the impact of his unease in his body: a body that was either denied (as, for example, when he ignored how tired he felt or the fact of his eczema), or it was triumphed over (as when he ignored risks to his physical well-being when he went skiing off-piste and placed himself at significant risk). In this respect, it became clear to me that if Mr B. had not been in analysis, and more particularly, if he had not had to confront using the couch, we might have skirted around these issues unproductively for a long a time. As it was, the first encounter with the paranoid quality of these primitive anxieties was immediately alive in the room as we negotiated the use of the couch. The anxieties he voiced about the couch included feeling trapped under my 'gaze from behind' such that he could not see me and keep an eye on me.

Despite his anxieties, Mr B. eventually made the transition to the couch and here is an abridged version of the first session on the couch (approximately seven months after he started the analysis).

As soon as Mr B. lay on the couch, he was seized by panic. He said he felt his throat constricting, his heart racing. For fifteen minutes he could not speak. He then told me that he felt like he was drowning. There was enough of an intact ego to allow him to manage the anxiety without having to act on it by getting off the couch, but his anxiety was palpable in the room.

He eventually told me about the fantasy that dominated his mind as he lay down: he was aware of scrutinizing every noise that came from behind because he anticipated that I would physically strike him and he had to be prepared. He said his head felt especially vulnerable and that he felt 'crazy' for even having these thoughts because he knew I would never harm him, that this was a 'preposterous idea', and yet he was gripped by the conviction that this is what would nevertheless happen.

I thought it premature to make a transference interpretation and more important to remain silent, and give him the space to ground himself in his bodily experience as the basis for understanding the object relationship that was being activated and that was so disturbing to him. I was mindful too that any intervention on my part could readily be experienced as intrusive.

Mr B. went on to describe how he imagined me raising my hand to strike him, but then he added, 'strangely your hand relaxes and then strokes my head and then you touch me ... this is not a nice touching ... it feels more like you are looking for something ... something wrong ... it's like a kind of grooming but not done with love ... I don't know, I can't explain it ... '

As he spoke I was aware of being struck by his choice of the word 'grooming', which had perverse sexual connotations in my mind as if I was experienced by him as a kind of paedophile. It alerted me to the possibility of being drawn into a more sexualized relationship and of the likelihood that my attempts to understand him could be readily perverted along these lines.

Near the end of the session, I said that he was not anticipating a loving 'grooming' but more an intrusive inspection.

Mr B. became quietly tearful at this point and said that he did not know why he was crying. He then recalled being on a beach with his mother when he was aged seven or eight and she insisted that he lay on the sun lounger with her. He said he could still feel the 'stickiness' of her skin against his as it was hot and there was barely enough room for her 'large' body and his. She encouraged him to sit in the sun because she believed this would clear his skin, but he hated the heat and felt upset that he had to expose himself to it in order to look better *for her*. He felt she had been very preoccupied with his appearance as she was with her own.

In Mr B.'s experience his mother's apparent concern for his skin was felt to be a kind of lie. Significantly the screen memory of the beach conveyed the way that he had felt that his mother's skin and body took him over quite literally, encroaching on his body and physical space: he was stuck to her and crushed by her large body. On another occasion he described how his mother had been very invested in rubbing into his skin the various ointments for his eczema when he was a child, a task that she never delegated to the father. He recalled that she would spend a long time doing this. Alongside this appropriation of his body, Mr B. also reported feeling that she had been critical of his appearance, especially the condition of his skin. He thus seemed trapped between his mother's colonization of his body and her consequent humiliation because he was not 'perfect' in her eyes.

The couch mobilized these anxieties powerfully. In his dreams during this time I often featured as a 'large' figure impervious to his needs. Spatial metaphors abounded. Significantly there were only ever two characters in these dreams, underlining the missing third/father.

In my mother's house: skin and its vicissitudes

Images of the discomforts and perils of close bodily contact dominated Mr B.'s early narratives and provided me with food for thought about the possible link with his eczema. I knew from our first consultation that he had suffered with eczema since his early childhood. However, it was striking that Mr B. seldom mentioned it as a problem thereafter despite the fact that this was evidently an ongoing issue for him as his skin often noticeably flared-up.

Anzieu (1989), developing Bick's (1968) ideas about the skin, proposed that the ego is primarily structured as a 'skin ego'. He suggests that some skin problems may be understood as resulting from either an excess or a deficit in the early skin-to-skin contact with the maternal object. In Mr B.'s case I gained the impression that his eczema expressed the complications that can arise as a consequence of the impact of a felt-to-be intrusive, undigested excess of maternal desire.

When on the couch Mr B. often scratched his skin; sometimes he dug into it and then lifted off the epidermis, thus creating small cracks in the skin. In the forced, often bloody detachment of his skin it seemed as though he wished to tear off the internal object, as if Mr B. felt his mother to be quite literally under his skin. His skin appeared to be both the place where he concretely experienced his mother's intrusion and where he tried to reclaim a sense of separateness by digging her out and so reclaiming his body as his own. During adolescence this had also taken the form of tattooing his body (see Chapter 1 for a discussion of the 'reclaiming phantasy') – an action that had deeply angered his mother, he recalled, but which we eventually understood to have been his attempt to stamp his skin as belonging to him, not his mother.

For many months in the analysis, however, it felt like Mr B.'s eczema was a no-go area between us and inside himself. I felt that I had to 'mind' his body for him rather than present it to him so that we could think about it together. I was confronted with the dilemma that if I took this up, he would most likely feel intruded and I risked enacting an all too familiar dynamic with his mother. But if I said nothing I risked becoming the impotent father who never intervened. This scenario was ripe for enactments, as illustrated in a Wednesday session that took place towards the end of the first year of analysis.

Mr B. arrived looking very red in his face. His skin was noticeably flaking and I detected two small lesions on his left arm. He was vigorously scratching his arms. He said he was not feeling well and that he thought he should see a doctor.

It was not clear what he was concerned about in relation to his health so I asked him. He was silent. I felt uneasy, concerned that I had been drawn into becoming intrusive rather than waiting to see how he might have elaborated his associations.

Mr B. eventually replied that he felt tired all the time. He wondered if he had some viral infection and spoke in some detail about this without, however, making any reference to the evident flare-up of his skin.

I said that his skin also looked like it needed attention, but that I thought this was hard for him to bring to me as something that might be of concern and that we might think about together.

Mr B. told me, matter-of-factly, somewhat dismissively, that this was 'just a skin condition, like bad teeth ... what can I do about it'.

I said that I thought he had felt intruded upon by my focus on his skin and that this was dangerous territory – something neither of us could safely approach. I added that behind his manifest resignation I sensed a deeper hopelessness.

Mr B. then said that he had just learnt to live with it, that it was not always bad, that he knew stress made it worse, but that he was not too worried about it. I sensed his irritation with me. He was scratching himself a lot on his arms as if I had now become the irritant under his skin.

He was silent for a while and then changed the subject and spoke to me about a party he was due to attend later that week. He was expecting that a woman he had once had a relationship with might be there and that this might be awkward. He had ended the relationship in a brutal manner that he now regretted, but he had not known how else to do it at the time. He hoped that now he might handle such a sensitive situation differently. But at the time he just felt the need to end it and get away. She was a kind woman – maybe I would think this was in fact the kind of woman he should go for – but back then he felt like recoiling because she was 'too available'; it scared him, as if she would just want to get married, settle down, have children. She made him feel suffocated though he could now see that this probably said more about him than her.

I said that when I had brought up his eczema, he had experienced my interest in his body as intrusive, suffocating, as if I was taking him over and wanted to tie him to me forever. And although in a part of his mind he was hanging on to the possibility that my intentions were benign – just like he could now see his ex-partner's intentions might also well have been – a terrified part of him felt the need to push me away.

At this point Mr B. became tearful. He was silent and then recalled that his mother had once told him, 'I gave birth to you in pristine form and look what you have done to it [the body].' He felt that his mother struggled with his eczema: she used to take him to lots of doctors, but instead of feeling this was done with care, Mr B. had experienced this as her urgency to hide something she could not bear to look at.

I heard this change of affect, and his associations, as a validation that there had been some movement in the session, between us, that now we could both look at what his eczema meant rather than cover it up, as he felt his mother had done. But I felt, too, that his recollection of the mother's insistence that she had 'given' him the perfect body that he had now spoilt and that it was her exclusive right to nurse his skin, was a powerful reminder to me that my care and understanding could so easily become perverted in his experience and become the kind of intrusive 'grooming' he had referred to in the session when he first lay on the couch.

From the outset Mr B. impressed on me both his difficulty in tolerating closeness and of bearing the pain of separateness. He both feared the object's takeover and yet could not tolerate its separateness and longed to reunite an ideal self with an idealized other. The way this was most concretely expressed early on in the analysis was through his experience of arriving for his sessions, as can be discerned in a Tuesday session two years into the analysis.

Mr B. started by saying that he hated the 'arrivals and departures', but especially arrivals. He said that he could see that as he pressed my doorbell he was 'invested in the fear of being abandoned' to such a degree that he could then not dislodge himself from that internal reality.

He said that on those occasions when he had come for his session and not found me, and hence he had been 'left out in the cold', this had been 'mostly' due to the fact that he had come at the wrong time [which he had a habit of doing regularly in the first year of his analysis].

I took up the way that he was being very careful not to be overtly critical of me and yet I sensed that in his 'mostly' he was letting me know that he felt I was responsible for his experience of being left out in the cold when he turned up at the wrong time.

Mr B. replied that he knew it was his confusion, but that when I 'changed the time of the session' this only added to his confusion.

As I listened I knew that I had only once changed his time. Yet I also felt that he needed to keep me in the position of 'the one who always wronged him'. I eventually said that in a part of his mind I was forever not there for him when he needed me to be.

Mr B. followed this up with a dream he had a few nights previously:

He was at a concert in which two people were singing together a cappella. The sound, he said, was eerily beautiful and then something terrible happened: one of the singers was gripped by a bout of coughing and this interrupted the singing. The singer drank water but could not stop. His face became all red and he had to leave the stage. In the dream Mr B. said that he felt pained as he looked on. He had found it most unbearable to watch when the singer left on the stage welcomed another colleague to join him, replacing the coughing singer.

As we explored the dream together Mr B. told me that he recalled how his mother hated it whenever he was ill. She especially hated the sound of coughing, but more generally he felt that she did not like anything messy that disrupted the surface appearance of things being in their place. I thought that the dream and his associations captured the tyranny of being part of an idealized couple, in synchrony, where anything that was more 'messy' had to be split off – a synchrony that in the dream breaks down into a physical spasm that cannot be controlled. This spoils the beauty of the joined voices and one partner has to leave the stage and is replaced.

I took up with Mr B. how he longed for the two of us to be in synchrony, and that it was this compelling phantasy of a perfectly timed couple that was in his mind as he pressed the doorbell. But no sooner had he pressed it, the phantasy was punctured by the inevitable delay between his desire and my response – we could never, actually, be in perfect synchrony.

Much of the work in this analysis focused on exploring this dimension of Mr B.'s experience, through the transference, which I think can be discerned in the session just described, namely the way the expulsion from the idealized couple was felt to be painfully shaming. Like the coughing, and significantly *red-faced*,[1] a cappella singer who has to leave the stage, Mr B. readily felt easily supplanted in the object's mind by a more desirable Oedipal rival. His skin was felt to be the damaged organ, the surface on which he had felt the touch of desire only to then feel brutally rejected when he could not satisfy his mother's desire. Her look of disgust was deeply imprinted on his skin.

Mr B.'s dual preoccupation with his own desirability and the other's availability and desire for him made some sense in the context of his feeling that his mother remained 'haunted' by the very late miscarriage of a baby not long before Mr B.'s own birth. This 'fact' only emerged in the analysis in the second year. But even before this disclosure Mr B. had frequently referred to his mother's 'narrow mindedness'. I then wondered to myself how much space his mother could have had in her mind for him as a baby separate from the rawness of the loss of her other baby, such that her mind had perhaps been both hungry for the solace of replacement, and also 'occupied' (Rhode, 2005) by the loss of the wished for perfect baby that Mr B. could never assuage. The internal grievance this gave rise to in Mr B. trapped his objects/me in a kind of time warp where I was forever rejecting, leaving him to lick his wounds off stage, whilst someone more desirable replaced him in my mind's eye.

This internal scenario also prevented Mr B. from reflecting on his own triumph over his father in particular, who was never given residence in the 'mother's house'. In turn, this left him bereft of an internal father who could help him to dilute the intensity of the relationship with his mother. One of his associations to the coughing singer in the dream was of a memory of his father ill with a chest infection and he said his father had looked 'pathetic'. I thought that the expelled singer was also a version of his father, expelled and humiliated by Mr B. as he joins the mother (in identification with her) as a duet in her house/body.

The skin and necrophilic fantasies: reversing narcissistic mortification

The extent of Mr B.'s sensitivity to feeling shamed and to being easily supplanted by a more desirable rival, became even clearer and more dynamically specific when we eventually started to explore his sexual fantasies in the third year of his analysis.

It was around this time that Mr B. decided to turn down a series of jobs in order to commit himself fully to the analysis because up until then he often had to cancel sessions due to work-related trips. However, he now felt that he had sufficient funds to be a bit more discriminating about the jobs he took on, not least because he paid no rent as he lived in his 'mother's house'.

At first, along with him, I viewed this move as a positive step reflecting some reduction in the extent of his claustrophobic anxiety. With hindsight I did so too eagerly, enacting the kind of excited coming together that was so characteristic of the intense, if short-lived, relationships he had with women. Indeed, during this phase (but not for the first time, as this dynamic was clearly present from the outset), the analysis became the current, live version of 'my mother's house' as he settled into my room/mind, showing little desire to 'move out'.

Whenever I tried to take up the stasis that enveloped our work during this phase, Mr B. spoke of how 'dangerous' it felt to even contemplate a return to looking for work. Increasingly I felt the pressure of his need for an enveloping, unbroken, ideal skin that kept the world out and protected us as a united couple. This created a claustrophobic reaction in me and introduced a sense of deadness in the analysis as if he wanted to embalm us. I often felt sleepy and paralysed in my thinking. He would nevertheless comment on how much he enjoyed the 'stillness' in the room and that somehow he felt 'more himself' in this still space. He was very positive about the analysis and eager to impress on me how good I was in my role. Suffice to say that during this time we often found ourselves in an 'enclave' (O'Shaughnessy, 1997) – a psychic refuge that effectively replaced analysis.

No matter how idealized the transference, there were also moments when I could quickly became merged in his experience with a maternal figure of demand – a projective identification of his own possessiveness and demand. For Mr B. the 'object of desire' (Britton, 1998) partook of the insistent, nagging character of demand: an impossible internal object that could neither be satisfied nor relinquished.

As we approached these dynamics in the transference Mr B. began to reveal further Oedipal and early latency memories that exposed his profound fear of being rejected *and* humiliated by the object. His experience of humiliation had a clear visual dimension to it connected to the appearance of his skin. This was especially focused on his mother who could be 'cutting in public' and was felt by him to have made several negative comments about his skin in front of others who then 'stared' at him, leaving him feeling 'raw', as he put it.

The mother featured largely as the humiliating object, but his father was also conspicuously present through his absence and hence unable to help him to separate from his mother. An interesting dream he brought around this time helped us to make some inroads into these very complicated dynamics and the nature of the sexual fantasies they fed into.

Mr B. began this particular session saying he felt very troubled by a dream he had. He knew he needed to tell me about it but if he did so, then he would have to disclose other things that he would rather avoid thinking about. I said nothing and waited to see what he did with this dilemma. He eventually resolved to start by telling me the dream:

> *I am living alone in a dishevelled house out in the countryside. There is no one for miles. I go to my bedroom and under my bed there is a coffin. I made that coffin myself. I open the lid and my mother is inside. I look at her and she disgusts me. I can see the inside of her body. I then lie on top of her and have sex with her dead body.*

Mr B. said he felt sickened by the dream. It was a horrible image and he could not accept that his mind could produce such a disgusting image.

Mr B.'s discomfort was palpable and I simply acknowledged this. Mr B. said there was more. He struggled to speak but eventually managed to tell me that he had realized that he was very aroused by the fantasy of making love to his partner when she was asleep. He found the idea of her 'motionless', asleep, to be very arousing. He had touched her and then entered her a few times whilst she was asleep, inevitably then waking her. She had not liked it and said to him that she felt treated 'like I'm a corpse'. He had immediately felt reprimanded and disgusted at himself. He worried, however, that he could not shake off the urge; he managed this by simply using it as a fantasy in his mind when they made love rather than acting on it. The thought of her asleep, motionless, aroused him during sex, but when he spoke to me about it he simply felt disgust at himself.

I said the urge to make love to a woman who could offer no opposition because she was dead, as in the dream, or asleep, as with his partner, troubled him deeply and yet there was something compelling about the possibility of eliminating all risk of rejection and humiliation.

Mr B. said he was afraid of being humiliated, of not being 'man enough' to sustain an erection, but when he imagined his partner asleep he felt confident. He then recalled a dream he had as a child and which he had never forgotten because it had been a dream that had 'felt good and almost real'. In the dream he was inside a cave that had never been discovered by anyone before him. In the dream he looks very young and has perfectly smooth skin. Inside the cave he found gold treasures and filled many bags that he took with him, but he left feeling there was an even bigger treasure hidden away that he could not find and that he needed to go back for.

Mr B. laughed nervously and said he was really not sure why this dream had come to his mind now. He had not thought about it for years but in recalling it he noticed that it felt very pleasurable. The 'treasures' reminded him of the shiny pebbles he used to collect on beaches when he was a child.

I said that in his sexual fantasy as he entered his partner's sleeping body he could feel potent because he imagined a relationship in which rejection and humiliation were abolished – like in his childhood dream there could be no rival who had either been in the woman's body before him or who had skin smoother than his and he would *surely* be looked at with desiring eyes by her if she were awake.

Mr B. agreed and then returned to the first dream and how disconcerting it was to think about sex with his mother ... and a dead mother at that, he added. Mr B. now started to pick at his skin rather forcefully and a small trace of blood appeared on his arm. He said he had wondered what it might feel like to have sex with a corpse, but he never really allowed himself to run with that thought for very long. It was only when his partner made the comment about the corpse that he made the connection with his sexual fantasy about penetrating her when she was fast asleep. He added that when they made love 'normally' he worried about losing his penis inside her and when this thought entered his mind he was likely to lose his erection.

After a pause he then said that he hated his mother. In the dream she was repulsive because her skin was flaking off. 'In the dream,' he then added, 'I also take off her skin and mash it up in my hands until it becomes a kind of putty that I then spread all over me'. This made him think about how he hated his own skin.

I said it was interesting how he had at first omitted the part of the dream involving his mother's skin.

Mr B. replied that he had 'forgotten'.

I said that 'skin' was a sensitive subject between us and it was a sensitive area on his body as it was the site of shame.

Mr B. said that in the dream his mother's skin looked putrid and repulsive.

I said that he felt his own skin was repulsive too and that no one could find him attractive so he had to turn away from the gaze of the other or try to not be seen. I added that this anxiety was very alive between us, as it was me behind him looking at him, rather than the other way around.

Mr B. agreed. He then recalled the discomfort of our early sessions face-to-face. He had dreaded the couch too but at least he had been spared the agony of being looked at by me head-on. He added that basically there was no comfortable position. After a silence he said that he really did hate his skin and wished he could have a 'new' skin.

I said that he hated the mother that he experienced as being quite literally under his skin and that he wanted to pick her out and make some new skin that could be his own, but in fact in the dream he ends up recycling *her* skin. So he always ends up back in his 'mother's house'.

Mr B. was thoughtful and then added that it was hard to separate from her, to not feel she was 'pronouncing' on him and what he should be or should look like. He wished he could ignore her voice in his head, but he could see he felt stuck and that he now realized she was even at the heart of his sexual fantasies. He felt defeated by this realization.

I said he felt defeated now that he realized how compelling the fantasy had become because through it, as in the dream, he could reverse the experience of feeling humiliated: in the dream it was now him *looking* at his mother looking repulsive. I added that in the sexual fantasy he would not be looked at as the woman's eyes are shut – she is either dead or asleep. And that perhaps here too, between us, there was a wish that I would not look at him and see what was inside him.

Mr B. said he had not thought about it this way. He said it was true that he did not like being looked at during sex. It was easier if he entered his partner from behind. Although his partner had never made any disparaging comments about his skin, he was sure that she could not possibly find him attractive during the flare-ups. He thought he looked terrible and preferred it if she did not look straight at him during sex.

He then looked at his arm and slapped it, saying, 'I'd promised myself I'd stop doing this.' He said that when he made himself bleed he felt better but he knew this was a 'bad habit'. He said his own flaking skin made him think of disease and death. His mother's skin in the dream looked like he sees himself: defaced by the flakiness. He then added: 'I feel flaky, like I'm not able to stand on my own two feet. It's like I'm missing something,' and he began to cry. When he recovered himself he said he often feared he would one day let go of all the pretence and 'fall to pieces'.

I said that perhaps, like in his childhood dream, he had a sense that there was a hidden treasure somewhere that he cannot access, a treasure that might provide this missing part that would help him to have a new skin to hold himself together without pretence, that he could trust that his own skin could protect him and not expose him.

There were five more minutes left of the session and Mr B. was silent.

Living in one's own skin

Many clinical presentations are characterized by interpersonal patterns driven by a primary concern with maintaining optimal distance from the object. The predicament they share in common is that to be intimate is to risk engulfment and to be apart is to court intolerable aloneness. This leads to a variety of psychic compromises, revealing anxieties pertaining to distance and closeness, as well as the phantasies defending against these anxieties. Along these lines Glasser (1979) identified an internal scenario – the core complex – characterized by the wish to fuse with the object, but this fusion is felt to present a danger of total engulfment, and hence has to be aggressively resisted. I believe that Mr B. struggled with anxieties of this nature. He experienced profound castration anxiety typical of the phallic-narcissistic phase (Edgcumbe and Burgner, 1975) in which the individual fears envious appropriation of the narcissistically invested phallus, which gives rise to shame and humiliation, not guilt as would be the case where the anxiety is characteristic of the phallic Oedipal phase. This kind of anxiety was relieved through the necrophilic fantasy.

The analysis with Mr B. focused primarily on understanding the unconscious meaning and function for him of living in his *mother's* house. I understood this to designate a place in his mind, and experienced quite concretely in his body and manifesting as eczema, in which he felt trapped, with nothing to dilute the dyadic enmeshment with a felt-to-be intrusive, oppressive and demanding maternal object/body. Of course, this is how he experienced it: as the analysis unfolded it became clearer that he had not only felt projected into by his object, but that he also forcefully projected into it.

Rey (1994) has described a primitive universal position of claustrophobia and agoraphobia, which he roots in the body:

> Claustrophobic space is the result of projective identification of the body and its inner space into the outside world ... It is therefore the child inside the mother's body who becomes claustrophobic inside the inner space of his mother projected into the outside world.
>
> (Rey, 1994: 267)

Mr B. was trapped both literally and metaphorically in his 'mother's house'. In the analysis he recreated with me a version of 'my mother's house', bringing alive in the immediacy of our relationship both the grievance that underpinned it and the seductions it held. Over time, as we both got stuck in his 'mother's house', I came to understand the underbelly of his anxiety about being intruded upon, namely his wish to get right inside the object and be at one with it, effectively killing off the father in his mind, and retaining the omnipotent illusion of complete control over the object of desire.

The necrophilic fantasy, as I suggested at the outset, fulfilled a number of functions for Mr B. The attacks aimed at the mother's body, and as vividly depicted in the dream where Mr B. can see 'inside' her dead body before having sex with her, could be understood as expressing the wish to exclusively possess and explore the interior of the mother's body and its contents without any opposition (Calef and Weinshel, 1972) or any 'takeover' by the mother's narcissistic needs. The wish to get right inside the mother's dead body, however, might also express a desperate search for the father's penis inside her (Gillespie, 1940) without encountering any impediment from her in the form of her desire. The phantasized paternal penis here is thus not simply an object of castration, but also a source of something sustaining to the self, perhaps representing the hidden treasure that Mr B. could not find in the cave of his childhood dream and that he so urgently needed in order to create a stable body boundary impermeable to his mother's projections.

The necrophilic fantasies revealed not only how Mr B. viewed the corpse as a safe object that offered no resistance, thus eliminating all risks of either humiliation or unwanted intrusion – it is he who intrudes at will – but importantly too it was the receptacle for the dread of annihilation by the maternal object that so terrified Mr B.: in the fantasy it is the mother who is dead, *her* skin peeling off. The dead mother enabled him to evacuate an inner deadness, so that he then could become manically alive, filled up with 'treasures' instead of an inner emptiness.

The final function of the necrophilic fantasy that I now want to turn to is the way that it averts the humiliation felt concretely at the level of the body-self. My countertransferential claustrophobia and sense of feeling 'sleepy' when Mr B. seemingly took up residence in the analysis rather than working with me, and specifically my sense that he wanted to 'embalm' us, might perhaps be understood as anticipating unconsciously his eventual disclosure of his necrophilic fantasies. Even though these had not been yet explicitly declared at that point in the analysis, we might wonder if I was then already being exposed to his pleasure and sense of safety about being with an object that is asleep and thus cannot actually 'see' him. Of course, a non-seeing object might also be experienced as one that cannot deflect his projections – a container who cannot protest or retaliate. But I want to draw attention here to the specifically *visual dimension* rather that the more metaphorical meaning of a non-seeing object, which are of course not mutually exclusive.

The dream in which Mr B. has sexual intercourse with his dead mother is important on many levels, not least in how it reveals the eroticization of the *visual revenge* on the object who is humiliated. The corpse can be looked at, but does not look back with critical, shaming eyes. It is now Mr B. looking at a flaking, decomposing mother. With a corpse the living body is always the voyeur with no threat of a humiliating comeback. Hanna Segal (1953) indeed emphasizes the aggressive aspects of the necrophilic fantasy, understanding the choice of a helpless object as a means both of denying the subject's own sadism and of nullifying the risk of retaliatory aggression on the part of the object.

Mr B.'s graphic description of the skinning of his dead mother to make 'putty' that he can then use to create another skin for himself, before he has sex with her, is also significant. Mr B. desperately wanted a new skin that was whole and his own, impregnable to the other, but in the dream, in identification with an intrusive, devouring object, he skins the mother and steals her skin to remodel a new one for himself. In doing so, of course, he does the very thing he wants to avoid: he literally wraps himself inside the mother's skin, forever trapped in his 'mother's house'. We might well speculate as to whether Mr B.'s experience as a child of his mother smoothing cream onto him contributed to a phantasy that she was actually smoothing a layer of her own skin over his.

Bick's (1964) work on the proto-mental functions of the skin and her fine-tuned understanding of fear as a basic affect that requires containment by the object are invaluable to understanding the predicament of patients like Mr B. In particular her work vividly elucidates the function of the skin as both the container and the point of contact with the other, that is, what is seen and touched by the object.

According to Bick the experience of the skin forms one of the most primitive experiences of being passively held together, without which the rudimentary self would feel like it was falling to pieces. The subjective experience of skin is an amalgam of the infant's own skin and that of mother obtained through handling. The internalization of this function provides the infant with a primitive notion of a body boundary. Early failures in first skin containment, Bick suggested, can lead the baby to a defensively active use of his body to confer a self-generated sense of being held together in the face of severe anxieties, a primitive defence she termed a 'faulty second skin formation' (Bick, 1968, 1986).

The origins of Mr B.'s eczema are most likely over-determined, but his subjective experience of his skin suggested a failure in the first skin containment described by Bick. His damaged skin was both felt to be appropriated by the mother through her nursing and investment in it *and* it was also the site of her rejection and humiliation. The necrophilic dream and the necrophilic fantasy more generally reverse this narcissistic mortification.

Conclusion

The neurotic equivalents and derivatives of necrophilia do not necessarily denote the same kind of malignant psychopathology as necrophilia per se (Calef and Weinshel, 1972) and I would argue that this was so in the case of Mr B. He was clearly not aroused by the fantasy of an actual corpse and the fantasy of sex with a woman who is asleep, though compelling, was not essential for him to reach orgasm. Even so, the fantasy was perverse in the sense that his quest for sexual excitement through the necrophilic fantasy, when active, revealed his underlying incapacity to relate to the other as separate from the self and not as a narcissistic appendage.

Perverse fantasies invariably defend against anxiety. This anxiety may be related to both libidinal and destructive forces (Glover, 1933). Indeed it is not uncommon to find necrophilic fantasies that are driven by both of these currents. Mr B. shifted from normal (i.e. non-perverse) sexual fantasies to necrophilic ones partly as a reaction to a perceived threat of engulfment or humiliation. His own libido thus mobilized anxiety, and his turning to a perverse rather than a neurotic solution was in part because he felt locked in a relationship with a suffocating and humiliating internal mother.

In this chapter I have suggested that such necrophilic derivatives appeared in three patients whose bodily integrity and separateness from the primary object (the mother in all these cases) was experienced as compromised in some way. More specifically they shared in common an experience of a hypercathexis of the body-self in early development, as I hope I have illustrated in the case of Mr B. The eroticized colonization of the body by the object contributes to an internal scenario, as described by Glasser (1979), where fusion with the object heralds the threat of engulfment and hence has to be defended against and yet separation is also terrifying. However, I have also suggested that an important dynamic in these cases appears to be the experience of humiliation that is felt concretely at a bodily level and creates a hypersensitivity to being looked at by the object. It is the eyes that are felt to be castrating. In the necrophilic fantasy the object has no eyes and, for these patients, this is a compelling feature of the fantasy.

Note

1   The red face could also be understood not only as a reference to his shameful skin but also as the blushing shame of his Oedipal longings.

Chapter 3

An order of pure decision
Growing up in a virtual world and the adolescent's experience of being-in-a-body

In our advanced technological culture the body can readily be transcended rather than accepted as a cornerstone of reality. It can be corrected, transformed, or altogether bypassed, as we saw in the case of cosmetic surgery (see Chapter 1). In this sense so-called progress may fuel the fantasy that we can exist, to borrow Ewald's telling phrase (1993), in an 'order of pure decision'.

In this chapter I want to focus on a particular kind of technological development – the domain of cyberspace[1] – and to consider the fate of the body in cyberspace. More specifically, I will explore how retreat into cyberspace may be used by some young people as a way of bypassing the psychic implications of being-in-a-body and the related anxieties. This focus may help us understand clinical presentations during adolescence in which the young person is referred with an 'addiction' to cyberspace and in which anxieties rooted in the body – sometimes specifically focused on its appearance – may not be apparent at first assessment.

I will start by describing how virtual space can lend itself to being used as a psychotic enclave that become especially compelling for vulnerable adolescents due to the demands made on the mind by the physical changes of puberty. Through my work with an adolescent girl and an adolescent boy, I will then illustrate how virtual spaces allow the individual to manage confusion and distress about the real body. Here, the self's integrity is sustained through pseudo-representations of the body that are defensively experienced in terms of 'it's just a game' rather than as pathology, and that create obstacles to the invitation by the analyst to reflect on the function of cyberspace in the individual's experience, especially that of being-in-a-body.

Seductions and perils of technological embodiment

The term *cyberspace* refers to a computer-generated space that is viewed by the participant and responds to stimuli from the participant. It is populated by a range of cybernetic automatons that provide the individual a high degree of vividness and total sensory immersion in the artificial environment. Movements in virtual reality are not the same as movements in physical reality: for example, in cyberspace one can fly or go through walls, since the material constraints of the body do not apply. Most important, many of the games that can be played in virtual reality make it possible to assume new identities and to create whole 'new' worlds. Massively multiplayer online role-playing games (MMORPGs), for example, are highly dynamic and interactive, to the extent that the player can feel as if living inside an alternative reality where it is possible to control how characters look, how they behave, what they do, and what they say.

Cyberspace is indeed construed by its supporters as a space of unrestricted freedom. When the pursuit of such 'freedom' becomes compelling and all-consuming, this comes at a price: an important consequence of immersion in cyberspace is a corresponding shrinking of shared, physical space, and hence the loss of actual, physically mediated relationships (Robins and Webster, 1999) that provide a kind of psychic anchor – an anchor that is particularly important during the tumult of adolescence.

My aim in approaching this subject is not to demonize the virtual domain. It is all too easy to come across as a Luddite if one invites a moment's reflection on the very real progress made possible by technological development (Robins and Webster, 1999). From a psychological point of view, it has been suggested that cyberspace may in fact be construed as a kind of transitional space that facilitates helpful experimentation with new identities (Turkle, 1995, 2005; Suler, 2002, 2004; Allison et al. 2006; Dini, 2009), and that the imaginary possibilities afforded by cyberspace can be used therapeutically (Suler, 2008). It is also the case, however, that the techno environments of cyberspace are particularly receptive to the projection and acting out of unconscious fantasy (see, e.g. Wood, 2006; Curtis, 2007; Gibbs, 2007; Toronto, 2009), and like all 'good' things they may be put to less good use.

Moreover, because cyberspace forms part of the technologized landscape that is now a standard part of daily life across the world, this makes it easier, sometimes less conspicuous, for it to be deployed by young people as a refuge away from the demands of the reality of embodiment and its particular meaning for them. 'Playing' in cyberspace may then be used to bypass the arduous psychic task required to represent experience, giving way instead to simulation, with the attendant risk that the 'fake' can replace the real and become more compelling.

Of course, there are many ways through which one can escape from the body, for example, through a more exclusive focus on intellectual pursuits, making the body seem redundant. The question of why some young people become defensively 'bookish' while others turn to cyberspace is unlikely to yield any simple answers. However, unlike immersion in schoolwork, immersion in cyberspace, because of its very particular qualities (see below), can accede more rapidly to a state of disembodiment. This more immediate freedom from being-in-a-body, and the omnipotence it promotes, can be intoxicating for some. In this respect it is not dissimilar to taking drugs, with one important difference, however: computers are available everywhere nowadays and the use of games is socially sanctioned, whereas drug-taking remains less accessible to many young people, is illegal, and in general is not culturally sanctioned.

This begs the question of whether the widespread availability of cyberspace gives form to new pathological manifestations, or whether it merely aids the enactment of particular self-object representations (see Dini, 2009). My own clinical experience makes me sceptical of the view that the Internet per se 'causes' psychological problems. Rather, I am suggesting that it can provide a culturally reinforced and readily accessible vehicle for the enactment of conflicts related to our embodied nature that some adolescents are especially primed for given their developmental histories. This is consistent with evidence – sparse though it is – that those who misuse the Internet, for example, have pre-existing problems (Morahan-Martin, 2008).

Research in this area, however, is plagued with conceptual and methodological difficulties, not least the absence of agreement over what constitutes Internet abuse and whether it should be considered a disorder. What is clearer is that particular psychological factors are associated with the excessive use of various kinds of virtual reality; these factors include loneliness (Whang, Lee, and Chang, 2003), low self-esteem (Yang and Tung, 2007), and shyness and social anxiety (Pratarelli, 2005). There is also evidence to suggest that depressed young people are more likely to use the Internet more than their non-depressed peers (Ybarra, Alexander, and Mitchell, 2005). Research also suggests that socially anxious and lonely individuals are more likely than others to develop a preference for online social interaction over face-to-face encounters (Ervin et al., 2004), which is an important predictor of Internet abuse (Morahan-Martin, 2008).

The avatar is the perfect tool for titrating intimacy. Paradoxically, however, because of the illusion of the anonymity afforded by the mask that is the avatar, people often disclose a great deal about themselves online, far more than they would do normally. Because 'information' is more important than physical proximity in cyberspace, interactions online may then leave some vulnerable people feeling unexpectedly very exposed.

What this research also makes clear is that the young people who seek refuge in virtual worlds do not necessarily do so because they struggle with being-in-a-body or have problems with their body image. The compulsive use of cyberspace is over-determined, and may be driven by various unconscious conflicts, but my focus here is restricted to understanding those clinical presentations where its misuse is in the service of managing a disturbing experience of 'otherness' that is felt to be concretely located in the body. Where this is the central unconscious preoccupation, I am suggesting that cyberspace is ideally suited to being defensively used to bypass the psychic implications of an embodied self. This may be understood as in part a function of some of cyberspace's specific features[2] as follows:

It denies corporeality. Cyberspace defies the history, the transience, and indeed the very physicality of the body. Virtual space can be used to effectively suspend the history of the subject, and hence the link to the anchor of the past is eroded, especially as it is recorded in the body. Multiple identities can be adopted and discarded at will. We have, effectively, the creation of what Raulet (1991) has referred to as 'floating identities'. This could conceivably have some constructive uses if a more positive experience of a 'new' self in cyberspace can be integrated with life 'offline' (Turkle, 1995; Allison et al., 2006). But where this kind of integration is not possible, the potential for pathological splitting is considerable.

The exhilaration of virtual existence and experience comes from the sense of transcendence and liberation from the material and embodied world (see Wood, 2007). A vivid example of our yearning for this kind of transcendence can be found in Cameron's film *Avatar*, in which the main protagonist – a paraplegic ex-Marine – regains mobility through his avatar, never to return to his original, irreparably damaged body. The film is an apt illustration of the 'traffic ... between fantasy and reality' (Mendelsohn, 2010) that cyberspace can promote as the limitations and history of the physical body are suspended and may then be disavowed. This presents the individual the illusion of limitless possibilities – an 'order of pure decision'.

It abolishes the reality of difference and separateness. It achieves this in two ways. First, by promulgating the illusion of a disembodied self, the tyranny of the specular image need not apply in virtual space. Virtual reality thus promotes the fantasy that despite differences, we are 'all the same really'. It is this promise of *sameness* that makes cyberspace so compelling for some young people: it bypasses any exposure to an experience of difference, and to the sense of insufficiency we all must find ways of managing in ourselves. In virtual reality, however, the promise of sameness with an ideal (as projected into an avatar, for example) is forever such that the painful awareness of the given body and of bodily separateness may be sidestepped. This process is aided by the use of mimetic defences and the development of imitative identifications, which are primitive in nature and based on an appropriation of the other through imitation. Such imitations, as I suggested in Chapter 1 discussing cosmetic surgery, are fantasies of being or becoming the object. The aim is to *become* the ideal, and not simply to strive to *be like* it. This is especially apparent in virtual games in which people can look like and 'become' someone else according to their own specifications.

The second way in which the reality of difference and separateness is abolished is through circumventing the reality of geographical boundaries. Technology, starting with the advent of print and then telephony, has radically transformed our ways of communicating and our spatio-temporal organization externally as much as internally. These developments urge us to 'rethink space-time' (Doel and Clarke, 2006) as they introduce new forms of relating and hence of acting in the world with others (Thomson, 1995). Through the medium of representation we can now bring remote events and people near while experiencing them at a remove (Robins, 2001). This facility may be used constructively to connect with people who are geographically distant, as well as destructively to undermine a real emotional connection with others who are physically removed.

With physical presence no longer required to initiate or sustain a relationship, primary body presence is converted into pseudo-presence (Žižek, 2004). The reality and, I would argue, the *necessity* of distance and separation (Josipovici,

1996) are replaced by immediate communication, bypassing the otherwise painful psychic work required to allow for the mourning of the absent or lost object. Instead, the thrill of speed substitutes for the reality of a real other who can never be fully controlled by the self.

It promotes the illusion of interpersonal transparency. We can enter a world where there are 'no zones of disorder or darkness', as Foucault (1980: 52) put it. The strangeness and opacity of the other are circumvented because the other is effectively the self's creation. Here the object – who too is disembodied – can be fully known and hence possessed (Arias, Soifer and Wainer, 1990; Gibbs, 2007). For an illustration of this process, see the case of Sharon below.

It alters the relationship between internal and external reality. By offering an illusion of what is real, it bypasses the need for the psychic work necessary for understanding that inner and outer reality are *linked* rather than being either equated or split off from each other. In the virtual world the psychic equivalence mode of reality (Fonagy and Target, 1996) dominates – a mode whereby the internal world that is projected into virtual space is seen to correspond to external reality. The technological environment of cyberspace thus confuses the boundaries between internal and external worlds, creating the illusion that internal and external reality are isomorphic. In these conditions of existence there are no limits to what can be imagined and acted out. As the self becomes intoxicated with omnipotence, it loses all contextual referents – of which the body is one – that would otherwise lend meaning to experience. Thinking is attacked: as fantasy and reality collapse into each other, there is no space from which to reflect. Virtual space may thus be seen as providing a psychic reserve within which all wishes are gratified, as reality becomes an irrelevance and the individual reclaims the infantile illusion of omnipotence. As Freud (1930) put it,

> The hermit turns his back on reality and will have no truck with it. But one can do more than this: one can try to recreate the world, to build up in its stead another world in which its most unbearable features are eliminated and replaced by others that are in conformity with one's own wishes.
>
> (Freud, 1930: 81)

The body in adolescence

Anyone working with adolescents will recognize the importance of the body in mental life. The features of virtual space that I have outlined may become especially salient and compelling for the young people who struggle to adjust to the psychic demands imposed by the reality of the changing body that puberty forces upon them. During adolescence, when the wish to transcend the body is often at its peak for some young people, the desire to be somewhere other than *in* a real body finds a receptive space in virtual worlds where the body is superfluous, and where mastery, control, and the denial of otherness can be exploited. Immersion in cyberspace may then allow the young person to create 'synthetic worlds' (Baudrillard, 1986) in which the body can be dispensed with, history is frozen, and thinking is anesthetized, affecting the capacity to manage conflict and pain in reality.

The period of adolescence has been described by several authors as involving an identity crisis (Blos, 1967; Erikson, 1968; Briggs, 2002), but this requires some qualification: the psychic process of adolescence typically sets in motion an unsettling review of personal identity that is *rooted in the body*. Whereas at birth the mind may be said to develop from the body, in adolescence the body presents itself forcefully to the attention of the mind (Ferrari, 2004). Erections, masturbation and menstruation intrude into an oasis of relative calm in the physical domain characteristic of the pre-pubertal stage. For many young people the experience of an orgasm becomes a focal point around which a sense of reality of the genital can be further organized, accompanied by a sense of volitional control in the seeking of sexual satisfaction.

At the best of times puberty thus initiates a complicated and unsettling internal process: the physical changes that trigger changes in the body image and hence in self-representation are also accompanied by changes in relationships with others – all of these changes, in my view, are inextricably linked and impact reciprocally on each other. The demands made by this developmental transition, however, can for some young people be simply too much to bear (Laufer and Laufer, 1984; Bronstein, 2009; Flanders, 2009). For some this unavoidable development is experienced as 'catastrophic' (Bion, 1970). This is all the more so where the quality of early relationships has contributed to a fragile, undercathected bodily self, or to entrenched splitting such that body parts may have become identified with bad, terrifying objects. In such cases an internal or external organ can be experienced as an alien object residing within the body rather than as an integrated part of the body-self. Body sensations may then need to be kept separate from the image of oneself as sexually mature.

Meltzer (1967a) refers to the 'confusional anxiety' that he regards as typical for adolescents. Laufer (1968) focuses on the question of ownership of the body, an issue latent in so many clinical presentations during adolescence: is the body felt to belong to the young person or to the mother? In their detailed work on adolescence, Moses Laufer and Eglé Laufer (1984) have highlighted the need to change one's relationship to the body as the key task of adolescent development. Its outcome, they suggest, determines the final sexual identity on which the sense of self is based. As a result of the bodily changes due to puberty, the young person must now integrate into his sense of who he is the reality of the mature sexual body. This is inextricably tied to the resurgence of primitive anxieties about dependency and separation from parental figures, and of Oedipal conflicts.

When there have been deficits in the baby's earliest relationship with the mother and her body, this will compromise the child's relationship to his body, and hence to reality. By the time of puberty, the adolescent's fantasies related to his new body can become profoundly disturbing. The young person may fear losing control over his body and mind. This may lead to an experience of the body as a persecutor that must be attacked. It is not just that the young person must manage the reality of a body that can now actualize sexual and aggressive fantasies, both conscious and unconscious. He is also confronted with the reality of separation from the mother's body.

Under the pressure of puberty the young person who has not established a secure, positively cathected body imagining will struggle to manage the reality of his separate body in relation to the Oedipal couple. Instead there may be a need to create an idealized body imagining, which sustains an experience of fusion with the idealized pre-sexual body of the mother. It is only when the young person can feel identified with the mother's body that he can reassure himself against the threat posed by separation. This can then result in a disavowal of the reality of the sexual changes and a marked splitting off of the body (Laufer and Laufer, 1984).

The case examples that follow are meant to illustrate how for these two young people immersion in cyberspace became their solution to an inner turmoil connected with their experience of being-in-a-body. Both cases may be read as illustrations of how cyberspace can provide a means for escaping not just from the body, but also from thinking and feeling, which of course it does; as I have said, however, I understand body and mind to be inseparable, such that escape from the body can only mean escape from the mind as well.

A virtual body floating in psychotic space: the case of Sharon

Sharon was seventeen when I first met her. She had been referred to a public mental health clinic because she hated her appearance and was impaired in several aspects of functioning. On presentation she met the diagnostic criteria for Body Dysmorphic Disorder and was severely depressed.

Sharon came from a relatively deprived socioeconomic background. As far as she was concerned, it was only a lack of finances that presented an obstacle to her seeking cosmetic surgery: if she had the financial means she was clear she would pursue it to obtain for herself what she fantasized to be a 'normal' and desirable body. Perhaps because she could not find a solution to her intolerable predicament through cosmetic surgery, Sharon turned to cyberspace instead. There it was possible for her to sustain the fantasy of complete control over her self-presentation. I understood this as her way of managing the profound paranoid anxieties she felt when in touch with the reality of her body and what it unconsciously represented.

Sharon was the eldest of two. Her parents lived together, but their relationship was a violent one. Sharon said she hated her father. She felt closer to her mother, even though she experienced her as very inaccessible. The mother was often home, but like her daughter she was severely depressed. Sharon had seemingly always been anxious to maintain physical proximity to her mother and to be desired by her, but invariably she was left feeling that she could never enliven or impress her. Importantly, she believed her mother was more invested in her younger brother.

Sharon described feeling ugly for as long as she could remember, but this feeling took hold in a particularly vicious manner around the age of thirteen.

Menstruation had felt deeply unsettling, and she had hated this moment in her life. Around this same time, she said, her face had erupted in acne. Since then she had been especially concerned about her skin and the shape of her face. Her skin, she said, was now still blotchy and uneven. She could not say what was wrong with her face except that it was the 'wrong shape', that somehow it was 'too big'. She was, in fact, an attractive girl with exceptionally smooth skin, as far as I could see. Yet she spent several hours every morning applying makeup and changing in and out of various outfits before she felt able to leave the house, which was not often. This led her to drop out of college and to disengage from her peer group.

She spent long periods of time at home, lying in bed, playing games on a small Nintendo, visiting online chat rooms or immersing herself (often for seven hours or more) in a range of virtual games on her computer, where she acquired a new identity and new friends – in short, a new life. She created different characters and was especially concerned with their physical presentation. When she discussed this in therapy, it was clear she felt relieved and comforted by the transformations she underwent in her mind as she identified with her avatars, especially because she could imagine herself in a different and more desirable body.

It was hard to think with Sharon about her use of cyberspace. She dismissed what I said as irrelevant; the games were 'just a bit of fun'. The relationship Sharon developed with the computer itself was also important and similarly hard to think about. Interestingly, she was very possessive of the computer. Since she had to share it with the whole family, not least with her brother, access to it was often a source of heated rows. She described to me the way she enjoyed the feel of the mouse in her hand, and the pleasure she gained when she clicked and saw things happen on the screen, as if the responsiveness of the screen to her touch evoked a feeling of fusion with, and hence control over, the maternal object that the computer, I thought, and the privileged space it gave her access to, had become identified with in her mind.

Her descriptions of online relationships were revealing: once she rather excitedly told me about a girl with whom she regularly 'chatted', but whom she had never met: 'I know everything about her – I even know when she goes to the toilet!' This statement provides an important insight into one of the appeals of this kind of relationship: this disembodied other, about whom she paradoxically knew intimate physical details, was felt to be entirely transparent, knowable, and accessible. For Sharon this encapsulated the idealized, fused relationship she wanted to create with her mother. It expressed, I thought, the fantasy of getting right inside her body (she would even know her bowel movements).

Sometimes Sharon missed sessions because she had been on the computer and 'forgot'. When we would explore this it became clear that she had been immersed in one of the games. When she was playing or online she entered a state of mind that was completely disconnected from reality: time ceased to matter and 'real' others ceased to exist. She felt very involved in her games and hated intrusions into this idealized space: she responded angrily if either of her parents interrupted her and asked her to do something. She also felt angry with me for intruding into this space through my invitations to think with her about how she used cyberspace. These incursions into her cocoon gave way to rages as she felt brutally pulled away from the safety of a world of endless possibilities – all of them but a click away – back into a bleak reality of depressed, warring parents and of a felt-to-be-inhospitable body that left her feeling undesirable.

The missed sessions were also expressions of what she needed to avoid in our relationship. Coming to see me was experienced in the transference as being exposed to my undesiring, and hence felt-to-be-critical glare. She was often relating to me as someone who would reject her, so it was safest to withdraw and reject me first. Indeed this was a pattern of exchange between us that dominated much of the therapy: brief excursions into our relationship when we could think together were invariably followed by more protracted periods when she shut me out and comforted herself with the fantasy that she did not need anyone and hence would be hurt by no one.

If ever I took up in the sessions how she shut me out, she would shrug and say, 'I'm not in the mood today,' but more often she simply remained silent. Sharon did, however, sometimes bring dreams, and it was through these that we were able, painstakingly and over time, to begin to understand the encumbrance that was her body, and the way in which cyberspace allowed her to escape from the reality of her embodied self. I will illustrate this with clinical material over several weeks taken from the end of our first year of work together.

After missing two weeks of therapy because she had felt so low she had seldom left the house, Sharon arrived for her session irritable. She told me that she had had enough of therapy, that it wasn't helping, and that it was, to use her words, 'a waste of time'. She said that talking and looking at her dreams was not giving her any practical help. She had come only because she wanted to tell me that she was going to end the therapy. And yet as I listened to her I sensed that she had come because she was desperate.

I said that even though she had told me that talking and looking at her dreams had been unhelpful, I thought that she had nevertheless made the effort to come because she knew she was in trouble and wanted me to help her stay in the therapy. She remained immobile and silent for several minutes and then, as if in a trancelike state, told me of the dream she had the night before: 'I am in a dark cave and can't see anything. I try to get out but my body keeps bumping into hard things and I can feel blood gushing out of my leg. I felt sick and tired and I curled up in a corner hoping I would die.'

I said that she was in a lot of pain and that she wanted me to know this and help to shed some light on what was making her feel so bad. Sharon rolled up the sleeve of her cardigan and showed me some superficial cuts, as well as a new tattoo she had done the previous week – her only excursion out of the house. She said, without affect, and as she looked at her arm, 'It is painful … I guess.'

I said that her body bore the marks of the pain she felt inside and that perhaps, as in her dream, she hoped that if her body died, the pain would stop. Sharon replied that she hated her body and that she had spent the last two weeks wishing she were dead. She had only managed, she said, because she played a lot of computer games and that had taken her mind 'off it'.

I said that coming to see me must feel like having to switch thinking back 'on' and that this felt like me asking a lot of her. Sharon replied that she thought she was beyond help. I said that being in her body felt like being trapped in a dark cave she cannot escape from. She nodded and said she hated her body. I observed that when she played her games she could forget about her body. She nodded and said it was 'like being someone else ... being free. ... Claire [one of her avatars] is so cool ... she's pretty and smart and no one messes her about'.

The next session was a particularly tumultuous one because her computer had broken down that week and she had not been able to access her games for several days except on her Nintendo, which was not the same.[3] She was restless and highly irritable, impatient with my attempts to relate to her. She came across as less articulate than was usual for her; she was confused and struggling to form thoughts. I thought she had decompensated markedly in the intervening week, as if the loss of access to her virtual world had disoriented her, exposing her brutally to a real world she could barely relate to or think about.

She eventually told me that she had felt very 'bored' and that she hated not having something to do with her time. I put to her that perhaps she was feeling confused and frightened, which she called 'bored'. At this point her more dismissive facade gave way and she quickly became distressed, telling me that she had missed an interview to explore a place at a college (she had forgotten about it), and that her father had told her he would no longer support her, that she had to go out to work. She told me that she was not able to work, that she could not manage this. She then described in detail how unwell she had also been feeling, gripped by a gastric virus that had caused diarrhoea: 'I was out buying some gum and I thought I was going to lose it and shit everywhere,' she told me.

I said that she was letting me see just how dangerous it felt when she lost access to the only space in which she was relieved of this body that kept pulling her down: without that escape she feared that all her messy, shitty feelings would leak out everywhere. She nodded and said that it had all been made worse by waking up that morning to find her bedsheets soaked in blood.

At her worst, Sharon so disregarded the reality of her body that her menstrual cycle could catch her by surprise, as it had evidently done the night before. She told me that her mother had gotten very upset about this and shouted at her. Her father had taken one look and told her she 'disgusted' him. As she related this she sounded fragile and humiliated, and I became acutely aware of the physical, visual relationship between us. I said that she was bringing this powerful image of her bloodstained sheets as proof of just how difficult it was to escape this hated body, that somehow it always inevitably left its mark, exposing her to the harsh, critical glare of others including, now, my eyes that perhaps left her feeling exposed in my presence.

Sharon sat back in the chair and pinched the skin on her face: 'I hate this,' she said, and then pulled out of her coat pocket the Nintendo she often carried around with her. I said she had brought a lot of painful feelings today and that she was now retreating into the safe, predictable world of her games. Despite numerous attempts on my part to reach her, Sharon remained glued to her Nintendo until the end of the session. But watching her was in itself instructive: she tapped away furiously, engrossed in the activity, seemingly confident in her dexterity, and ultimately triumphant as she scored against feeling. I was left feeling redundant as I witnessed first-hand the seduction of the certainty that the machine afforded her and that pulled her away from real interaction with me.

It was clear that my attempt to take up the transference with her had not relieved her; rather, it seemed to turn me precisely into the kind of harsh, critical object she anticipated. As she shut me out I felt peculiarly exposed and became acutely aware of myself in my own body and very uncomfortable in it, as if I had now become identified with her felt-to-be-physically repulsive self and it was she who could now ignore me.

The next week she returned and told me this 'horrible' dream: 'I am floating ... I feel so light ... I look below and all I see are dots, moving around, close together and then they start to get bigger and bigger and they spread everywhere ... it's disgusting, like some kind of gluey mess.'

Sharon eventually went on to tell me that her parents had had a big row, that her father had hit her mother the night before and then left the house. She did not know if he would be back. She said she did not care one way or another. She was then silent. I said that when things got very difficult at home, and in her mind, she retreated into a safer place in her mind where she could escape from the physical reality of where she was – a 'higher' place from where big problems could seem so small, like tiny dots in the distance. And yet, as in her dream, these dots eventually grew bigger and bigger – they didn't simply go away, they left a gluey mess behind in which she felt stuck.

Unusually for her, Sharon replied immediately and more thoughtfully. She said that she hated living at home, that it was so hard to hear her parents arguing all the time and seeing her father hit her mother. She said that she had coped by putting her headphones on and playing games. When she played, she said, she felt 'peaceful, safe, like I'm not on my own anymore'. She then told me that she had had another dream earlier in the week in which she had had an accident and was on a life-support machine, with tubes doing all the work of keeping her alive. She said she could not recall anything else except that 'it felt good'.

When I asked for some associations to the dream Sharon said she had heard on the radio an item about someone who had been left 'like a kind of vegetable' after a motorbike had crashed into a car and that everyone was saying what a terrible thing this had been. Instead, she had thought to herself, 'Lucky bastard – this is better than being alive and having to do all this stuff for yourself – at least he is fed, changed, taken care of.'

I said that she had witnessed another terrible crash between her parents and this had left her feeling impotent and frightened, and that she did not know how to manage these feelings in herself. She felt her only option was to make herself not feel anything, to plug herself into her 'life-support' computer-machine, and though maybe there was another kind of life support that she longed for me to offer her, allowing me to help her was very risky. Sharon replied that there was 'no point to feeling because there's nothing I can change'.

I will not go further into this last session. Suffice it to say that these excerpts from three consecutive sessions are very representative of the first year of our work together. They illustrate the pain of thinking, the disturbing nature of being-in-a-body, and the hopelessness Sharon felt in relation to her predicament: 'nothing can change'. Faced with this feeling, cyberspace was a welcoming haven in which she could manipulate her world and her self-representation at will.

For Sharon, the body was an obstacle that had to be constantly managed and triumphed over, typically through its denial and the consequent retreat into the safe cocoon provided by cyberspace – the computer and the space it linked her into became quite literally a kind of life-support machine; that is, it supported Sharon in managing the demands of reality by providing an alternative to it. The images in her second dream of her 'floating' and feeling 'light' aptly capture the absence of a body weighing her down and rooting her in the hard reality that, by contrast, she painfully bumps into in the 'dark cave' of the first dream.

The image of the life-support machine is especially relevant to this discussion since it captures another feature of cyberspace I would like to draw attention to, namely, the way in which the relationship to the computer, and the space it gives access to, parallels the wished for pre-Oedipal relationship to a receptive, desiring maternal body that can be fully known and controlled. The computer's responsiveness could be understood as giving Sharon access to a good 'screen mother' – always there, except when it breaks down and then Sharon is once again 'dropped'. She feels enraged and then frightened, and her capacity to respond to the cues from her real body is severely undermined.

In the transference, the visual relationship between us became central, at times leaving her feeling at the mercy of what she experienced at best as my disinterest, and at worst as a more humiliating rejection because I had a more desirable other in my mind. Sharon evidently experienced herself as profoundly undesirable, in her mother's eyes in particular, which she felt were more drawn to her brother, but her father's eyes were also unavailable to her. Her body was felt to be messy, disgusting, always leaking and exposing her to the critical eyes of the object. She tried to counter this experience by searching for an alternative, more desirable image of her body through her made-up self in a virtual world, or through her fantasies of cosmetic surgery. These simulated versions of herself allowed her to temporarily create a connection to a fantasized responsive, desiring maternal body. I want to stress, too, the relationship to the computer itself, because as Sharon related it to me, and as I witnessed for myself in the session when she played with the Nintendo, the physicality of the machine and the way it almost moulded into her body – and became an extension of it – powerfully reinforced the fantasy of control/fusion with the maternal object/body with which it had become identified.

As will be clear, Sharon was a very depressed young girl who was on the edge of, or in, a psychotic state of mind much of the time. Cyberspace provided her an extension of the psychotic space into which she retreated in her mind. In this kind of space, the reality of the real world was disavowed and the quality of Sharon's painful experience was reduced to a kind of intoxication with the virtual promise of a disembodied self and other whom she could access when she wished. When she could not access this state of mind, she effectively broke down as the reality of the body violently intruded (as in her menstrual cycle soiling the sheets).

Being a no-body: the case of Paul

Paul was almost seventeen when his parents sought help for him privately. They were concerned that he had become withdrawn, spending long periods of time on the Internet, primarily playing computer games, but also using social networking sites. They had been very tolerant of this at first because they thought he would soon tire of it, but when he did not, and his time playing games increased, his mother in particular became worried.

Paul was an only child. Both his parents were gifted academics who devoted a great deal of time to their research and other interests. They prized independence and had adopted the stance that Paul would 'learn from his mistakes', that 'reason would triumph'. Like them, Paul was very cerebral; schoolwork had always proved easy for him. On meeting him, however, it was clear that he inhabited his body with less ease: he seemed awkward in his movements, his choice of clothes was very conservative and lacked any personal stamp, and his manner was tentative. He sat in my chair on our first meeting, perched on its edge for the whole session, without even taking his coat off on a hot summer day.

When I asked him why he had come, he replied that he did not want to worry his parents. He told me that they thought he worked too hard and did not go out enough with friends. With some difficulty he was able to tell me that he felt he was not amusing or entertaining like his friends were, and that he was 'awkward' in social situations. He did not have a girlfriend, and emphasized that he had no interest in having a relationship, but he chatted to a lot of girls on social networking sites. This suited him, he said, but he also added that sometimes he felt lonely – as far as I was concerned, this acknowledgement was the most hopeful statement he had made in this session. He rounded off this discussion with a pithy 'I'm a nobody'. At this stage he did not mention his use of the Internet.

As the months passed, the sessions developed a clear pattern: he came, he dutifully listened to whatever I said, and he left without making much of an impression on me; indeed I often found I forgot what he said or what I had said. The first important development took place around the ninth month of our work together, after he had fallen and sustained a cut requiring several stitches. His mother had left me a message to say she was deeply worried, as he had stopped eating, ignored his schoolwork, and now spent all his time on the Internet.

He came for his session five days after this incident, looking very downtrodden. At first he was very silent, and then he offered this dream: 'I am walking slowly and as I walk I see a house collapsing. There is dust everywhere and I get covered in this dust. I can't breathe. I fall to the ground and cannot get back up.' He gave no associations to the dream, but after a long silence he volunteered that he was fascinated by images of detonating buildings and that he often searched the Internet for these images. He had been gripped by the collapse of the Twin Towers. He was quick to add that his interest in this event was simply in the images of the fallen buildings, reduced to dust. Since the terrorist attacks he had avoided lifts and tall buildings, he said, and he added, 'Actually I have always been afraid of buildings collapsing. As a child I always read about earthquakes ... they fascinate me.' He then mentioned, almost in passing, that he had fallen.

I said that his fall had deeply unsettled him, as if it had reminded him that he had a body and that a body was like a building: it *could* collapse or explode and be messy, but he was now not dealing with an image of someone else's body or of a building collapsing – it was *his* body. Paul looked away, evidently uncomfortable with my mention of the body, and I commented on this. Paul said that he wished he could forget the body and 'have no body'. He said he far preferred 'being in [his] head'. I said that his body seemed like a scary place to be in, so scary that it was preferable to be 'a no-body'. Paul smiled furtively, as if he recognized my reference to what he had said in our first meeting and, I thought, felt understood.

He then proceeded to tell me for the first time that he had met a girl on one of the social networking sites he visited and had exchanged a lot of e-mails and text messages with her. After months of virtual exchanges, she had upped the ante and suggested that they meet up. It was, interestingly, after this suggestion that he had gone for a walk – 'to clear [his] mind', as he put it – and he had crashed into a lamppost, tripped, and fallen. When he saw the blood, he said that he had felt like throwing up, that it disgusted him. He said he had felt as if it was not his body he was seeing or touching.

I said that the thought of actually meeting this girl in the flesh had been deeply troubling; it had forced him suddenly into having to think about a real relationship – about sex – rather than a relationship he largely controlled in his mind. It was then that Paul told me he had never kissed a girl, let alone had sex, though he knew several of his friends who had. I asked him what he wanted for himself in this respect. He replied that the thought of kissing actually repulsed him. All he could see was 'an exchange of saliva', which disgusted him. When he was exchanging e-mails with the girl, he had told her he wanted to have sex with her, but he had not really meant it. In his fantasy he had imagined long talks with the girl, 'perhaps stroking her hair', he said, but it never went beyond this.

He then recalled being a little boy and spending summers in a mountain resort with his mother while his father wrote his books. His mother would read to him and stroke his hair. He became tearful as he told me this. It was the first time he had ever shown any live feeling in the session. I said he so longed to be this little boy, sitting with his mother, enjoying being alone with her and having all her attention. I said that it was this kind of image that he had in his mind as he communicated with this girl, but that as soon as she wanted to transpose their relationship into the real world of real bodies he became terrified.

Paul was silent, and I sensed his discomfort in his body in a very direct way. In my countertransference I became acutely aware of my own physicality and gender. I said I could see that as we spoke together about these things, the real world of real bodies was live in the room between us and that he felt very unsettled by it, not sure how to relate to me.

I will not go further into this session, but it is worth noting that where the denial of the body is central to the individual's psychic equilibrium, the sexual transference is typically avoided, and sometimes not just by the patient. It can indeed prove very difficult to take up, and even when it is, its interpretation can be resisted by the patient. Nonetheless, its eventual working through typically yields helpful developments in the therapeutic work.

Paul's feeling that he was 'a nobody' was an apt description of how the denial of the reality of his body – a no-body – was at the root of his emotional and social difficulties and his retreat into cyberspace. As the work progressed, it became clearer that as a young child he had enjoyed an overly close relationship with his mother. She had seemingly felt neglected by the husband's investment in his work and had turned to Paul for comfort. By the time he was twelve, however, she had resumed her career and Paul experienced this as being brutally cast aside. This expulsion coincided with the onset of puberty. This had left Paul profoundly confused about his changing body and the part it played in disrupting this more blissful pre-Oedipal union with his mother. To manage his internal confusion, he had to find ways of bypassing the body.

Over the Internet Paul could indulge once more in his fantasies of an uninterrupted closeness with a woman/mother. He could even write about sex without this posing a problem, at least until he was taken at his word. Then he literally crashed into something, tripped, and fell, and the sight of blood coming from his body was deeply disturbing to him. I thought that the 'crashing' into the lamppost, followed by his falling and the sight of blood, evoked his fantasy of sexual intercourse as a bloody exchange of fluids that disgusted him. Indeed, he told me in a subsequent session that he had 'felt sick' when one of his friends had told him about 'the blood when you have sex with a virgin'.

Paul's preoccupation with, and excitement about, detonating, collapsing buildings could be read in a number of ways, of course. His aggression and fear of the damage he could cause are evident. The buildings seemed to me to be a powerful metaphor for the maternal body – that fantasized house in which he lived tied to his mother, a house forever threatened with collapse by the Oedipal rival, and by his own hatred and attacks on the body that he felt had so brutally expelled him. The sexual imagery conjured up by the detonated building will be apparent: it was evidently exciting to him, and yet these images (actual or in his mind) were never used to masturbate, since Paul could not allow himself to do this. Even so, we were able over time to understand how his search for these images reflected his preoccupation with his sexual body – a body he feared and that he experienced as proof that he had lost his mother forever.

The fate of the body in virtual space

The denial of embodiment emerges as a strong current in discussions about cyberspace and the so-called post-human subject. Here the 'body is the original prosthesis we all learn to manipulate' (Hayles, 1999: 3) and it then becomes possible to add an infinite number of prostheses defying the limits of the given body.

Just as the invention of the car extended the human foot as a prosthesis, technology fundamentally changes us and our experience of our bodies, and hence of our selves as we interact with it. This is vividly captured in the words of one user as he describes his relationship to the computer and the simulated games he played on it:

> When I was away from the machine, I felt as though I had undergone some kind of terminal amputation. With this ability to dislocate functions of my body, with the mediation of my senses, and with this new prosthetic that allowed me to move to another place, I had stepped across *a mysterious and fateful line.*
>
> (Meadows, 2008: 95; my italics)

The 'mysterious and fateful line' that can be crossed in virtual reality is deeply seductive. Yet the rate of technological advances far outstrips the mind's capacity to reconcile the triumph of progress with the pain of the inevitable limitations of reality – and especially of our embodied nature. As nature is 'transformed into a field of human action' (Giddens, 1991) we have seemingly been freed from the idea that birth is destiny and believe that we can redesign ourselves at will. Many of the developments in cyberspace technology can feed into such an illusion.

Technology de-objectifies the human body, banishing the messy, internal body and its expelled or leaked fluids. It creates distance from our organic nature and limitations, protecting us from the crude reality, as Becker (1973) provocatively put it, that we are 'Gods with anuses'. From the point of view of the internal world avatars, for example, are pseudo-representations of a pseudo-self. For some young people they provide compelling visions of a more desirable self and conveniently bypass what would be a far less certain, messy and painful psychic journey.

The juxtaposition of the 'real' fleshy body in front of a 'hard' computer or a Blackberry invites pause for thought. Here the complexity of the relationship to the computer as an object of empowerment – its phallic 'hardness' – is exposed through the stark contrast with the softer and folded form of its static user whose body recedes in significance until it becomes superfluous in a virtual world that promises freedom from the constraints of the bodily self.

Focusing on virtual reality, and hence on virtual connectedness, raises the important question of the fate of the body in the mind as the very experience of intimacy is altered because virtual reality is a form of communication that is predicated on distance and a disembodied self. Anzieu (1990) has compellingly argued that today it is no longer sexuality that is repressed; rather, it is the sensual body, the body that comes into being through the other, the body that is denied by technology.

Just as technological advances promote the *necessity* of digital networks, and 'the circulatory systems of flesh and blood are now relegated as merely accessories of bygone times' (Heartney, 2004: 240), so a real relationship to the body, the self and with others can be opted in and out of with ever greater ease. Whilst communication between adolescents through texts and e-mails superficially may give the impression of close and intimate exchanges, in those young people for whom the body is felt to be terrifying, this virtual intimacy may paradoxically alienate them further from the reality of being-in-a-body. This may create greater difficulties in integrating the sensual and sexual body into a stable self-representation and into meaningful relationships with others.

The delicate and intricate processes that support the establishment of a secure sense of self confidently rooted in the body, and the capacity to reflect on experience rather than enact it on and through the body, may be undermined by the relentless emphasis on transformation, change, and triumph over the body now made possible by a staggering range of new technologies. I have suggested not that these external trends cause new forms of psychopathology, but rather that they may have an adverse impact on the course of the adolescent process in vulnerable young people, and more specifically on the young person's capacity to integrate the reality of the body into the self-representation.

Faced with the external complexity of the demands of the modern world (especially on young people), and the internal complexity and pain inherent in what is psychically required to develop a body and mind that feel one's own, it is tempting to retreat into virtual spaces where the reality of the body is either denied altogether, or where the body becomes solely an instrument for personal gratification, reassurance and comfort, not the basis for a connectedness with others. For young people like Sharon and Paul, immersion in virtual reality becomes psychically *necessary* in order to control an otherwise disturbing otherness that resides in the body.

Notes

1 I will be using the terms *cyberspace* and *virtual reality* interchangeably.
2 There is a degree of inevitable overlap between some of these features.
3 This was due probably to the fact that console games like Super Mario Brothers limit the user's control of the avatar. For example, the player cannot decide how Mario looks.

Chapter 4

Present without past

The disruption of temporal integration in a case of adolescent transsexuality

As an analyst I approach my task with the hope that whatever else the patient may take away from the experience of the analytic encounter he will at the very least understand experientially how present-day actions, thoughts, phantasies and wishes reveal a lifetime of experience that 'burns' through to the present – an image that was beautifully captured by T. S. Eliot in *East Cocker*. As analysts we are always witnessing or participating in, and thus hopefully facilitating, our patients' relationship to time past, present and future in order to help them to live *in* time.

Many psychopathologies have been conceptualized as reflecting 'problems to do with time and accepting change' (Birksted-Breen, 2009: 39). Some patients find it difficult to be in the present because they are stuck in the past; others, by contrast, struggle to remain connected with the past and are suspended in a so-called present that is effectively atemporal, that is, 'out of time'.

Living in time requires acceptance not only of change but also of continuity, that is, acceptance of what cannot be changed even with the passing of time (Boris, 1987, 1994). Nowhere is this challenge more painfully apparent than in the case of transsexual individuals who need to find a way of accepting the fact of having being born in a given body that is then felt to be odds with their subjective experience and is later altered through sex reassignment surgery (SRS).

In this chapter I will focus on the double meaning of 'given' body, that is both as the sexed body we are born into and the body 'given' to us de facto by our parents linking us indelibly to them irrespective of any changes we subsequently make to the given body. I want to examine the impact of extensive modification of the body on the 'temporal link' (Grinberg and Grinberg, 1981), which is an important feature of our identity as it provides continuity between different representations of the self over time.

I am focusing here on a subset of transsexual patients who start their transitioning in early adolescence. Transitioning is a dynamic process involving bodily as well as psychological adjustments. Children as young as 3 years of age may experience gender dysphoria and cross-gender behaviour; however, only 16 per cent of these children will continue to have persistent Gender Identity Disorder (GID) in adolescence and adulthood. In the group with profound and persisting cross-gender identification it is characteristic for severe distress to be exacerbated at the onset of puberty, due to revulsion towards unwanted physical changes. In addition to ongoing psychological support, pre-pubertal adolescents with persistent GID may thus be given hormonal treatment using gonado-trophin-releasing hormone analogue (GnRH) to suppress puberty once it has commenced, followed later by cross-sex hormone therapy to promote physical development in the affirmed gender.

When hormones are used in this way we can observe in some cases not only the desired suspension of physical time during which the body's given biological trajectory is artificially halted, but also of psychological time. I want to suggest that in some instances this biological and psychic detour can result in a marked distortion in the young person's relationship to time and impacts on their psychological adaptation following SRS, as I will illustrate through my work with Paula.

The time of the couple

Physical time is public time, the time that clocks are designed to measure. Biological time is an organism's circadian rhythm. Psychological time is private time and it is perhaps best understood as the subjective awareness of physical and body time. Our relationship to time is a pivotal feature of our capacity to manage reality. Where this relationship is disturbed many aspects of functioning are affected.

Several authors have rightly emphasized how primitive temporality is linked to biological rhythms punctuated by cycles of frustration and satisfaction (e.g. Hartocollis, 1974; Barale and Minazzi, 2008). The role of the maternal object in the construction of temporality has also been well developed in the analytic literature (e.g. Denis, 1995; Birksted-Breen, 2009) along with the important relationship between time and the foundations of the Oedipal structure (e.g. Fain, 1971). In this chapter I want to build on these contributions and focus on the specificity of the role of the *time of the couple* in establishing temporality *as rooted in the given body*.

The experience of time as it is rooted both in the body's potential for change and in its facticity highlights that it is not only change that has to be managed at the level of one's bodily representation, for example, because of the changes brought on by puberty or by ageing, but also the continuity of the given body and the objects it inevitably ties us to. This continuity overrides any actual changes the body may undergo over time because the continuity I have in mind here relates to the given body's link with the past and its origins.

We can manipulate the appearance of our body in more or less dramatic ways, and even change its appearance beyond recognition, but we can never delete the imprint of the other on the body. Another way of putting it would be to say that we have to accept that we cannot give birth to ourselves (see also Chapter 1). This psychic fact has to be somehow integrated into our sense of who we are and it is a core constituent of our orientation in time. Dependency on our objects has an intrinsically temporal dimension: it requires tolerating not only the object's independence and hence their absence in the present, but also the object's independent existence *prior to* our coming into being, that is, our absence in their past.

The transition from the intra-uterine to the extra-uterine state, which as Klein (1926) suggested was the 'prototype of all periodicity'[1] (99), is vitally important when we consider our relationship to time. However, from the outset and over the course of development, it is awareness of the parental couple – not only or even primarily the loss of intra-uterine state or of early dyadic unity – that structures the mind.

Our given body indelibly bears the trace of the mother whose body is shared in utero. But the body also serves as the most potent and concrete reminder of the reality of the parental couple that created it in the first place. Our orientation to reality has a temporal dimension that is related to these basic facts of life. In this sense we might say that the configuration of the body in the mind is intrinsically temporal: the body's very origins are concrete evidence of a specifically 'before-me' time dimension – before I was conceived, before I was born, before I was. Being cognisant of what I am referring to as *'before-me-ness'*[2] exposes us inevitably to an experience of exclusion and passivity relative to those who give us life through a union that not only excludes us, but actually creates us. In other words we have to bear the pain of exclusion *and* the envy of the couple's creativity. This is the basis for establishing the Oedipal structure in the mind and hence respect for the differences between generations. A capacity to live in time requires tolerance of the time when we did *not* exist – when our body was a 'no-body' – and would never have existed were it not for the parental couple.

When all goes well the fact of *before-me-ness* is integrated with an experience of 'as-I-am-now', in the present, to form a stable representation of the self rooted in the body. Crucially the body representation, despite the inevitable physical changes the body will undergo over time, retains nevertheless a core stability – a sense of our body that both integrates its indebtedness to the parental couple along with the idiosyncratic fashioning of the body that marks it as also separate from the primary objects.

Working with transsexual patients invites us to consider interesting questions about time because where the body is extensively modified (i.e. altered from how it was 'given to me by my parents in the past') the individual's relationship to time is sometimes also affected. This is so when the modification is aimed at deleting what the body unconsciously represents for that individual.

These considerations are especially relevant to current debates about the practice of delaying puberty through hormone treatment, giving the patient the time to make a permanent decision later in their teens. In some cases, I want to suggest, this pubertal/physical limbo, followed for some young people with a radical transformation of the body through SRS, warps the relationship to time, fuelling an omnipotent state of mind characterized by a severance with the reality of *before-me-ness*.

Living on a cloud: the case of Paula

Paula was an MtF transsexual who had undergone SRS very young and whom I first met when she was about to turn 19. She had held the conviction that she was a girl trapped in a boy's body from as early as she could recall. She sought hormone treatment to suspend puberty aged 13. She started cross-sex hormones aged 16 and then pursued SRS just before turning 18.

Paula was an only child; she had one half-sister from her father's first marriage with whom she had very little contact. Paula's father left the family home when she was under a year old and she retained very infrequent contact with him. He was described as a very religious man with conservative attitudes. He had moved abroad, remarried and started another family. He was not supportive of her sex change and struggled to accept what she had done. Her mother, by contrast, was felt to have been very supportive after the initial 'shock'.

Paula was a very bright, attractive young person who passed convincingly as a woman. She was referred for help because she felt depressed and was struggling to resume college after the time she had taken off due to the SRS and the complications that ensued. Additionally she had moved out of the area she had lived in all her life up until that point so she could have a 'fresh start'. This meant adjusting to a completely new social environment with her new identity as a 'girl' whom no one would know had undergone SRS. She was struggling to adapt to her new environment, finding it difficult to make friendships and feeling very awkward, especially around boys. As a result she was missing most classes and spent increasing amounts of time at home seeking proximity to her mother.

The geographical disruption aimed at erasing Paula's past in order to aid her integration following SRS appeared to have contributed to a profound sense of dislocation and triggered a breakdown. She developed various somatic complaints that enveloped her and literally kept her in bed for weeks on end, nursed by her mother as if she were a newborn needing to be looked after round the clock.

Both Paula and her mother had seemingly viewed the suspension of puberty, followed by SRS, as a process of giving 'birth' to a new self: Paula had to grow up again from scratch. As such Paula's orientation in time was profoundly disturbed: she appeared unanchored in the past and consequently lived in a very particular kind of present without history. This was a striking feature of her presentation that alerted me to the way the past had to be effectively deleted so as to accommodate the present-day reality of her new body and identity as a woman, but paradoxically because of the severed link with the past she could not be 'present' in the present either. This also impressed on me the difficulty we would encounter in our work since thinking itself is impossible without any reference to the past.

Paula's life prior to her sex change was hard for me to picture. I use the word 'picture' advisedly because, of course, I could not even picture what she looked like before her sex change. My difficulty, I thought, was related to how she could not keep alive in her mind any picture of herself prior to the surgery. She was indeed very vague about how life had been up until that point, as if it had all been wiped out and along with it all temporality. Consequently her story came across as very disjointed, with a marked absence of references to the past prior to her starting hormone therapy aged 13. At that point she appeared to have entered a phase of suspended animation whilst she waited for the body she felt she could inhabit more comfortably. She recalled this time as 'the beginning' and it brought relief to her acute distress. Sexuality of any kind had been put on hold – she told me that she never masturbated and regarded her then penis as alien to her, nothing that could bring pleasure. She said she had no interest in either boys or girls at that stage.

As she spoke about her family Paula barely acknowledged her father: it was me who brought him into the picture by asking her directly about him. More to the point she seemed to exist in a place in her mind where there was no parental couple. She told me she knew nothing about how her parents got together and showed no curiosity in this respect. She was similarly sparse in her account of why they had separated, as if focusing on their separation would require acknowledgement that they had once been together. She was also disconnected from any sense of extended family history such as grandparents and became irritable when I enquired about this, all of which left me with the peculiar impression that there was literally no past before her, just as there was no past prior to the sex change.

First encounter

The first time I met Paula I was struck by her relationship to her lateness. She arrived 15 minutes before the end of her scheduled appointment. She did not seem fazed by this and she did not make reference to it. When I observed that we had very little time left she looked surprised and replied that she had forgotten the actual time of the appointment, she had guessed it was around the time she arrived, that the letter I had sent her got lost so she had not been able to check it anyway, 'But I am now here', she added somewhat provocatively. She said all this rather dismissively, leaving me feeling as if I was the one enslaved to a clock that was ticking away, whilst she existed outside of the constraints of time.

This first encounter, like so many, contained the seeds of what we eventually came to understand about Paula's relationship to time and how this tied in with her relationship to her given male body. As I listened to her in this first brief meeting I felt as if the 'now' moment – 'But I am now here' – was a triumphant display of how the past was redundant, that it could offer no perspective and hence her lateness was of no consequence. As such I caught a glimpse of what I later understood to be her existence in a time warp that had been concretized through the artificial suspension of puberty when she was 13, but which I speculated had most likely been a feature of how she functioned prior to that time too.

The suspension of puberty and the anticipated bodily transformation from male-to-female had functioned in her case as a kind of psychic and physical hibernation during which she was effectively waiting to be reborn according to her own specification thereby obliterating any awareness of the couple in her mind. This anticipated rebirth created a stasis in which the present was a form of waiting unanchored in a past. However, once the surgery had taken place she remained stuck in this time warp. This stasis laced the analytic relationship and effectively functioned as a defence against making links with the past, precluding working through the relationship to the given body and hence interfered with her adaptation to her 'new' modified body.

In a discussion of technique Denis suggests that,

> the transference which makes the past present modifies the unconscious causing it to become temporal or giving it back a temporality in the sense that it allows the unconscious to exist in time by bringing it out of a past without a present.
>
> (Denis, 1995: 1110)

This very valuable observation needs to be considered alongside the importance in cases such as Paula's where the aim of working in the transference, we might say, is to allow the unconscious to exist in time by *bringing it out of a present without a past*. This proved to be the challenge I encountered in my work with Paula, which I will now illustrate with two sessions taken from different phases of our four-year-long psychoanalytic psychotherapy.[3]

Session 1: 9 months into the therapy

The first session I will report followed a session when Paula had arrived outside my room 15 minutes early, unannounced by reception, just as my previous patient was leaving.

Paula arrived 20 minutes late following the previous week's event. She made no reference to the lateness, by now a rather characteristic way in which she wiped out the constraints of reality. She sat quietly, averting her gaze, and then she spoke in a rather detached manner about an incident at college when a girl had made some 'stupid' remark about her appearance that had left Paula feeling irritated with her.

I observed that she was describing an incident that had been difficult and yet she sounded rather detached. Paula shrugged and said she had a lot to do for college and was not meeting deadlines. I detected a twinge of anxiety as she admitted that she was so behind on her coursework that she might fail. She added that she was tired, too tired to think, and she then went on to describe how she had smoked a large joint the night before and enjoyed losing all sense of where she was.

I said that was the state of mind she wished she could be in right now instead of having to think with me about her lateness to her session, her lateness with her coursework or the painful comment made by the girl at school.

Paula said nothing at first but then went on to recount a dream she had a few days previously in which *her maths teacher had set her a complicated piece of work and had given her a very tight deadline. She had put the work in her bag but on her way home had stopped by a lake and thrown the bag with all its contents into the water.*

In her associations she told me that she enjoyed watching objects sink to the bottom of the water. She liked the way they disappeared 'out of range' so that no one would know they had ever existed. As a child she recalled how she enjoyed scribbling over figures she had drawn until it was impossible to discern the original drawing. She then spoke about a forensic detective series she had been following on TV where they often fished out dead bodies from lakes as part of the investigation. She liked this series and was especially taken with the lead female forensic scientist whom she thought was 'very smart'.

I said that [her] being in the session today felt like being pressurized to do complicated homework and that she preferred to wipe out of her mind difficult thoughts and feelings so that they were safely kept out of our 'range' of exploration. I made no reference to the association to the forensic series but I was encouraged by it because it suggested to me that a part of Paula needed me to not be distracted from the task of 'fishing out' the drowned thoughts and feelings, which like the dead bodies on TV series, needed to be kept alive, in my mind at least, so that we could carefully investigate them.

Paula went on to say that she was fed up today because she was not responding to the hormones and her breasts were still too small. She was angry with her doctor who would not yet refer her to have the surgery done 'for free' and was encouraging her to keep taking the hormones instead.

I said that perhaps she was upset that the hormones had not managed to successfully wipe out all traces of her boy body. I wondered aloud whether the girl's 'stupid' comment about her appearance, and about which she had not yet given me any detail, might have stirred this anxiety.

Paula said that the girl had said she was 'too skinny' – nothing about her breasts. She paused and then said maybe being told she was skinny had left her feeling like 'less of a girl'. She envied curves even though she knew that some people would kill to be as skinny as she was. She added that she never actually thought about being a boy. She recalled how 'excited' she had felt when she had been put on GnRH (to halt puberty) because she then knew she could get out of her boy body.

I invited her to help me to understand how that time had been for her. Paula replied that it had felt like her boy body was gradually slipping away, 'like shedding skin', she said, and a new skin could then grow. Now she had thrown away all photos of herself as a boy. She could not even recall what she looked like and could not see the point of doing so 'because I *am* a girl', she added.

I said it was a bit as if she had scribbled all over her boy body and it was now impossible for her to even see its contours in her mind.

Paula said she did not like to think about that time. I said it had been a very difficult time. She nodded and said she really could barely recall it and she then added: 'I want to look forwards, not backwards. There's nothing before the operation. My life was shit. I've lost so much time already because of the operation and the recovery.'

I said the past was a time of feeling trapped and of despair and she had now moved out, quite literally, not only from the area she had once lived in as a boy and from her boy body, but also from a place in her mind that stored memories of being a boy because they disturbed her. Paula said rather forcefully that being a boy did not feel like her; it had never felt like her.

I said that today I had started to draw the contours of her boy body, reminding her of it and she wanted to scribble over what I was saying, just as she scribbled over other things that happened between us, like the fact of her lateness today, or arriving early the week before, because these were also things she did not like to think about.

Paula said she had seen someone coming out of my room the previous week. She was not sure if this had been another patient; or it could, she added, have been my teenage child for all she knew.

I reminded her that this had happened because she had not in fact reported in at reception when she arrived but had come straight up to my room, early, not at her time but during someone else's.

She said she had not known that she should always report to reception. I said I thought she knew very well that this was the routine, but that perhaps a part of her was curious to see what went on in my room before she was able to come into it.

Paula said she was not really interested in whom else I saw; it had been an accident: she was always getting her times wrong. It was 'no big deal', she said; she thought I 'went on about our session times a lot'.

I said she was angry about my focus on time and that it left her feeling criticized. Paula said she did not like to follow anybody's rules – if she had followed rules then she would have followed the rule that said 'You should accept the body you are born in' and she would now be very unhappy. That's what her 'stupid' father had said to her some years ago.

I observed that she thought I was stupid too, forcing her to think that her given time with me was not the only time in which I existed, but that there were other times – like the time with my previous patient or with the child she imagined I had – that excluded her. I said that maybe she did not want to think about anything or anyone that came before her in my mind.

Paula went very silent and was fidgety in her chair. After some time she said that she was struggling with maths at college. She had never been good at maths. She added that she just felt it was 'all gobbledygook', that she could not even add up properly.

I said that she was letting me know that what I had just said was 'all gobbledygook', that she simply could not follow what I meant when I said that she did not want to think about anything or anyone that came before her in my mind. It felt perhaps like I was asking her to add up difficult ideas and feelings all at once and this was turning out to be like a complicated maths problem.

Paula looked at me intently and nodded as if she felt recognized somehow but she was not quite sure what she thought about anything that I had said. She was then silent for the remaining 5 minutes and unusually thanked me as she got up to leave.

Session 2: 26 months into the therapy

By the time of this session Paula had privately secured breast augmentation surgery.

She began the session speaking briefly about some housing difficulties and then reported the following dream:

> *I am suspended on a cloud. I feel light. Nothing moves around me. The clouds are still. I can see the world below but I am not part of it. A woman is standing below in a field, shouting. I think it's because she thinks I will fall through the cloud and break my bones. I can hear her voice, loud at first, then it becomes dimmer and dimmer until I can just see her mouth moving but no sound comes out. She looks so small ... My father then appears and pushes right up against her from behind. The woman looks kind of surprised but does not seem to mind. He mouths too but no sound comes out. They both look like cut-out figures ... funny (laughs).*

I invited Paula to say a bit more about the dream. She said that when she was a child she would look up at the sky and wish she could travel into the sky and sleep on a cloud where there would be stillness around her. She recalled a children's story she used to like in which a man lived on a cloud and from up there he decided if it would be sunny or cloudy or rainy or cold on any given day. She then added that as a child she had believed that storks delivered babies. When she realized that she was *'really'* a girl, she imagined her girl body must have been delivered at another address and she fantasized about one day finding it.

I said there was a way in which she still liked to live up in the clouds where everything stands still, even time, and she could then be in control of everything – like the weatherman – whilst others, like me or her parents, were cut down to size, little people with no voice.

Paula said she thought her father cut a pathetic figure but her mother, she felt, meant well and had helped her through the hard times. But she could not understand how her mother had ever got together with her father. She did not like to think about that time in her mother's life because her mother had told her she had been unhappy due to the 'bad fit' with her father. She did not like to think of her mother as being unhappy.

I said that perhaps it might also be difficult to think of a time before she was born when her parents, however mismatched she might think they were, did nevertheless come together and created her.

Paula said the thought of it repulsed her. She added disparagingly that they were such a bad fit that she could only have been born into a 'badly fitting' body.

I said that the 'right' body in her mind seemed to be one that had nothing to do with her parents whatsoever.

Paula replied that she had simply restored her body to what it should have always been.

I sensed that she had felt criticized and I wondered whether I had been too forceful. I was by then familiar with the challenge of titrating my interventions with Paula because of the extent of her defences against reality; it was all too easy to err on the side of exposing her to too much too soon, which would shut down her thinking. And yet remaining largely supportive in my interventions without any challenge felt as if I was joining her up in the clouds and suspending reality. The risk of badly timed interventions was therefore large.

I went on to say that perhaps she was feeling criticized by me. She said nothing. I added that she had perhaps felt that I could not take in how strongly she still believed the story of the stork delivering her real body to the wrong address and how this story had helped her through some difficult times.

She nodded and was then silent for over 5 minutes. When she resumed talking she told me how after her session the previous week she had been listening to her iPod on the bus and an older man had complained about the noise. She had felt very angry with him; instead of turning the volume down she told him, 'Who do you think you are?' and then went to sit on the upstairs deck.

I said she seemed to feel outraged because he had intruded into her space, not her into his. She replied curtly that he had been intrusive and that no one upstairs had minded the volume. She said it was better to sit upstairs anyway because on the 'lower deck' you were more likely to meet 'weirdos' who always had a complaint.

I said that she had experienced what I had been saying today as intrusions into her mind – as if I was somehow complaining about her and pointing the finger at her – and she just wanted to drown my voice out. She replied that sometimes I said helpful things but today she just felt what I said was 'irrelevant'.

I said that when she did not want to hear something she retreated to a place in her mind that felt like being up the clouds or the upper deck of the bus where she did not have to play by anybody else's rules. I added that this was a familiar and safe place.

Paula looked thoughtful and after a few minutes said it was hard to be her. When she was first started on hormones she felt her problems would be over and then she could start her life. Now she felt stuck. She quickly added she had no regrets about the surgery, but she also quickly returned to how lonely she felt. The days at home 'drag on forever', she said, and she did not know what to do with her time. She could see people at college having 'a good time'. As I listened to her I felt she was more emotionally present in the room and I was more connected with how painful it was to be her.

I said that at one stage in her life being suspended up in the clouds felt like a better and safer place to be, but that perhaps it was now getting in the way of life down below, where time now dragged on and she felt very out of step with her peers who were living in time.

After a brief pause Paula asked me, for the very first time, how much time we had left in the session.

We were very near the end by now. I acknowledged this, adding that she seemed to have become aware for the first time of the passing of time in our session and that this might make it harder to end today.

Paula nodded and the session ended in silence – a silence that, for the very first time, felt very rooted in time and hence in a reality below the clouds.

The temporal link

Paula, like other transsexual individuals I will discuss in the next chapter, endured many years of pain and loneliness because of her gender dysphoria. Unlike many such individuals, however, she is representative of a newer group of transsexuals who can access earlier intervention than once used to be the case. In some respects such advances could be said to reduce distress. There is some evidence to suggest, for example, that when a strict assessment and clinical protocol is followed, hormone treatment to suspend the development of puberty is associated with a good outcome and a low rate of regret (Delemarre-van de Waal and Cohen-Kettenis, 2006; Cohen-Kettenis et al., 2011; Steensma et al., 2011).

However, when we consider a case such as Paula's we are alerted to the complexity of such assessments because we are inevitably dealing with both conscious and unconscious motivations that lead young people to request such interventions. Indeed such cases necessitate a thorough *psychodynamic* assessment in order to understand how the suspension of puberty may impact on the young person's psychological development and the capacity to integrate the reconstructed body with the given body. This way we can support the young person to consolidate a stable sense of identity, which is an essential requirement for the capacity to live in time.

Time, as Kant grasped, is a 'mode of representation of myself' (Kant, 1787[2007]: 12). How we relate to time reveals a great deal about how we experience ourselves in the world and about our internalized object relationships. Indeed from a psychoanalytic perspective we might add to Kant's insight that time is a *mode of representation of the self-in-relation-to-an-other(s)* and as such it is centrally related to our sense of identity.

The development of a sense of identity, as outlined by Grinberg and Grinberg (1981), is the outcome of a process of continued interaction of three lines of integration, namely the spatial, temporal and social. Along with others they underline how the experience of time is a binding activity in which, at best, past and present and future can have a mutual influence (e.g. Loewald, 1972).

I want to focus here on the Grinbergs's (1981) notion of the *temporal link* that refers to the continuity between different representations of the self over time. This establishes the foundations of a sense of continuity of the self. Indeed it was the link of temporal integration that was disturbed in Paula and which I am suggesting most likely accounted for her poor post-operative adjustment.

Paula's dream image of living *suspended* in the clouds from where, like the weatherman, she could control everything, evocatively captures the omnipotent, timeless state of mind she retreated into. This made it very hard for her to live in time because she was otherwise painfully confronted with a past that she could not integrate with the present.

From up above in the clouds the parental couple (and me in the transference) became 'irrelevant', laughable mouthpieces. As in her dream image, the 'noise' of the primal scene (the voiceless father forcefully entering the mother from behind) was turned off in her mind, reducing the parental couple to cut-out figures over whom she triumphed. Living in real time required of Paula that she face the accusation 'Who do you think you are?', which she had levelled in outrage at the man on the bus, that is she had to re-own the projected shamed 'weirdo' self with a complaint, namely her grievance against the parental couple.

In the dream – reported over two years into the treatment – there is also, however, the woman/me who wants to protect her from falling out of the clouds and breaking her bones, perhaps reflecting a dawning awareness of the costs of her defence and her awareness of me as a potential figure of help.

During puberty Paula lived in suspended animation waiting to find a new body that she could inhabit comfortably whilst she 'shed the skin', as she put it, of her male body. Interestingly the dream image of her suspended in the clouds captures not only the suspension of time, as I suggested earlier, but it is of note too that she renders the clouds immobile – 'The clouds are still' – capturing perhaps how she could not allow any intercourse and movement in others or in herself.

As the past became a wasteland Paula lost a temporal context that could support her through the psychic impact of the modification of her body. In this respect the challenge for Paula was not that of integrating the subjectively felt-to-be-'real' body in the context of the body she was born into; rather it was a case of taking on wholesale a new identity and then being on the run, as it were, from anything or anyone that might reconnect her identity in the past. Unsurprisingly this led to a severe breakdown in functioning with marked somatization as one of its features and a disruption in the temporal link. Paula's fantasy of an actual rebirth was powerfully reinforced by the geographical move after SRS, which cut off all physical and temporal links with the past. Her position was clear, as she summed it up, 'There's nothing before the operation. My life was shit.'

In the first session reported here, however, we might also understand her early arrival to the session as prefiguring, in action, a dawning awareness of a past 'before-me-ness', as if this was the only way she could begin to explore this temporal dimension in our relationship. If this is so, this might also recast my understanding and response to her in the session when I take up how she did not want to think about anything or anyone that came before her in my mind, to which she replies by making reference to how maths feels like 'gobbledygook' to her. If Paula had indeed started in her own way to explore what went on in my room/mind before her by arriving early, my intervention failed to acknowledge this and hence was indeed a kind of 'gobbledygook'.[4]

As I suggested in the last chapter, the body in adolescence presents itself to the attention of the mind (Ferrari, 2004). In normal development the advent of puberty, with its dramatic physical changes, necessitates the integration of the sexual and aggressive urges of the post-pubertal body into the representation of the body, and so of the self. In an adequately prepared pubertal boy, for example, erection and orgasm bring a focal point around which not only can a sense of reality of the genital be further organized but also a new sense of time in the rhythm of sexual needs and in the seeking of sexual satisfaction can be discovered.

However, when such changes are suspended artificially there is an inevitable psychic corollary: instead of development and the requirement to integrate the changing body's rhythms (which have a temporal dimension) into the young person's existing representation of the body so that it can be 'updated', there may be stasis. This may be accompanied by a rupture with past representations of the body in the mind. This scenario carries the inevitable risk that omnipotent phantasies about self-creation are reinforced as the body's natural trajectory is bypassed and along with it there is a bypassing of a mourning process about that which cannot be changed.

The 'given' bodily configuration, even if at odds with subjective experience, informs the representation of the body in the mind and needs to be somehow integrated into the experience of the self. The transsexual feels that s/he does not inhabit the 'true' body and responds to this experience by developing a parallel body image. In turn this needs to be actualized because it is invested with the power to bring greater cohesion and relief. But this 'new' edited body is *always* a reconstructed body with a history. This is the area that requires considerable and painful psychic work. We can add breasts where there were once none, we can take away a penis where there was once one, but it is impossible to obtain the original genitalia of the opposite sex, that is, the acquired genital, and hence the 'new' body, is always in the wake of a body that once was (Lemma, 2012). What can be achieved through SRS is a closer alignment between the outward appearance with inner experience. This undoubtedly brings relief to some transsexuals – I have no doubt of that – and it makes a difference to their quality of life, but history and hence loss cannot be bypassed without psychic consequences (Quinodoz, 1998).

Concluding thoughts

Working with Paula helped me to better understand how the suspension of puberty and SRS are unlikely to be followed by successful adjustment unless the individual can integrate the modified body into a psychic dwelling in which the parental couple can also comfortably reside. If, as was the case with Paula, the fable of the stork is the dominant birth fantasy, then the modified body remains dislocated from its origins and the temporal link is disrupted. The work we undertook was aimed at helping her to find a place in her mind on the 'lower deck', as it were, from where the clouds could then perhaps be seen not as immobile (as in the dream image) but could be allowed their own independent movement and fluidity, their joined-upness, if you like, as they 'float and drift and join together and part and reform for eternity' (Ryan, 2007: 12).[5]

I want to be clear that I am not suggesting that hormone therapy during adolescence should never be considered; rather if it is, those involved in the care of the young person need to be mindful that such hormonal manipulations have psychic implications that may impact on the young person's adjustment to transitioning via a disruption of the temporal link.

How this treacherous internal course is negotiated, and the extent to which the temporal link can be maintained between the given body that once was and the hormonally suspended/post-surgery body that replaces it, makes a significant difference to post-operative adjustment. Pursuing surgery may be the only way to live, but the state of mind one has in relation to the surgery and what it can deliver is crucial to the quality of relationships the individual can then establish through the newly reconstructed body. There are no shortcuts to the disturbing and painful psychic work necessary to secure a sustaining dwelling for the psyche in the body.

Notes

1. This may need to be reconsidered in light of the foetus' intra-uterine experience, which may already provide 'prototypes' based on the mother's bodily rhythms.
2. This term that arose out of my work with individuals who have extensively modified their bodies.
3. The therapy was conducted in a public health service setting, face-to-face once weekly.
4. I am grateful to Harry Smith for his reflections on this exchange.
5. Rob Ryan is a British paper cutter artist who specializes in paper cutting, screen-printing and drawing and painting. Ryan's first book, *This Is for You*, consists of a fairy tale told through his paper cut-out art and explores themes of love and loneliness.

Chapter 5

The body one has and the body one is

The transsexual's need to be seen

> I got sleepy while driving and pulled in under a tree at the side of the road. Rolled up in the back and went to sleep. How long? Hours. Darkness had come. All of a sudden I was awake and didn't know who I was. I'm fully conscious but that doesn't help. Where am I? Who am I? I am something that has just woken up in a back seat, throwing myself around in panic like a cat in a gunnysack. Who am I? After a long silence my life comes back to me. My name comes back to me like an angel. Outside the castle walls there is a trumpet blast and the footsteps that will save me come quickly down the long staircase. It's me coming! It's me!
>
> But it is impossible to forget the fifteen second battle in the hell of nothingness a few feet away from a major highway where the cars slip past with their lights on.
>
> Tomas Tranströmer (2006)

In this visceral short piece aptly called 'The Name', Tranströmer captures the challenges of embodiment in the absence of the receptive mind of an other who can lend meaning to, that is, 'name', the baby's sensory-motor experiences from the moment he 'wakes up' to the external world and engages with it.

'Where am I? Who am I?' asks the protagonist. A sense of who we are – of our identity – evolves out of sensory-motor experience, which is inseparable from the interpersonal fields in which it is embedded. Because we are embodied beings we can become trapped in the body – *'like a cat in a gunnysack'* – unless what is experienced at a bodily level can be mentally represented.

In the best of circumstances the experience of *me*, as Tranströmer puts it, evolves out of the repeated exchanges with a caregiver capable of mirroring back the child's experience contingently and in a 'marked' manner (Fonagy et al., 2002). But if the experience mediated by the body cannot be mirrored back and named, the self's experience of being-in-a-body may feel like *'the fifteen second battle in the hell of nothingness'* because there is no capacity to mentalize bodily experience (Gergely and Unoka, 2008). For many transsexual individuals the experience of gender dysphoria[1,2] is one of a living hell that painfully spans longer than 'fifteen seconds'. On the contrary, for many, time is measured in decades before, as they describe it, being freed from a body that does not feel their own through sex reassignment surgery (SRS). Some will have experienced high levels of distress pre-operatively and/or post-operatively (Green and Fleming, 1990; Di Ceglie, 1998; Dhejne et al., 2011).

Transsexuality remains controversial within the psychoanalytic and public consciousness. All too often pathologized within psychoanalysis[3] and at times heavily politicized in the feminist and queer literature, clinical and theoretical discussions about transsexuality appear to evoke rigid, binary thinking and positions (e.g. the biological vs the social or the normal vs the pathological). Interestingly, such binary positions parallel the so-called rigid state of mind that has been observed in transsexuals (Hakeem, 2008, 2010; Jones et al., 2011; Di Ceglie et al., 2014).

Irrespective of the aetiologies of transsexuality – and I want to emphasize the plural here as there are likely to be several pathways – what transsexuality is not, in my view, is *only* a medical or *only* a sociocultural problem (Dean, 2002), making a psychoanalytic account redundant. Understanding the internal world of the transsexual individual is essential (Layton, 1997; Elliott, 2001) so as to throw light on the subjective experience of embodiment.

Working with transsexual individuals typically confronts the analyst with powerful countertransference responses to what can feel like a disorienting 'visible' otherness and which often presents as such. There is indeed something inherently disorienting about sexuality such that those individuals who stray off the normative heterosexual path act as reminders of its inherent fluidity, as Freud (1905) disconcertingly revealed to us through his understanding of sexuality.

In turn, how we 'look' at the transsexual impacts on their experience. Our theory about transsexuality will lead us to see particular dynamics in the transference while obscuring other features. Given the likely heterogeneity of pathways to transsexuality we are best served by a range of perspectives because some theories may be more or less useful in understanding the distinctive particularities of transsexuality in each of our patients. Importantly we need to understand the function of a transsexual fantasy in the psychic economy of each individual.

The aim of this chapter is to contribute to the ongoing debate about how we can understand transsexuality. I contextualize the struggle *some* transsexuals convey within a necessarily speculative developmental framework rooted in object relations and attachment theories. This developmental account is a hypothetical formulation focusing in on a particular dynamic feature of the transsexual experience, namely that of 'being seen', of being taken in (or not) visually and mentally by the other in a state of incongruity. It is not intended as an all-encompassing explanation of transsexuality: as with any theory, by honing in on one dimension of experience it neglects features that other theories will highlight. I present it here thus as one alternative way of looking at some of these patients' experiences relative to, say, how an analyst approaching transsexuality through the theoretical filter of 'perversion' might approach these patients' predicaments[4] (e.g. Socarides, 1970; Limentani, 1979; Argentieri, 2009).

I illustrate my hypothesis through a qualitative study involving interviews with eight transsexual individuals and through a five-year-long, once-weekly psychoanalytic psychotherapy with an MtF transsexual who underwent sex reassignment surgery (SRS) during this time.

The study

Writing in 2005, Ethel Person suggested that 'psychoanalysts would do well to follow Freud's example and supplement information gleaned from the couch with information garnered from the street' (Person, 2005: 1270). I want to begin by sharing some observations on transsexuality 'garnered from the street', as it were, and analysed using qualitative methodology, to describe salient dimensions of transsexual experience that emerged out of my interviews with eight transsexual individuals at different stages of transitioning, before and after they took part in a four-part TV series about transsexuality. I had been asked to screen them psychologically in order to assess their psychological suitability for taking part in the documentary.

This series involved them coming together as a group to share their experiences of transsexuality. As such the TV series can be considered to be a kind of 'intervention'. The interviews pre and post offer an unusual opportunity to reflect on how the changes observed may be understood psychoanalytically in relation to the experience of taking part in this programme. The narratives of the transsexual individuals provide the data from which I formulate some hypotheses about the developmental deficit that may be present in *some* transsexuals and which maps onto my clinical experience with this group of patients (Lemma, 2012).[5]

The embodied self and the experience of being seen

The first theme to emerge from the interviews concerned what participants variously called a 'gap', 'disjoin' or 'incongruity' between the given body and the body they identified as their 'true' physical home. Moreover this experience, which I shall refer to from now on as one of *incongruity*, was precisely what several of the participants reported as being difficult to communicate to key attachment figures during childhood and adolescence. The second theme concerned the experience of being seen, of the self as a visual object. The core of the experience of the transsexual is indeed located in the visual order. They inhabit an internal *and* external scopic economy as their incongruous appearance invariably draws the gaze of the other towards the self.

Winnicott grasped the challenge imposed by our embodied nature when he reminded us that it is easy 'to take for granted the lodgement of the psyche in the body and to forget that this again is an achievement' (Winnicott, 1988: 122). This 'lodgement' – or as Winnicott (1970) elsewhere referred to it through the somewhat poetic image of the 'psyche in-dwelling in the soma' – brings home the rootedness of mental structures in early sensory and affective experience (Freud, 1923). It also speaks directly to the experiences recounted in the interviews I conducted in which the search for a receptive physical 'dwelling' for the self resonated throughout. And yet the other 'dwelling' that was also strikingly absent for many was that of a receptive mind that could house the experience of ambiguity, confusion and uncertainty felt to be lodged in the body.

The plight of the transsexual exposes in possibly the most extreme manner the developmental challenge we all have to negotiate and to which we all find compromise solutions, namely how to transform the body one *has* into the body one *is*, or to use a Winnicottian (Winnicott, 1970) term, how to 'personalize' it. For the transsexual this core developmental challenge is further complicated by an experience of embodiment, which for biological and/or psychological reasons, is felt to be intolerably confusing and painful.

The transsexual individuals I interviewed described their experience in such terms as, for example, *'feeling in pieces'* or *'I feel like a jigsaw you can't complete'* or *'a stranger to myself'*, underlining a disturbing discontinuity in the experience of the self, which leads them to search for their 'true' body – one that is anticipated to relieve them of this intolerable experience. In the study the extent of the investment in SRS, and hence the extent to which the participants were focused on the materiality of the body, distinguished them. This seemed to be strongest in those who reported hostile, absent or misattuned responses from caregivers during childhood and adolescence to their subjective experience of incongruity between their body and their gender identification.

The participants' consciously reported experience with others is one that I have also encountered, albeit in its greater complexity and unconscious dimension, through my analytic work with these patients. It manifests in the transference as an invitation – and indeed at times as an urgent, forceful pressure – to 'be seen' and taken into the mind of the analyst in the body's state of incongruity. I would like to suggest that one way of conceptualizing the experience of *some* transsexuals might thus be in terms of exposure to a repeated failure of contingent mirroring and mentalizing of the child's felt incongruence at the level of the body, regardless of its aetiology.[6] In these instances transsexuality may be thought about as a disruption in identity coherence.

If one's bodily experience can be represented in the mind of the other this will make a difference to the development of a coherent sense of self that is rooted in the body. By contrast a child who experiences his body as incongruous with his internal experience, and is repeatedly not related to by the primary object as a separate and intentional being with contingent marked mirroring, is at risk of developing an 'alien self'. This is a self-state based on the misattuned mental state in the parent (Fonagy et al., 2002). Through a process of introjection it becomes part of the core self structure, yet remains alien to the child's authentic state. The breakdown in an early mirroring process of an experience of incongruity felt to be located in the body may help us to understand how the child is then exposed to an intolerable internal experience of feeling dissociated from the given body, which feels 'unreal' and remains unintegrated into a coherent experience of the self. This may then lead to the search for the 'right' body that is anticipated to guarantee relief from the pain of incongruity.

The case of Ms C.

Through the case of Ms C., with whom I worked once weekly, face-to-face, for 5 years, I want to illustrate the experience of incongruity and the failure of mirroring as reported by the patient in her early relationships and as it played out in the transference. I selectively focus on the importance of the visual relationship between the analyst and the transsexual patient to illustrate how the patient's physical presentation may be used to forcefully impress on the analyst the experience of something that is felt to be fundamentally 'alien' and incongruous at the level of the bodily self and how the analyst, in turn, needs to represent this experience in her mind so as to mirror it back to the patient before further other explorations are possible, such as work on unconscious conflicts.

Ms C. was an MtF transsexual in her late twenties who was referred for help as part of her decision to seek SRS. At the time she was feeling depressed and suffered with panic attacks associated with being in outside spaces. By the time I met her she had been living as a woman for over two years. Her physical presentation was the first thing that hit me. I use the word 'hit' advisedly to denote a powerful visual dynamic that is present in this work. Interestingly, in the service of passing, and hence accompanied by the need to 'edit' the given body, many transsexuals often adopt a caricatured/stereotyped 'feminine' or 'masculine' look that tends to result in an outward appearance that does the opposite of what it is consciously intended to do[7]: it actively *draws attention to* an incongruity between the biologically assigned gender and the gender of identification. The 'excess' it betrays struck me forcefully with Ms C., as it has done in other cases, as if a possible (unconscious) function of this incongruous visual presentation[8] was precisely to draw my gaze towards the self's condition of incongruity, to take it in and digest it for her.

An only child, Ms C.'s early life was a miserable experience punctuated by frequent and at times violent rows between her parents, both of whom appeared to have been emotionally unavailable. Her mother had severe problems with alcohol. Her father was described as a distant, irascible man who died in her late adolescence. Neither parent was felt to have been physically affectionate.

She recalled dressing up in her mother's clothes from about the age of 4. She said she could identify the moment when it became clear to her that she was a 'girl' around the age of 5. Her cross-dressing remained a largely secret activity, in which she often indulged when her mother was asleep after her frequent alcoholic binges. This activity was comforting, but she denied any sexual arousal associated with it. I gained the impression that at times the cross-dressing had functioned as an attempt to create on her skin the loving touch of a fantasized mother, which replaced the actual mother who would not touch her.[9]

Ms C. told me that her mother did see her cross-dressing a few times and she recalled that the mother seemingly ignored this. However, she also related one instance when, aged 6, her mother saw her wearing her clothes, told her she looked 'ridiculous' and laughed. Ms C. recalled feeling very ashamed of her body.

Whatever her actual mother may have done or not, the mother was felt internally by Ms C. to have either not responded at all to her perception of an incongruence between her expectation of what Ms C. should look like and Ms C.'s experience of her own body, or to have actively ridiculed her when faced with this incongruence. This left Ms C. not only filled with shame, but also with an unmetabolized experience of a profound incongruity at the level of her bodily self.

As I listened to these accounts I obviously had no access to external information that would allow me to corroborate them so my focus is on what they convey about Ms. C.'s internal world. I was struck by the painful misattunement reported by Ms C. in her exchanges with her mother which resonated countertransferentially with the way in which I felt unusually conscious of how I looked at her and of the words I used, as if not understanding her would be catastrophic.

Ms C. recalled always feeling at odds in her given body. She had felt estranged from it, as if it 'belonged to someone else'. She did not 'hate' her male body but neither did she feel at home in it. At school she had been drawn to friendships with girls and disliked playing with boys. As she grew older she felt that she was going to 'explode' under the pressure of the reality she had to conceal from all: she felt she was a woman in a man's body. At 18, shortly after the father's death, she left home. She remained thereafter in sporadic contact with her mother.

Ms C. was ill at ease in her body, which tragically looked as if it belonged to someone else because her visual presentation jarred: she wore very short skirts that exposed her very athletic and unmistakably 'masculine' physique. Her breasts, enhanced by hormone treatment and other aids, were very much 'on display' but looked incongruous with the rest of her body. There was nothing sexual in her presentation. Rather, her body felt shut down, turned away from anything alive, like a ghost dressed up with nowhere to go. I understood this to be, at least in part, a consequence of a lack of early bodily cathexis by either parent, leaving Ms C. without recourse to an experience of a desiring gaze or touch directed towards her that could provide a bridge for the organization of her own pleasure in her body and the elaboration of her sexual desire.

As these sessions were face-to-face I sensed that a great deal was communicated and enacted between us through our respective gazes. For my part I had to take note of how I would look at her: I found her incongruous physicality hard to take in. At times I found myself exposed to something more forceful in the way she presented herself to me and looked at me, as if I was being made to look at the damage imprinted on a body that felt alien to her and that I, in turn, experienced as very 'other' to me. In truth I struggled to take her in visually and not infrequently I found myself wishing she were lying on the couch and not sitting opposite me. It was important to take note of this powerful countertransference reaction because it helped me to gain some understanding of that which could not yet be put into words between us.

Very quickly Ms C. developed an intense transference towards me. She became preoccupied with the sessions and what was in my mind about her. She found the gaps between sessions very difficult, but as she was being seen in a publically funded service she could not have more than once-weekly psychotherapy. In the early years I sensed her hunger, quite literally, for space in my mind. I took this up in the transference on many occasions. Her response to transference interpretations during this stage was interesting and was itself a manifestation of this 'hunger': I felt that she settled into the intimacy and immediacy of a transference interpretation instead of being able to make use of it – the so-called 'here-and-now' became a comfortable, gratifying home that seemingly reassured her that we were very close, only to then feel brutally ejected when the session ended.

Ms C. often prefaced what she said with 'I guess I'm not explaining this clearly' or 'You won't understand this because I'm putting it so badly.' Either way it seemed as though she felt she was communicating the incommunicable and I, in turn, would not understand her. Not infrequently I had the strong impression that we both 'talked' but never actually met. There was something rather sterile in our exchanges. It was only when I took her in visually, or when I became aware of her looking at me, that something more immediate, if disturbing, transpired. But it took time before we could 'look' together at the experience of looking and being looked at.

In the first year the transference was a rather idealized one during which time I often experienced her as wanting to fuse with me and effectively become me. This fantasy of becoming me was concretely actualized when she arrived for one of her sessions dressed in a manner that was evidently trying to copy one of my 'outfits'. Even her long hair had been styled like mine. Over time we explored her imitation and appropriation of me in this very concrete manner. This led her to recount the long stretches of time when she was left alone in the house as a child with her inebriated mother, dressing up in her clothes, wearing her high heels, as if trying to conjure up an experience of closeness with her mother through imitating her – and quite literally stepping into her shoes.

However, there was another dimension to my experience of her imitating me that took us in a fruitful direction. The sight of Ms C. wearing a copy of my outfit had a curiously disturbing impact on me. I found myself looking at her, recognizing the vestiges of my outfit, but it now looked ill fitting. I anxiously thought: 'I don't look like *that*!' as if I needed to distance myself from what she was exposing. I also felt ridiculed through her impersonation of me – an experience perhaps not dissimilar to how she had felt when her mother laughed at the sight of her cross-dressing. In other words I reacted as if I was being misrepresented in some way, and shown a distorted and denigrated image of myself that I was struggling to take in because it felt alien: that was not how I saw myself or wanted to be seen.

As I reflected on this exchange I thought that Ms C. had somehow turned the tables around and exposed me to an experience of not being accurately mirrored by her in my bodily state. It was not possible there and then to take this up because I needed time to really understand this. It also required repeated experiences of different kinds of misattunements in our relationship before we could find a language together for her experience of not feeling accurately mirrored by others and for feeling shamed.

This perspective was eventually helpful in also shedding light on her panic attacks and agoraphobia. Ms C. subjectively experienced public spaces as a 'hall of mirrors', as she put it. When outside her home she described feeling haunted by the prospect of catching sight of her reflection in shop windows or being looked at by other people. In those mirrors, she explained, 'I look all wrong.' At such times she described feeling dizzy, desperate to flee back to the safety of her dark flat. It was as if when in the grip of her panic attacks she entered a nightmarish experience of being forced to look at a body that did not hang together.[10] Outside spaces were seemingly equated with distorting reflective surfaces, perhaps not dissimilar to the inebriated eyes of her mother, or the absent eyes of her father, in which she could not find her self.

It became very important in our work to focus on her deep-seated expectation that her objects could not bear to look at her as she was and take in her experience of a 'bad fit' at the core of who she was – one that was visibly apparent in her bodily presentation. This understanding of the 'what' of her experience, as opposed to the 'why'.

In the two years leading up to surgery, during which time she was under the care of a specialist unit for transsexuals, we spent a long time thinking together about it through the transference experience. Ms C. related to SRS as 'the' solution, with a conviction that reinvigorated itself every time she experienced me as unavailable to her. In these moments we came to understand how the fantasy of the 'true' female body she would one day accede to, became her way of reconciling herself to her separation from me, perhaps just as she had done as a young child when she lost her mother repeatedly to alcohol. At such times, in her mind, she comforted herself with the fantasy of giving birth to herself and inhabiting a body that was whole, self-sufficient and a direct replica of an idealized maternal body and mind she felt deprived of – except in this fantasy the body became a 'copy without originals' (Baudrillard, 1988) as the mother was effectively obliterated.

In this state of mind the given body became a ghost of a body that ceased to have any reality or origins: her penis was experienced then as an alien 'thing' that had nothing to do with her and needed to be cut off. By contrast her 'new' breasts became the reassurance that she needed no one. The anticipated surgery ceased to function as potentially opening up the possibility of a better life more congruent with her subjective experience of herself, but became instead the means through which she enacted a profound grievance towards her mother.

The grievance she harboured was also aimed at a parental couple felt to have been wrapped up in violent fights that secured a physical closeness she felt deprived of. Interestingly their fights were accompanied in her mind by a fantasy (but possibly also a reality) of an excited sexual reconciliation, which healed the fracture between them, leaving her alone with an experience of something in pieces inside that neither father nor mother had seemed able to help her with. This was painfully alive in the transference, especially during holiday breaks, when she imagined me having a good time with my family and dropping her from my mind.

Over the five years of our work together Ms C. became more receptive to our explorations of her wish to effectively 'become me/mother' so that she could avoid the painful experience of separation, which felt to her like a traumatic expulsion from the mind of the other. However, this did not impact on her strong feeling that she was more at home in a woman's body and I should add it was never my therapeutic aim to change this. I considered my role to be that of helping her make sense of her experience.

After just over two years of therapy, Ms C. underwent SRS. As the date approached she fluctuated between anxiety and mania. She anticipated how the surgery would finally lay to rest her experience of feeling at odds within herself and in her body. She imagined she could finally allow herself to have a sexual relationship because the body she would reveal to a partner would be the body she really was.

Post-surgery she experienced several physical complications, which led her to feel depressed and desperate that her body would never feel right. Once again, I became very aware of the visual relationship between us. I felt she needed me to take in with my eyes and mind this reconstructed body she felt was still in pieces. It was as though she needed a witness to this process – one that was willing to look and not shame her. The castration she had effectively subjected herself to was hard for me to imagine and I felt she sensed this in me, but as she looked intensely at my face I also felt the urgency with which she needed me to take in this reality.

Ms C. was angry with the surgeon for doing a bad job. 'I still look and feel wrong,' she would say with some reproach. She was painfully aware that even though she no longer had a penis and had a reconstructed vagina, she still looked more masculine than she wished. This proved to be a very painful time, but it was essential for Ms C. to face the decimation of the fantasy that SRS would take away the pain so concretely located in her body.

A dream she reported around this time involved buying a large antique mirror, which she carefully hung above her mantelpiece. During the night it fell and shattered into pieces. We came to understand this dream as a communication to me about how she looked into my eyes for a mirror that would reflect her back whole and reassure her that surgery had done the trick, but each time she looked she felt she could only see herself still in pieces. I was intrigued by the 'antique' nature of the mirror. I took up with her how this might express a wish for me to reflect back her 'old' body too, to keep it in mind that is, when she struggled to do so because her body and its history were still a part of her. Ms C. became tearful, and said that she could not bear to look at any old photos. She then composed herself and in a very detached manner said that she was toying with the idea of shredding them. I said that she was letting me know how hard it was to remain connected with her 'old' body and that she now wanted to literally tear to shreds my interpretation, which had perhaps felt like me forcefully exposing her to the reality of her old body and the pain that she carried inside her and which she had hoped the surgery would 'cut out'. I also thought, but did not interpret this at this time because I did not think she was in any state to take this in, that she recognized the violence she had inflicted on her body – that she had literally 'shredded' it through SRS – but that to acknowledge this now left her feeling in pieces again.

Recognizing the 'original' body is important psychically. This requires painful work that involves facing loss and acknowledging dependency. How this treacherous internal course is negotiated makes a significant difference to post-operative adjustment. Pursuing surgery may be the only way to live, but the state of mind one has in relation to the surgery and what it can deliver is crucial to the quality of relationships the individual can then establish through the newly reconstructed body.[11]

In the wake of the disappointment about the surgery it was important to think together about her experience that I had what she wanted and that I had kept it all for myself. At first I took this up in terms of me being the woman she wished to be, but I realized eventually that this was not right: my sex and my gender were red herrings. What Ms C. envied most was her perception that I inhabited a desired body and that it could desire. Indeed she spoke about her perception of me as 'alive' and at ease in myself. These sessions heralded a slow and gradual shift in her state of mind towards what we could regard as more depressive functioning.

This development was apparent some months later when in an important and spontaneous gesture she brought photos of herself as a boy to show me how uncomfortable she had looked in this 'old' body. I thought that as well as trying to reassure herself that she had done the right thing by pursuing surgery she was also beginning to *look* at a ghostly part of her, as captured in these images of her body from childhood, which was still within her despite the SRS. This helped us understand that part of her adaptation to her post-surgery body could only succeed if *she* was able to look and take in the male body she once inhabited and what it was consciously and unconsciously associated with in her mind.

A year post SRS Ms C. began a sexual relationship, the first in over 10 years, with a man who appeared troubled but who was loving towards her. There was respect for the otherness of the other. She was able to tell him her story and felt accepted by him. She slowly started to come to life and relate to her body as a potential source of pleasure. Inevitably, perhaps given her early history, she remained sensitive to slights from others and could easily feel shamed, but she could also understand this better in herself. Her panic attacks subsided significantly and she obtained work. It seemed as if her body not only in the context of her new relationship, but also more generally in her experience of herself in the open spaces of life that she had once so feared, was one of greater potentiality. Significantly she started to wear clothes that were better fitting to her actual physique, thereby diminishing the earlier visual incongruity I remarked upon. I began to discern feminine contours in her appearance alongside her more masculine features that somehow looked more of a piece than at odds with each other. When we ended our work Ms C. remained clear that SRS had been the right thing for her and that therapy had helped her to 'come to terms' with who she was.

Pathways to transsexuality

As I reflect on the experience of working with Ms C. and what helped her, I consider that what may have made some difference to her adjustment was the experience of 'being seen' as she was and to experience her incongruous body and fragmented self represented in my mind. This helped her slowly to feel more coherent within herself and as this stabilized she was able to become more emotionally connected with the losses associated with the decision to pursue SRS even though she did not regret it. However, it was also important for her to be in a relationship with someone who not only mirrored back this experience and contained it, but who could also hold in mind the hatred she felt towards her objects and her attacks on the object via the body.

In some cases of transsexuality, as I hope I have illustrated through my work with Ms C., we can discern in the patient's history, and in what is elaborated in the transference, developmental experiences that might account for how a cross-gender identification evolves and its defensive functions. Here I have selectively focused on early mirroring of body states as crucial in the development of a coherent sense of self.

The primary object's capacity to mirror the child's experience has long been recognized within psychoanalysis as a vital factor in determining the quality of internalized object relationships. Winnicott (1956) proposed that when the baby looks at the mother what he sees in the mother's expression is his own self-state. Here the mother's mirroring function is seen as essential for the establishment of the baby's self-representation. From a different angle Bion (1967) effectively elaborates on the function of mirroring by emphasizing the developmental importance of an actual mother capable of absorbing (i.e. containing) *and* retransmitting the infant's psychological experience in a metabolized form, thus supporting the gradual internalization of a thinking function.

Winnicott's and Bion's theories underline respectively the importance of mirroring and transformation of the child's experience as mediated by the primary object's capacity to accurately reflect the child's internal experience[12] whilst indicating clearly that s/he has a different experience (i.e. the mirroring is 'marked'). This process facilitates the 'mentalization' of experience (Fonagy and Target, 2000). This line of thinking represents a point of convergence between psychoanalysis and contemporary elaborations of attachment theory and mentalization, notwithstanding their different epistemic assumptions (Fonagy, 2001).

In Ms C.'s case her parents failed not only to mirror back her experience of incongruity at the core of her subjective bodily experience and gender identity but in a more general sense they also failed to mirror her emotional life. However, in the transference it was her bodily experience and appearance that I felt she needed me to look at with urgency and to represent in my mind, which is why I have focused on it in this chapter. In proposing a failure of mirroring as central to understanding Ms C.'s transsexuality I have in mind the impact of repeated experiences of feeling 'not right in my body', which remain unprocessed and hence become concretized in the body.

Projective identifications into the child's body by the parent(s), or the parent's inability to mirror a child's experience of their body state may contribute to developmental distortions that can manifest clinically as disturbances in sexual development and gender identification. If we are to understand these clinical presentations we need to take into account not only the projective processes that underlie the way the body and gender as perceived and experienced by the parent is mirrored back to the child, but also how the introjection of these experiences involves varying degrees of distortion and idiosyncratic elaboration. Ms C. had unconsciously identified with a ridiculing, distorting object and this became apparent in the transference when she arrived wearing a facsimile of my outfit.

A focus on mirroring emphasizes the developmental importance of real-life relationships. However, such a relational focus is not psychoanalytic unless we also consider the role of unconscious phantasy and conflict in the development of the mind. Nowhere is this more important than in relation to an understanding of sexuality and gender identifications. Sexuality is not simply an instinct and behaviour; it also organizes intrapsychic experience and phantasy. In other words, early attachment relations provide the interpersonal context within which the experience of embodiment, and hence of our sexuality, unfolds (Schilder, 1950; Diamond and Blatt, 2007; Weinstein, 2007) and infantile sexuality is in turn shaped by these interactions (i.e. external experience with others is relived as autoerotic activity). In our work with transsexual patients we need to understand the patient's experience of *sexuality in infancy* but this is not the same as *infantile sexuality*, the residues of which are to be found in the unconscious (Scarfone, 2002).

Additionally, it is also important to incorporate into our analytic formulations the systemic cultural forces that frame the experience and expression of sexuality and gender (Dimen, 1991; Goldner, 1991, 2011; Harris, 1991, 2011; Benjamin, 1998; Suchet, 2011) so as to challenge more simplistic equations of biological sex, gender and sexual desire (Foucault, 1976; Butler, 1998, 2003). Approaching transsexuality thus requires a wide-angled lens so as to formulate the interpersonal and intrapsychic processes that give rise to a highly idiosyncratic experience of the child's gendered embodiment.

In Ms C.'s case it is impossible to know with any certainty whether her early feeling that she was a woman in a man's body is best explained with reference to biological and/or psychological factors. In her particular case a psychogenic account of her difficulties is compelling given the early history of emotional deprivation and especially the way the 'absence' of her mother, and the hatred for her father who had abandoned her to this fate, appeared to have been managed through a feminine identification that supported a fantasy of symbiotic fusion with the mother (Ovesey and Person, 1973) and obliterated the father.

In other cases it proves harder to identify a deficit or trauma in early childhood. In such instances we need to remain open to the possibility that there may be biological factors that influence the cross-gender identification.[13] This is not to say that such factors, even when present, operate independently of either psychology or social forces.

Conclusions

Although transsexuality is often conceptualized as if it were a unitary 'condition' afflicting a homogeneous group of individuals, it would be more correct to refer to transsexualities to capture the heterogeneity of pathways to, and of the functions of, a transsexual identity and the body modifications it can entail.

I have suggested that transsexual experience may be in some cases approached not simply as a matter of gender and sexuality but as a disruption in identity coherence. I have focused in particular on the transsexual's experience of incongruity, suggesting that an unmentalized incongruity experienced at the level of the body-self may contribute in some instances of transsexuality to the search for the 'right' body, that will relieve the incongruity through the certainty it imparts that the image in the mirror (literally and metaphorically) will match the subjective experience of the body. The search is fundamentally for the receptive mind of the other through a modified body anticipated to 'guarantee' relief from the incongruity.

A focus on the relevance of an intersubjective mirroring process in relation to body states, and as one of the foundations for the development of identity, provides another lens through which it may be possible to approach the transsexual's experience in the transference–countertransference matrix. However, I would like to suggest that marked and contingent mirroring of the self's bodily experience is most likely, for us all, a vitally important feature of the development of a coherent sense of self firmly rooted in the body.

Notes

1 This refers to the belief that one's 'true' gender identity (i.e. whether we think of ourselves as male or female) is the opposite of both chromosomal sex and bodily habitus.
2 This chapter focuses on individuals whose gender identity is felt to be at odds with the 'given' body. They feel trapped in what feels like the 'wrong' body and hence seek to acquire through SRS the body congruent with their subjective experience. I am therefore not addressing here the question of transgenderism, which is a much broader term encompassing individuals who transgress gender norms but are not necessarily seeking surgery. Neither am I addressing transvestism, which refers to sexual arousal associated with cross-dressing.
3 There are some notable exceptions to this. Recent North American contributions that counter this trend include some excellent papers by Harris (2011), Goldner (2011) and Suchet (2011). In the UK, see Hakeem (2008, 2010).
4 I am drawing here on Tuckett's (2011) reminder that 'a good theory makes distinctions that are practically useful' (1372).
5 Notwithstanding the conscious nature of this data the themes that emerged from the interviews mapped onto my clinical experience with this group of patients – and specifically with a particular feature of the transference and countertransference dynamics that I have encountered with these. As such they provide some triangulation of data from the couch with data 'off the couch' and they have thus informed the ideas I present in this chapter.
6 Approaching sexuality from the standpoint of attachment and mentalization, Fonagy (2006, 2008) underlines that 'a key facet of psychosexuality is a sense of incongruence with the infant's actual experience [that] disrupts the actual coherence of the self' (Fonagy, 2006: 17). At the core of this view lies the difficulty the mother has in mirroring the infant's sexuality – an adaptive failure that structures psychosexuality, indelibly inscribing in the mind the need for an other who makes it possible to experience our sexuality through their elaboration of it.

7   I am referring here specifically to the choice of clothes and the way makeup is used.
8   I say this because not all transsexuals present in this more exaggerated manner.
9   Ferenczi indeed noted how bodily self-stimulation could be understood as a substitute 'on one's own body for the lost object' (1938: 23–24).
10 I considered whether Ms C. might be suffering from Body Dysmorphic Disorder (BDD). This may well represent another group of individuals who present as transsexuals but are in fact better understood as suffering from BDD. However, it is important to note an important phenomenological distinction between the two, namely that in BDD the body part that needs excision is typically regarded as 'ugly', but this is not often so in transsexuals, who tend to view the genitalia as incongruous with their gender identity or as 'not belonging' to them, but not necessarily as 'ugly' or flawed. Ms C. did not see her given body as 'ugly'.
11 The transsexual's relationship to sexual difference also represents an important dimension of their experience. It is beyond the scope of this book to develop this theme. However, it deserves some mention because the reality of sexual difference and the meaning this acquires in the patient's experience will be an ever-present preoccupation for both patient and analyst in this kind of work. Being sexuated means biologically differentiated not at the level of the genitals per se, which can be grafted on or removed at will, but in terms of the biological function of the 'original' genital. We are 'sexed around reproduction' (Mitchell, 2004) – this is a fact. The painful reality for the transsexual who undergoes SRS is that they become biologically castrated. The traumatic realization that one cannot give birth or contribute to the biological creation of a child has to be managed internally and requires a process of mourning.
12 I want to stress here that this includes mirroring of the somatic reactivity and excitability stimulated by early physical exchanges between mother and baby.
13 As with analytic hypotheses, there is *some* evidence for biological ones (Zhou et al., 1995; Garcia-Falgueras and Swaab, 2008) but this is by no means a consistent finding or the findings are themselves limited in a number of respects (for critiques see Chung et al., 2002; Hulshoff et al., 2006; Nieder and Richter-Appelt, 2009).

Chapter 6

Trauma and the body
A psychoanalytic reading of Almodóvar's *The Skin I Live In*

In all the preceding chapters I have illustrated different manifestations of psychic pain that are played out on the body, as it were – desperate attempts often to 'cure' the pain through changing the body. In all the cases described, the body was the site that exposed developmental deficits as well as the site for the enactment of psychic conflicts.

Like shedding layers of skin, Almodóvar's latest narrative painfully unravels to reveal the rawness of losses that cannot be mourned. The skin – that 'scrim' on which we project our fantasies and fears (Mifflin, 1997) – is used here to good effect to examine deeply psychoanalytic themes that are very relevant to our understanding of the body.

The title of the film takes its central character's profession – Dr Robert Ledgard (Antonio Banderas), a tormented plastic surgeon – and turns it into a metaphor for exploring two central themes: the complex relationship between the given body and our identity and the particular use made of the body, namely the projection into the body of the object – the use of their body *by proxy*, as it were – in order to manage traumatic events that cannot be represented in the mind.

In characteristic Almodóvar fashion, as in *Tie Me Up! Tie Me Down!* (1989), *High Heels* (1991) and *All About My Mother* (1999), this most recent offering emphasizes the human body as the site for the negotiation of identity and its traumatic collapse. *The Skin I Live In* is a timely film that gives pause for thought given contemporary culture's preoccupation with the body as a project (Giddens, 1991) within which it can be manipulated at will and without conscious acknowledgement of the developmental history imprinted on the body – one that, as this film powerfully reminds us, can never be erased no matter how extensive the transformation of the body (see also Chapters 1, 4 and 5).

The film's story is based on a French novel by Thierry Jonquet, *Mygale*, which was eventually turned into a horror film by Georges Franju (*Eyes Without a Face*), a surreal classic in which Dr Génessier (Pierre Brasseur), a plastic surgeon, becomes obsessed with grafting the faces of abducted Parisian girls onto his daughter who was disfigured in a car crash.

Almodóvar has imaginatively elaborated Jonquet's tale of perversion and relocated the narrative to Spain in the beautiful surroundings of Ledgard's minimalist and elegant home, El Cigarral. This is the stage for a private medical clinic with its own operating theatre: a stylized, sterile yet deadly version of Frankenstein's workshop of 'filthy creation' (Shelley, 1818). Ledgard is a hubristic scientist, a man who transforms nature 'into a field of human action' (Giddens, 1991), freed from the idea that birth is destiny and that death is its inevitable destination. As well as addressing contemporary tensions about the potential misuse of technological and medical advances, Ledgard's character powerfully represents the human tendency to reshape the world according to our own needs and desires rather than accomplishing the more messy internal psychic work required to accommodate reality, not least when trauma is its hallmark.

Ever since his wife was horrifically burnt in a car crash, Dr Ledgard has become preoccupied with creating an impregnable skin grown genetically from human and pig DNA. It is resistant to any assault – so strong that even a blowtorch cannot penetrate it – but it remains nevertheless sensitive to touch. It is this new skin that has completely replaced a beautiful young woman's epidermis, piece by piece. Ledgard refers to this woman as Vera (Elena Anaya), one of his patients on whom he has performed plastic surgery. Vera, however, is effectively his prisoner, locked in a room supplied with everything she needs through a dumbwaiter sent up from the kitchen by Ledgard's devoted housekeeper, Marilia (Marisa Paredes) – the woman who looked after him since the day he was born. If Vera appears resigned to her captivity, the walls of her starkly furnished room tell a very different story: they are covered in small writing tallying up the days since her imprisonment.

Vera is not only physically imprisoned in a room and in a 'new' body that we slowly discover she has been forcibly given by Dr Ledgard, but also in his mind where she has taken up residence as the object of his obsession. He has no regard for her existence as independent of his omnipotent wishes and fantasies. As he gradually remodels her body to uncannily resemble that of his deceased wife, we are exposed in a most disturbing manner to repeated and violent projective processes/ surgeries through which Dr Ledgard manages the unbearable losses he cannot mourn. The surgical precision with which he pursues his goal of perfecting Vera's new skin and body gives some clue to the way in which this obsessional, violent pursuit holds him together and presages how it will eventually also destroy him.

Ledgard's narcissistic and perverse but still recognizably human character is played with chilly precision by Banderas, allowing us at times painful glimpses of the multiple traumas he has endured and of the impenetrable perverse solution he has found to his predicament. Despite his traumatic past Ledgard remains emotionally inaccessible to us. His inaccessibility conveys how the perverse character structure convinces both the self and others that there is no inner life, that there is nothing to think or feel about, hence propelling Ledgard into a vicious cycle of deception and violence.

The perversion of loss

The narrative of the film, with all the painful developmental denouements for the central protagonists, emerges slowly from a pieced-together series of flashbacks and scenes from the present day. As in Hitchcock's *Vertigo*, the past and present exist in a loop. This movement powerfully captures the mental to-and-fro from past to present and from present to past that is so characteristic of traumatized states of mind, at times collapsing the two into an imprisoning 'present moment' from which no escape seems possible except through violence.

Gradually we learn that Ledgard is a man who has faced numerous losses, not least the loss of his birth mother, Marilia, who we discover some way into the film, unbeknownst to Dr Ledgard, gave him up at birth after conceiving him with her then employer, whose wife was infertile. Marilia effectively raised Ledgard 'undercover' as the housekeeper, never disclosing to him her true identity as his mother, yet this secret is live in their exchanges. In a scene that sees Marilia return to El Cigarral after a period of absence to resume her role as housekeeper to Ledgard, we can discern the deeply rooted familiarity between them as she accepts without question what he tells her about his so-called patient, and in his apparent comfort when he smells that she has cooked him his favourite potato croquettes – a moment when one feels connected with Ledgard's boyish self in the presence of a woman who knows him only too well, their complicity lingering in the air like the smell of the potato croquettes. This scene provides a potent backdrop for the intergenerational nature of the trauma that cannot be spoken about: a mother who has to renounce her child and raise him as if not her own and a child who is deceived about his own bodily origins.

As an adult Ledgard faces more losses when his wife abandons him first to a lover (who turns out to be his half-brother) and then commits suicide after catching sight of her face deformed by the burns she sustained in a car crash with her lover. Further losses await him: no sooner has his daughter, Norma (Blanca Suárez), started to make a recovery from the trauma of witnessing the mother's suicide, she breaks down again after a sexual incident at a party with a boy called Vincente (Jan Cornet) that leaves her unconscious. She subsequently becomes phobic of men and especially of her father, who was the first man she saw as she resumed consciousness, and she now appears to associate him with being the perpetrator of the assault. Ledgard is thus left filled with this projection: Norma equates him with the assailant and, in turn, he identifies with the aggressor.

Ledgard's psychological and physical intrusiveness emerges as the hallmark of his relational repertoire. In a painful scene Ledgard visits Norma in the psychiatric clinic and desperately wants her to respond to him as her father. Instead we see her recoiling away from him in fear until Norma has no option but to hide in the cupboard and he is asked to leave the hospital. The scene poignantly illustrates Ledgard's intrusiveness into the object: Norma has to create quite literally an impregnable cupboard-skin to keep him out.

As in other scenes punctuated with unremitting loss, Ledgard is unable to bear the pain of this rejection and immediately converts it into accusations and violent rage: he becomes angry with Norma's psychiatrist and criticizes his care of her, his grievance perhaps not insignificantly focused on why the psychiatrist does not encourage Norma to put on some nice dresses instead of leaving her in a white nightshirt all day that indeed makes her look like the patient she *is* and that Ledgard wants to deny. Here as elsewhere we witness one of Ledgard's primary defences: he wants to 'make over' reality, changing the surface of the body in an attempt to distance himself from the painful reality that is inscribed on it.

From the outset there is no doubt that Ledgard is engaged in dubious scientific activities or that Vera is *not* a consenting partner to his experimentation on her body. However, it is only some way into the film that we discover that Vera is in fact none other than the young boy, Vincente, now castrated and trapped in a surgically reconstructed woman's body. Ledgard holds him responsible for Norma's breakdown because he apprehended Vincente leaving the scene of the party during which his daughter was sexually assaulted.

Unable to manage the loss of his daughter to her breakdown and withdrawal from him, Ledgard abducts Vincente and takes him back to El Cigarral where he is chained and fed like an animal. During the period of Vincente's captivity, Norma, like her mother, also commits suicide. This further loss is simply too much for Ledgard. During her funeral he attributes her death to her psychiatrist's incompetence and threatens to sue him. Here we begin to get a sense of how Ledgard's projection of his impotence and failure hold him together. In this paranoid-schizoid state of mind fuelled by grievance, he returns to El Cigarral to perform a vaginoplasty on Vincente, enacting a surgical rape on him.

As Ledgard scrubs down and dresses in his operating theatre attire ready to castrate Vincente we get a chilling close-up of the violent work of destructive identification and revenge. Ledgard is a man who lies with ease: he lies to the medical community about his experimentation with a new skin and he lies to his surgery colleagues about the sex reassignment operation he is about to embark on: Vincente, he tells them, is a consenting young man who has only ever wanted to be a woman. We might wonder how Ledgard's evident corruption and dubious medical ethics relate to his identification with a deceiving, lying object: both his two mothers (the birth mother, Marilia, and his adoptive mother) never disclose to him the truth about his origins – the kind of secret that only serves to create uncertainty and doubt and corrupts internal and external relationships.

In a not dissimilar fashion to *The Skin I Live In*, the novel *Frankenstein* by Mary Shelley (1818) also traces the fate of losses that cannot be mourned and the consequent use made of the body of the object through the creation of a physically monstrous creature that is then abandoned at birth.

Aged 17, following the death of his mother, Frankenstein leaves home to attend university where he becomes overly preoccupied with the possibility of creating a new being using the parts of deceased bodies that he collects through digging out graveyards. Frankenstein becomes intent on circumventing the significance of the mother in reality, and in his mind, as he pursues feminine Nature to her 'hiding places' to appropriate for himself the maternal role, allowing him to create a new species without the intervention of woman.[1] In this respect we might say that Ledgard also omnipotently becomes mother as he gives violent birth to 'Vera'.

The way Frankenstein puts together the creature's body out of decomposed tissues – the vestiges of former lives now dug out of their graves – provides a disturbing portrayal of the signs of an absence already inscribed on the body at birth. In Frankenstein's mind the creature's body is a composite figure of faded lives whose loss cannot be mourned, just as we can discern in Ledgard's relationship to Vera's body.

Ledgard's predicament (like Frankenstein's) illustrates the *breakdown or perversion of the capacity to mourn* – a dynamic that is central to understanding how a traumatic event may impact on the mind (Lemma and Levy, 2004). Traumatic events, as this film powerfully depicts, typically involve irreparable losses. There is considerable pain and guilt associated with such losses. Often the experience is too much for the individual to bear: instead of a normal grieving process, there is a breakdown, where the individual identifies with the lost person in a particularly cruel and relentless way (Freud, 1917). Such identifications can be very concrete and literally located in a body part in one's body or in the body of the object.

Freud (1917) emphasized how the relationship with the lost object determined whether normal grief or melancholia would follow. Where ambivalence or hostility towards the lost object dominates psychic functioning, mourning is impeded and a melancholic state follows. In this respect it is significant that Ledgard has to psychically manage his wife's serious burn injuries, and then her subsequent suicide, in the painful knowledge that she has betrayed him with another man – betrayal and loss layering on each other in a tormenting spiral. Ledgard's vigil over his dying wife, followed by his obsessive preoccupation with keeping her alive and creating the perfect skin, is not born of love towards her but of his hatred for what she has done to him. She is kept alive as his appendage, a shadow of her former beautiful self, a woman now so defaced by her burns that no one could be attracted to her. It is her disfigured self that guarantees that she is only his and effectively becomes his prisoner – until she frees herself of his control through the act of suicide. The 'alien' self (Fonagy et al., 2002) that is lodged within has to be expelled: killing the body becomes the solution to the psychic torment. Indeed suicide as a means of escaping the bad object experienced as concretely lodged in the body recurs as a leitmotif in the film: his wife and daughter kill themselves and Vera too attempts suicide twice to escape from Ledgard. But in true sadistic fashion, Ledgard needs to keep his objects alive because he needs them to suffer. The pain he inflicts on them is the insurance against knowing about his own pain.

In both normal and pathological mourning, the loss of the loved object elicits hatred towards it. Klein (1940) described this process in terms of the individual's grief that the object is not part of the self. This reality is difficult to bear. The melancholic, instead of facing this truth, takes into himself/herself a concrete representation of the lost object. It becomes part of the self and therefore there is no loss. Ledgard's predicament epitomizes this dynamic: he denies the reality that his wife and his daughter are lost and not under his control. Ledgard fought to keep his wife alive against the odds and despite the knowledge that she would remain severely defaced. The guilt of survival, the guilt of triumph and the pain of separation are all abrogated. Despite the phantasy that pain can be done away with, however, this denial is costly to the self. The dead and the living are now fused in a concrete identification dominated by hatred as the film chillingly portrays.

We can link this type of identification with a collapse of symbolic functioning where the ego's capacity to know about and think about the self as a separate agent is reduced. This breakdown is one of the most devastating consequences of trauma (Segal, 1986; Garland, 2002) because it prevents a secondary order representation of the loss such that it cannot be psychically processed. Ledgard is indeed unable to distinguish his feelings from action: he feels rage about his wife's affair and her death, rage about the sexual assault perpetrated against his daughter and her suicide, but he can only assuage this by himself identifying with the aggressor and enacting his violent fantasies of revenge on Vincente's body and specifically on his sexuality: when he castrates him Ledgard has projectively identified his own impotent self into him. This collapse of the capacity to symbolize properly powerfully illustrates how a form of symbolic equation comes to dominate his functioning in this area.

From a developmental point of view the transition from symbolic equation to symbolism proper typically involves a shift from the psychic experience of concretely possessing the mother, to one where a representation of the object is appreciated mentally or symbolically (Segal, 1986). An awareness and acceptance of this separateness is one of the psychic achievements of the depressive position: the baby comes to 'know' that its real mother is not actually inside him, but external and separate from him. Where there is recognition of difference between the internal object and the self, then the capacity for an inner dialogue is acquired. Segal described this process as symbolic functioning, the essential forerunner of all communication, in particular verbal communication.

Segal emphasizes the important function of the caregiver in facilitating this crucial process. She pays particular attention to Bion's (1962) work around the container/contained, the relationship between the baby and his primary caretaker. From this perspective, symbolic functioning has its origins in the mother's and baby's earliest interaction, in particular the mother's ability to contain her infant's emotional states and the infant's ability to be contained. In Ledgard one senses a man who has no such internal capacity (no good internal object) to contain emotional experience without being overturned by it. Projective identification becomes the modus operandi: when we see Ledgard looking through his surveillance cameras at close-ups of Vera we discern how she must be kept both at a distance but also very close – this is an essential requirement of projective identification.

A traumatic experience thus impacts not only on the capacity to relate, to feel, but also on the capacity to think in a symbolic way. This, in turn, makes it more likely that the body is used to enact what cannot be mentally represented. This is most powerfully evident in Ledgard's inability to put feelings into words, to construct a narrative that could lend meaning and substance to his experiences. When Marilia mentions the death of his daughter, Ledgard tells her firmly that he does not want to think about this. McDougall (1989) describes this process as the alexithymic condition, where words lose their value, and the relationship between feeling and language is abrogated. In a trauma scenario an alexithymic process takes shape. The link or dialogue with an internal object who is both receptive and resilient, who is historically able to withstand assaults and attacks, is often severed. It is as if there is a regression to a state where words have no meaning and where the capacity to communicate in a meaningful way is severely curtailed. This is not to say, however, that emotion itself is truncated. On the contrary, emotional states, now no longer bound by the containing function of meaningful, expressive language, run rampant in the psyche. These kinds of emotional states, described by Bion (1962) as beta elements, can assume destructive proportions, at times leading to violent behaviour towards others or to assaults on the self, and not least on the body.

The survival of the good object

A major trauma impacts on the person's internal and external relationships. Klein (1937) viewed the infant's experience of love, loving and being loved, by both the internal and also external good object, as a critical determinant for psychic integration. We might say therefore that the mind's capacity to manage traumatic impingements depends on the quality of these earliest attachments.

Perhaps another way of understanding how trauma impacts on relationships would be to talk about levels of *resilience.* Resilience in this sense denotes the ability to withstand stress in terms of either internal or external encroachments that threaten the integrity of the self. Levels of resilience are closely connected to the nature and quality of early attachment relations (Fonagy et al., 2002). Secure attachments foster a greater ability to endure and to prevail under extreme pressure. Insecure attachments often undermine the development of resilience or foster a 'false self' structure which pertains to this ability without much authentic substance. If there is a predominantly secure internal scenario, however, then these attachments hold the self like a ballast, providing an internal template, which is not easily overturned. This is poignantly illustrated through Vincente/Vera's capacity to prevail under the extreme circumstances inflicted on him by Ledgard. Indeed if *The Skin I Live In* can be read as a story of loss that becomes perverted into revenge through manipulation of the other's body, it is also a story about the way the good internal object can prevail under the most extreme circumstances. It is in essence a story about inner resilience that transcends the actual changes perpetrated on Vincente's body.

Vera, wearing nothing but a full-length flesh-coloured bodystocking, spends her days watching wildlife documentaries, practising yoga, writing on the walls of her prison-room and creating little busts inspired by the work of Louise Bourgeois. The Bourgeois figures that Vera becomes fascinated with evocatively conjure up broken, malformed bodies made out of gunny sack, sewn together, just like her. And yet in the very act of creating them, one senses that Vera asserts the reality of her mind – of who 'she' really is – over her sewn-up, unreal body and so restores a sense of unity within her self.

In order to cope Vera turns to creativity and she also immerses herself in yoga after watching a yoga class on her TV, during which the teacher explains how yoga can help to create a safe place within. This 'safe place within the mind' is then graphically represented on the wall in a drawing of a naked woman's body whose face is enclosed by a house: Vincente's true masculine self, we might say, is protected in his mind even if his actual body now *looks like* that of a woman.

Vincente's resilience shines through in his responses to Ledgard's repeated attempts to mould him in his image. Along with food, Vera is sent women's clothes and Chanel makeup through the dumbwaiter. The dresses are ripped to shreds in defence of his true masculine self. The makeup – the tool that Vera is encouraged to use to identify with her imposed 'female' identity – is used subversively instead to inscribe on the walls the days of his imprisonment and statements like 'I can breathe'. Writing on the wall, that other hard surface on which, like a skin, Vincente writes his story, acts as a reminder to himself that he can still breathe through the skin imposed on him by Ledgard.

What keeps Vincente alive in Vera's body? From the outset Vincente believes that his mother will be searching for him. Indeed we are shown scenes of his mother not believing the police when she is encouraged to accept their version of events: Vincente's motorbike was found near a cliff and his body was washed away at sea. She says that this cannot be the case: she tells the police that she knows he is still alive. One has a sense that Vincente has a good enough object inside him who has not forgotten him: a mother who knows that he would always call her and not just disappear as the police seem to suggest he has done.

Vincente is given a new skin/body and becomes Vera in Dr Ledgard's image, but he never ceases to be Vincente in his mind. To this extent he continues to live in his own skin, not the one artificially layered on his body by Ledgard, impregnated with his narcissism. When 'Vera' sees a photo of missing people in the paper 'she' catches sight of himself as Vincente. At this stage, we may be looking at a beautiful woman, but we are in no doubt that this is a man shaken to his core. He reconnects with himself as he kisses the photo before returning to the bedroom where Ledgard is waiting to have sex with Vera, and kills him, freeing himself of his captor. In the moment he shoots Ledgard, he reclaims himself as Vincente and returns to look for his mother. In a poignant closing scene that sees Vincente return to the chic boutique selling vintage dresses run by his mother, we are struck by the way nothing has changed. It feels as if time has stood still, reflecting both a sense of the mother's state of suspended waiting for her son to return and the way that beneath the dressed-up woman's body that is at first unrecognizable to his mother, Vincente's true self has not changed.

Concluding thoughts

There are limits to how much suffering people can endure and also limits to our capacities to control the seductive and defensive power of hostility and attack.

Through Ledgard we can see how hatred (in all its forms) offers a retreat, an exciting analgesic to suffering. This 'analgesic' is offered to us by Almodóvar in the form of horror that unfolds within the confines of apparent style and beauty. Indeed the real horror of this film lies in its seductive aesthetics. As our gaze is intoxicated with the beautiful physical surroundings of El Cigarral and of its prisoner – the stunningly beautiful Vera whose skin is flawless – we are jolted by the reality that Vera's beautiful skin masks a body that has been brutally cut up and redesigned against 'her' will. Beauty frames the horror and the horror is all the more brutal against this surfeit of beauty, which is but a corruption of the reality it masks. Vera's flawless skin, which conjures up unreality in its perfection, covers up a profound traumatic injury, which unlike the new skin perfectly grafted onto her by Ledgard, can never heal in Ledgard's mind.

There is something poignant in the belief that enough trips to the cosmetic surgeon can prevent the ruin of the body, or that looking young somehow enures us to other physical and psychic catastrophes. Vincente's fate makes it clear that changing the surface of the body does not erase or change identity; it cannot change reality. Yet, in our advanced technological culture, body images appear to be infinitely mutable, promulgating the fantasy that by changing the body we can change who we are and how we feel. Nowadays self-identity has become a global product. Specifically, as Giddens (1991) has helpfully articulated, it is far more 'deliberative', and we are witnessing an ongoing 're-ordering of identity narratives' in which a concern with the body is central (Giddens, 1991; Featherstone, 2000). In this kind of external world, psychoanalysis allows us to understand that the real challenge is how to stand up to the seductions of identification with a narcissistic, omnipotent object, as Almodóvar's film illustrates.

Note

1   The male birth myth is central to *Frankenstein*'s narrative, but it features a great deal in horror films:
> In his attempt to create life, the male womb monster of the horror film re-creates an intrauterine mise-en-scene, a maternal landscape, which is symbolically his womb, his birth giving place. He gives physical form to an unconscious memory of his first home. (Creed, 2005: 42)

Chapter 7

The body of the analyst and the analytic setting

Reflections on the embodied setting and the symbiotic transference

The analytic setting or frame[1] is generally thought to include the establishment and maintenance of the physical setting and of the psychoanalytic contract, which includes negotiation of the time, frequency of sessions, use of the couch and money, and the role of the analyst (Winnicott, 1956; Bleger, 1967[2012]; Langs, 1998). Some analysts also include within this notion the delineation of 'the data of analysis', namely the patient's free associations (Busch, 1995) and the analytic attitude. Many would also include the analyst's internal setting, that is, the setting as a structure in the mind of the analyst – 'a psychic arena in which reality is defined by such concepts as symbolism, fantasy, transference, and unconscious meaning' (Parsons, 2007: 1444). Others still bring into the notion the analyst's theoretical leanings (Donnet, 2005). In this chapter the term 'analytic setting' denotes both the pragmatic parameters and the analyst's internal setting as defined by Parsons (2007). It is this definition that provides the basis for the elaboration of the 'embodied setting'.

The function of the setting has been written about extensively. It has traditionally been understood to be the essential 'background' that provides the necessary containment and stimulus for the gradual unfolding of the patient's transference. Within an object relational model one would add that it allows for the emergence of the unconscious phantasies that give the transference its dynamic specificity. Accordingly the role of the analyst is to be the custodian of the setting. This requires that the analyst not only pays close attention to how the patient reacts to the setting (the unconscious phantasies and resistances it may generate), but also carefully monitors her own internal processes, which can both facilitate (through free-floating attentiveness) or hinder (through the analyst's own resistances and 'blind spots') the unfolding of an analytic process.

In this chapter I will not review the vast literature on this subject; rather, I will restrict myself primarily to the seminal paper by Bleger (1967[2012]), whose conceptualization of the setting adds an important dimension because he highlights that we are always working with *two* settings: the one provided by the analyst and the one brought by the patient (what he called the 'meta-ego'). His ideas, I will suggest, are especially helpful in understanding the particular way that patients who develop a symbiotic transference, and whose core primitive anxieties relate to non-differentiation from the object, need to relate to the analyst's body as an *invariant* part of the setting, as if it were part of the background and silent; for this kind of patient any sign of aliveness and separateness in the analyst's body heralds a catastrophe which cannot initially be reflected upon. I will illustrate these dynamics through my work with a patient – Ms D. – who started three-times-weekly sessions on the couch for two years and then moved into a four-times-weekly analysis for a subsequent five and half years. I will focus on how Ms D. first related to my body as a 'non-process' (Bleger, 1967[2012]) and only later as a dynamic feature which she could make use of to understand her need to fuse with the object in a destructive symbiotic tie.[2]

I am also taking the opportunity to initiate an exploration of whether there may be some merit in conceptualizing the body of the analyst as a part of the setting. I am using the term 'embodied setting' in two ways: (a) to denote the way that the analyst's physical appearance and presence – their sensoriality, if you like – provides an embodied form of containment such that changes at this level may mobilize particular anxieties and phantasies in the patient and (b) to underline that the analyst's somatic countertransference is an important cornerstone of her internal setting, that is, the analyst also uses the body's free associations to listen to the patient, not least as they may relate to the patient's 'embodied phantasies' (Bronstein, 2013).

In the tradition of the single case study (Hinshelwood, 2013) I am focusing on one patient in detail. However, one case alone cannot be demonstrative of the thesis I am interested in: I am using it merely to illustrate the ideas outlined above as the basis for stimulating further thinking and to engage with colleagues in considering whether this focus is specifically relevant to particular patients, such as Ms D., or may have broader applicability.

The embodied setting: revisiting Bleger

Bleger described the psychoanalytic situation as comprising of

> phenomena that constitute a *process* which is what we study, analyse and interpret. However, it also includes a *setting*, in other words a 'non-process' in the sense that they are the constants within the framework of which the process takes place.
>
> (1967[2012]: 228)

The setting is thus the background against which the analytic process unfolds. Because the setting's 'rules' provide a sense of security, it is ideally suited, according to Bleger, for serving as the depository for the patient's symbiosis. It is only when the setting is altered that the symbiosis, which may have been 'mute' until then, is thus exposed.

He considered symbiosis to be a developmental stage and primitive mode of relating which results from a way of experiencing reality in the *'glischro-caric'* position. In this position the ego is not yet differentiated from the object: it is the '*agglutinated nucleus*' or '*ambiguous nucleus*'. The symbiotic core coincides with the psychotic part of the personality and is characterized by a failure to distinguish between inside and outside, between the self and the object. In the mature personality a nucleus of this primary undifferentiation persists. From an object relational point of view, the agglutinated nucleus is an archaic position – a very primitive level of functioning – that precedes the paranoid-schizoid and depressive positions. Bleger was indeed primarily concerned with patients who presented with a marked split between neurotic and psychotic parts of the personality. In his view this had implications for technique in terms of the kinds of interpretations that the patient could take in – a point we shall return to later in the discussion.

Bleger gives the name 'symbiotic link' to the projection of the 'agglutinated nucleus' into a depository. He points out that at this level of functioning there is an urgent and indeed omnipotent need for depositories in order to feel safe. He likened the symbiotic relationship to a kind of 'pact' between two people, each using the other as a 'depository for parts of themselves' that cannot be integrated (Churcher and Bleger, 2012). His is not only an incisive analysis of symbiotic dynamics, but also a reminder of how the patient's setting or '*phantom world*', as he would put it, and which he also referred to as the '*meta-ego*', is a key part of the unspoken pact established with the analyst in his/her own mind. In his view it is the setting and its management by the analyst that allows this primitive and undifferentiated relationship to the object to emerge with the aim of facilitating a gradual process of differentiation from symbiosis.

This process, in my experience, is especially delicate when one is working with patients who need to create a symbiotic fusion with the object in order to maintain their psychic equilibrium. Work with these patients often evokes powerful somatic countertransference responses in the analyst, which invite us to consider how the body of the analyst is being unconsciously used by the patient. The challenges I have encountered in my own work have led me to be curious about the way that these patients appear to relate to the body of the analyst as a kind of 'fixture' in the analytic setting that must not be changed, thus revealing their own setting; this, in turn, may leave the analyst feeling intruded upon and controlled in their body. When the analyst's body reaches the patient's awareness *because* of a more obvious change (e.g. pregnancy, weight fluctuations, a visible injury, change in hairstyle), it mobilizes primitive phantasies and related anxieties in the patient. Importantly such physical changes, like any change, signal the analyst's separateness and patients who experience difficulties with differentiation from the object are especially sensitized to this and it provokes their hostility.

Bleger's (1967[2012]) ideas and my work with patients like Ms D. have, in turn, led me to speculate about the potential usefulness of conceptualizing the 'embodied setting'. This position draws on ideas about pre-symbolic sensory levels of experience developed by a number of analysts (e.g. Rosenfeld, 1987; Ogden, 1989; Ferro, 2003; Lombardi, 2005; Fonagy and Target, 2007; Civitarese, 2008). It also draws on the seminal work by Lakoff and Johnson (1999) on the embodied mind and the work by Gallese et al. (2007) and Iacoboni (2008) on mirror neurons, highlighting how the mirror neuron system generates pre-reflexive empathic reactions (see also the Introduction, this edition). Focusing on our embedded nature reminds us that our first perceptions and phantasies are sensory in quality and content (Isaacs, 1983). The analytic setting can evoke a range of phantasies, including pre-symbolic ones (Bronstein, 2013), both through the patient's experience of sharing a physical space and the analyst's physical presence.

Civitarese (2008), informed by both Bleger (1967[2012]) and Ogden's (1989) ideas about 'sensation dominated experience', underlines the *sensory* qualities of the setting: 'A particular function of the setting is precisely that of providing a "skin" still in adhesive contact, with the role of integration' (Civitarese, 2008: 28). The use of the word 'skin' incisively captures the importance of the body of the analyst as part of the setting that our patients come to expect.

The analyst's physical appearance and the way she inhabits her body and physical space in the room – the way she sits in the chair, breathes, moves in the room, speaks, dresses and so on – could be said to constitute core sensory features of the setting that contribute to the containment provided by the analyst. We might say that several aspects of the setting are indeed embodied. Our nods or glances as we greet the patient or the way we stand up at the end of sessions are part of the rituals or frame parameters embodied as 'constants'. All of these become expected features of the setting.

These are, however, 'constants' that by virtue of their embodied nature are hard to keep reliably constant, such that the patient may react to this aspect of the setting more strongly and more frequently than they do in relation to other parameters of the setting. By 'reacting' I do not just mean that the patient consciously reacts to visible changes in the analyst's body; rather I have in mind how the analyst's body acts as a powerful stimulus in the patient's internal world, as will become manifest in the patient's associations, enactments and so on, as well as impacting on the analyst's countertransference, all of which allows us to infer the patient's unconscious phantasies and internal objects.

The body of the analyst, however, is not typically considered to be a 'constant' part of the analytic setting, perhaps precisely because of the body's inherent changeability. Nevertheless there is a relevant and rich literature that addresses the use of the analyst's body by the patient and the 'reciprocal observation' of it by both patient and analyst (Zanardi, 1995; Tintner, 2007; Burka, 2008; De Toffoli, 2011). This literature coalesces largely around two strands of work. First, the work of analysts with adult psychotic and perverse patients who have also formulated the significance of their bodies as part of the work of differentiation (Bleger, 1967[2012]; Chasseguet-Smirgel, 1990; Rey, 1994; Lombardi, 2005), including the way the psychotic patient projects *into* the analyst's body (Goldberg, 1979; Lombardi and Pola, 2010). Second, the work of child analysts who have long suggested that the setting may be experienced by some children as synonymous with the analyst's body (Isaacs-Elmhirst, 1988; Davies, 1989). Work with autistic children in particular touches on this and illustrates well the child's need to control the therapist's body (e.g. Rhode, 2005) – a dynamic prominent in my work with Ms D. as I will now illustrate.

The somatic countertransference and the somatic 'cautionary tale': first encounter with Ms D.

The sensory features of the analytic setting are most likely important to all patients. The way a room is decorated may give rise to feelings of warmth and phantasies of being taken care of, or quite the converse: a patient may feel that a room is too 'bare', which may give rise to a phantasy that the analyst is depriving him. Similarly, the body of the analyst sets a particular sensory tone to the setting and mobilizes particular phantasies: their voice may be experienced as 'warm' or 'cutting'; their choice of clothes may be too 'cold' or intrusively 'colourful'. These phantasies, which as Bronstein (2013) notes could be understood as 'embodied phantasies' not yet accessible to representation, may nevertheless be communicated non-verbally to the analyst, leading to powerful *somatic countertransference* responses in the analyst.

Those patients who have difficulty in establishing and maintaining a stable differentiation from the object typically present with marked difficulties in symbolization and may powerfully project into the analyst's body, as analysts working with psychotic patients and autistic children also often note. The analyst's somatic reactions may be understood to result from projective processes that bypass verbal articulation and that are deposited in the body, as it were. The patient's 'bodily states of mind' (Wyre, 1997) inevitably impact on and are impacted on by the analyst's bodily states of mind: the patient communicates through his body and the analyst receives such communications in their body. This cannot, however, be considered to be an identical reflection because in the process of being received by the analyst what is projected is also modified by the analyst's own internal world (Arizmendi, 2008).[3]

The scope for enactments is always wide since we are here in the realm of pre-symbolic functioning in the patient *and* potentially also in the analyst, whose capacity for symbolic elaboration of their own bodily experience may be temporarily disrupted. Such bodily experiences need to become 'thoughts with a thinker', to play on Bion's (1967) turn of phrase, and eventually shared with the patient in order to support the development of a capacity to symbolize. However, with these patients the analyst's 'sensory acceptance' (Lombardi and Pola, 2010) of the patient's projections may be an essential prerequisite before interpretations can be helpful.

The importance of the somatic countertransference was vividly brought home to me in my work with Ms D., an intelligent, attractive and professionally capable twenty-eight-year-old woman who was nevertheless very disabled emotionally. She had longstanding eating problems that oscillated between periods of moderately severe anorexia and bulimia. Ms D. was the eldest of two; her sister was several years younger than her. Her mother died when she was in her late teens, deteriorating very rapidly due to an aggressive tumour. Her father was described as an irascible man who drank heavily. Ms D. recalled a happy childhood until the death of her mother. She described a very close relationship to the mother whom she felt understood her 'perfectly'. When Ms D. started her analysis she had been in a long-term unsatisfactory relationship with a man.

I want to begin with my very first observations of Ms D.'s body, of how she related to the physical space in the room and my somatic countertransference, because this revealed a great deal about the patient's psychopathology and what was to unfold in the transference. Taken together they represent, in my view, the somatic counterpart to Ogden's (1992) 'cautionary tale', which he understands as the interpersonal narratives the patient brings in the first session that communicate the patient's unconscious anxieties about developing a relationship with the analyst. I am suggesting here that the non-verbal narrative communicated sensorially, through the patient's relationship to the physical space and to the body of the analyst, impacts on the analyst, and is a central feature of the cautionary tale. Indeed Ogden (1997) has emphasized how the analyst's reverie may be a general feeling state that comprises of primarily physical sensations.

As Ms D. entered my room for the first time she stood by the door and looked around very carefully, she then turned towards me and scanned me with her eyes. This was uncomfortable for me because it felt intrusive somehow and it left me feeling ill at ease in my body. As I watched her move towards the chair I was very struck by how her body carried excess weight relative to her petite frame, which made her seem even smaller than she was, as if she was somehow crushed under her weight. She was mildly overweight but came across as somehow heavier, as if 'weighed down' by something. There was also a marked slowness in her movements, which conjured up in my mind the peculiar impression that she walked standing still, as if her body was attached to a string pulling her back to the starting position.

Ms D. did not so much sit on the chair opposite me as sink into it. As she did so she dissolved into an amorphous physical heap such that it was hard to distinguish her face from the rest of the body or from the chair. She spoke in a very slow, flat manner, which left me feeling rather flattened and I noticed the shallowness of my own breathing as I listened to her. It felt effortful to be with her in a way that I could not quite understand there and then, but I had the distinct impression that I needed to make a lot of effort to make contact with her even though she ostensibly appeared interested in what I had to say. I noticed, however, that she agreed with all that I said without hesitation in a manner that felt unconvincing. I was aware too that when I spoke the volume of my voice lowered; I half-finished my sentences, tapering off into a kind of untypical murmur as my words met with Ms D.'s very deep, loud and frequent inhalations. My voice merged with her breathing and disappeared.

Ms D.'s loud inhalations were at first irritating and disconcerting in equal measure: they had an enveloping, suffocating quality. All this left me with a powerful sense, as I wrote in my notes at the time, that 'my words are sucked into the vortex of her breathing'. I was thus alerted early on to a difficulty around differentiation that manifested itself very concretely through her relationship to the physical setting, in how she physically merged with the furniture and in my visceral claustrophobic experience of being flattened out and suffocated by her breathing.

Despite her otherwise softly spoken and agreeable manner I felt Ms D. had already given me some sense of the aggression that lay behind this facade and of the pull towards something dead and hard to reach within her. Agreement between us seemed to be imperative whereas genuine understanding, which might expose differences between us, felt perilous.

The first two years

After the initial consultation Ms D. took to the couch easily in the same manner as she had used the chair: she sank into it, lying virtually immobile, speaking softly. As I looked at her from behind she reminded me of a corpse lying in a coffin. In the long silences that characterized the first two years of our work, I frequently felt that we breathed the air of death. I noticed that I often yawned and that this, in turn, had a kind of enveloping, still quality – a somatic reaction that could be understood as a way of insulating myself from her by retreating into a kind of sensory narcissistic cocoon, but which might also offer some insights into how she enveloped herself in a similar, 'still' state where time stood still and loss and separation could thus be averted.

Ms D. also spoke softly, such that I often struggled to hear her. I found that I had to move my body closer to the edge of the couch to catch her words. As I leaned over I noticed that I gripped the side of my chair very hard, as if I feared losing my balance and falling onto the couch. It alerted me to my urgent need to 'grip on' to my chair/analytic role as if what she was exposing created some resistance in me. This made me wonder about the strong homosexual current that was present in our relationship, as if she was luring me into the coffin/couch with her where she could be at one with me. At this stage these remained thoughts in my mind that it seemed important to contain and not interpret prematurely.

Throughout this time my physical movements felt constrained and stiff and, as I came to understand later, this mirrored how my mind was not always as free to accompany her where she needed me to go. Indeed during this phase my interventions often missed the patient, whose primitive level of functioning, though understood by me intellectually, was nevertheless sometimes resisted by me emotionally, most likely because symbiotic processes are not easy to bear and invariably lead to enactments and impasses to which both the patient's and the analyst's unconscious contribute.

In the transference I had the peculiar experience of there being 'no transference'. My attempts at interpretation were met with barely disguised, if courteous, indifference or were simply ignored altogether, as if there was nothing relevant in my attempts to understand what was happening *between* us. And indeed herein lay the problem as I came to understand it: there was no 'between us' because this presupposes a space, some separation or differentiation between self and object, and this is what Ms D. could not tolerate. Instead it felt like she related to me as part of the furniture in the room (i.e. not only that the furniture was experienced at times as an extension of my body, but also that my body *was* furniture), all of which functioned as a kind of umbilical cord between us. She would often comment on how comforting she found it that my room was always the same and she could also rely on me to be 'the same'. She did not elaborate on what she meant by me 'being the same'.

At this stage Ms D. seemed to respond best to interventions that described her states of mind without making explicit links to the transference.[4] Interpretations that focused on tracking how she used my interpretations seemed to destabilize her. At best she made use of analyst-centred interpretations (Steiner, 1993). Bleger (1967[2012]) referred to these as 'interpretations without splitting' and considered these necessary in order to manage the agglutinated nucleus, incrementally helping the patient to recognize an 'outside' and eventually enabling them to make use of the 'split interpretation', which is not dissimilar to Steiner's 'patient centred' interpretation (Churcher and Bleger, 2012). Ongoing processing of the transference and countertransference in my mind was nevertheless the internal compass that helped me to formulate when she might be able to take in more from me at any given point.

I would now like to illustrate the function of the invariance of the embodied frame in her psychic economy by selecting a few instances when Ms D. reacted to changes in my appearance and bodily state.

On one occasion during the first year of our work Ms D. arrived for the Thursday session, the last session of the week for her, and stared intently at me as she came into the room, her facial expression betraying what can best be described as confusion. After a few minutes on the couch she remarked irritably that I looked 'different'. I was aware that I received her comment as a kind of urgent and intrusive injunction to not look different and immediately I scanned myself in my mind to think *how* I might seem different. It then occurred to me that I was indeed wearing a more colourful shirt that day than was usual for me as I was due to attend an evening event straight after the session.

Ms D. devoted the next fifteen minutes to talking, in what felt like furious detail, about her maternal aunt whom I knew she did not like. Amongst several accusations levelled against this aunt, Ms D. dismissed her as someone who dressed in an 'outlandish' manner that made her 'stand out'. She was unpredictable too, Ms D. told me: the aunt had never settled down into a stable relationship; instead she had been 'promiscuous'.

I thought that my colourful shirt – the colour of sex in her mind – had been registered as evidence of my separate life from her, most likely also fuelled by the upcoming weekend break. Ms D. seemed deeply troubled and aroused by my 'outlandish' shirt, as if my deviation from the dress code she was accustomed to was experienced as a sign that I was promiscuously involved in my mind with someone else over the weekend, and she was furious about this. My body was now also evidently exposed as separate from hers and she could not tolerate this separation: she appeared to be communicating to me that I should settle down and marry her. As I listened I started to feel curiously constricted by the waistband on the trousers I was wearing – a somatic countertransferential reaction that could be understood as responsive to my experience in the transference of Ms D.'s colonization of my body. I eventually simply said to her that what she perceived today as something 'different' about me had outraged her.

Ms D. did not engage with what I said; she remained rigidly stuck in discussing her aunt. I thought that Ms D. really could not make use of her experience of my slightly altered appearance to represent her anxieties and phantasies of displacement, as might have been the case with a less disturbed patient who could have 'played' with the intrapsychic implications. By contrast, the setting in Ms D.'s mind, which included me looking a particular way, needed to remain unchanged so as to preserve the symbiotic tie.

Some months later when I developed a bad cold and cough, she was similarly perturbed by this physical change. On this occasion, after I coughed several times, she recounted a story about a colleague at work whose face was asymmetrical. She said that she felt sorry for this woman because she imagined she must be very bothered by this as it meant everyone looked at her. After I coughed again, she said somewhat irritably that the cold made my voice sound 'different, as if it's not really you'. At first I again felt controlled by her and this made me acutely aware of my cough, which only worsened, perhaps betraying the hostility mobilized in me. Then, as this feeling subsided, I recalled what she had previously told me about the day her mother died. She had described how the mother had become progressively unconscious and I now imagined her in my mind sitting by her bedside, looking at her mother, and feeling 'it's not really you'. Perhaps the difference she heard in my voice altered by 'illness' destabilized her not only because it mobilized feelings associated with the loss of her mother, but also because the cough had altered my voice and changed me, and this was experienced by her as something that had come between us, like death, imposing a boundary that disrupted the longed for symmetry and togetherness.

Ms D. often spoke about her mother, describing how she had always felt close to her and enjoyed the physical proximity between them. She had shared a bed with her mother until she was ten. She told me that when her parents had violent fights, after the rows Ms D. would close the door to her mother's bedroom so as to keep out her father whilst her mother regained her composure. She described how the mother would get into bed with her, wrap herself round her and caress her skin. Of course these memories did not provide evidence as such of what the mother may or may not have done, but they contributed to the evolving picture in my mind of Ms D.'s object relationships and of what may have been transpiring between us.

The long and the short of it: the impact of the analyst's haircut

Towards the end of the second year of our work we increased to four-times-weekly sessions,[5] which I considered necessary if we were to make progress. Ms D. eagerly welcomed this increase. At this stage I understood that one of the unconscious functions of the analysis was to embalm her relationship with her mother/me. In her mind the increase in frequency served to consolidate a symbiotic tie to the object, which was the only kind of relationship she could establish with me at that point. I was clear that she required my engagement with her at this primitive level, that this was an essential part of the analysis.

Towards the start of the third year of our work a significant event took place, which in my view furthered our work. With hindsight I think this was mobilized by a change in my appearance (a visible haircut) and the enactment that ensued. In this session Ms D. walked into the room and stared at me, looking clearly at my face. Her own face showed confusion and shock. There and then I was not sure what she was reacting to so strongly. Significantly *I* felt very confused and disoriented, experiencing a peculiar sense of dizziness as if I had stood up suddenly.

As Ms D. lay on the couch I eased myself into my chair. I registered my relief but also noticed that I was gripping the sides of my chair with considerable pressure. This alerted me to the possibility that what Ms D. had reacted to had shaken her deeply and she may have powerfully projected into me an experience of disorientation that, in turn, I experienced as dizziness and the related need to cling to my chair, a gesture I was of course familiar with (see earlier). As I regained some capacity to think I remembered my haircut and wondered if this is what had so shaken her. Clearly this was my association, as Ms D. made no direct reference to my haircut, so I could not be certain that this was what she had reacted to. Instead she lay silent on the couch, rhythmically twisting strands of her long hair. I found myself almost hypnotized by this movement and began to feel sleepy. I must have lost track of what she was saying for several minutes. I was only brought back into the room when I heard her say that she had nothing of importance to say today. After a pause she added that she did not want to be in the session, that she thought the analysis had stopped helping her. She then said that she had no desire to meet a friend later – this friend lived 'a long way out' and she always got lost when visiting her. Her words came out slowly and in a manner that felt disjointed. She sounded disoriented and this now resonated with my temporary sleepiness and loss of concentration, as if I had lost my bearings in relation to her and had moved out of the analysis in my mind, like the friend who lived a 'long way out'. This had led to a breach in the continuity of our contact, which had left Ms D. feeling stranded in a place she no longer recognized or felt safe in. I had indeed temporarily left her, perhaps as a defensive retreat from something disturbing that was transpiring between us which I had not yet understood.

A long silence ensued during which I sensed she felt anxious. She then said she fancied something sweet to eat. She had been dieting but she was finding it hard to stick to the diet and had bought some chocolate on the way to the session. Her body weight had always fluctuated, she said, and it was disconcerting to see pictures of herself when she was anorexic compared to how she looked now: 'It's like two different people: Dr Jekyll and Mr Hyde.'

The image of Dr Jekyll and Mr Hyde triggered in me two associations: one to the experience of becoming sleepy and losing touch with her, as if the Dr Jekyll-me had left the room, exposing her to a Mr Hyde-like frightening object; the other association was to how she had played with her own hair and the fact of my own haircut. I then recalled a child I had seen at the hairdresser the previous week who had been very distressed, refusing to have his hair cut. At the time it had reminded me of a kind of torture. One cannot exclude the possibility that by now I was pursuing an 'overvalued idea' (Britton and Steiner, 1994) in my mind with respect to the haircut, but as far as I could determine it was my free associations, in so far as they can ever be 'free' (i.e. my internal setting), that led me back to the hair and its possible significance, especially now the link with something cruel imposed by an adult onto a child. The association to the child's haircut now raised the possibility that I might have enacted a cruel 'cutting-off', becoming Mr Hyde-like, an experience that Ms D. was especially sensitized to, and that she might indeed have invited me to participate in.

All these thoughts led me to eventually say that she had been confronted today with a totally different picture of me and she was not sure if she was now in the room with Dr Jekyll or Mr Hyde. Ms D. replied that she could not hear me well because of 'some noise outside' and could not follow what I was saying.

I thought to myself that she was accurately responding to a 'noise from outside' (i.e. my own unconscious reaction to her that led to my sleepy withdrawal) that had disrupted our relationship earlier on. Perhaps the haircut too was a 'noise from outside' intruding into *her* setting and it had stimulated phantasies in her of a cruel cutting off of the symbiotic link that she needed to preserve with me, which I had then enacted by becoming Mr Hyde-like.

Ms D. fell into a deep silence that seemed to shut me out. She eventually spoke in a dreamy manner of her mother's long hair and how the mother would use it to caress her face when they shared the bed together. She found this soothing and it put her to sleep. She told me that at times of stress she used her own hair in this way. As she spoke Ms D. forcefully pulled her long hair across her neck.

I said the memory of the mother's hair was soothing but I also made her aware of the fact that she was now wrapping her hair around her neck and pulling at it rather forcefully. Ms D. said she had not realized she was doing this.

I said perhaps she wanted to tie herself very close to the me-who-once-had-long-hair, just like her, and not let me go.

Ms D. then suddenly sat up on the couch and turned to look at me. She appeared confused and then crumpled, tears streaming down her cheeks. She had not cried like this before. Then she lay down on the couch and was silent.

I said she had experienced my haircut as me cutting loose from the close relationship she wanted to preserve with me, leaving her stranded on her own. This was terrifying for her.

Ms D. nodded and I sensed she was more receptive than usual. I added that any change in me destabilized her and left her exposed in her mind to something very frightening and confusing. Ms D. nodded again and said she could not talk about 'it'. I was not sure what she meant by 'it' but it did not feel timely to press her.

Here, for the first time, I felt that my body and its changed appearance could be used to begin to approach her experience even if it could not yet be verbalized. It had become part of the process that we could slowly reflect on together. In the following session she brought a disturbing story about a doll she played with as a child. She had stripped the doll naked and imagined that the doll was being raped. It took several more sessions before Ms D. told me that when she shared the bed with her mother, the mother would sometimes touch her vagina. She reported other instances of her mother literally lying on top of her, at times immobile, at other times stroking her skin. Ms D. described how heavy her mother was, such that she could not breathe, but she did not dare disturb her because she longed for this closeness and dreaded the rejecting manner that her mother sometimes adopted with her. I was very struck by the image of my patient suffocating under the weight of her mother's body and its intrusion into her. This reminded me of my initial somatic countertransference of feeling suffocated by her loud inhalations and my initial perception that her small frame seemed crushed by what I thought was the 'excess weight' she carried.

Symbiosis, the analyst's body and the analytic setting

Despite her high level of professional functioning Ms D. was a very troubled woman who lived on the edge of psychic death much of the time. By the end of her analysis she had nevertheless made significant progress. I have not focused in this chapter on her eating problems, her representation of her body in her mind or her sexuality, but these were some of the important issues we worked on over the years. The analysis of the homosexual transference was central to this work. In this discussion, however, I will focus selectively on how we might understand what may have helped this patient with respect to the embodied setting.

With less damaged patients than Ms D. the transference relationship, and the body of the analyst in particular, provides the impetus for a range of phantasies and the emergence of the patient's instinctual capacities. As Bollas put it: 'if all goes well he or she comes into a new-found body-experiencing in the analyst's presence' (Bollas, 1994: 578–579). Here the body of the analyst is a *dynamic* variable between them (i.e. part of the analytic process) which can be used or 'played' with by the patient to further the exploration of her own body and mind. The development of Ms D.'s capacity to make use of my body in this way was at first severely undermined because this required acknowledging that there were *two* separate bodies. This capacity appeared to have been gradually and painstakingly facilitated by the 'crises' prompted by her perception of changes in the setting as represented by physical changes in me, which mobilized primitive phantasies and anxieties as the symbiosis (her setting) was interrupted and brought to light. This, in turn, led at times to enactments between us that illuminated some aspects of her internal world and created a bridge between pre-symbolic experience and its representation in the context of the transference.

Focus on her strong reactions to my bodily changes and her relationship to her own body, is an aspect of the work that I think enabled her over time to discriminate the boundaries of her own body-self, which were very confused, as was apparent in her sexual relationships. As Lombardi put it, the perception of the body is 'the decisive element of differentiation and a first principle of reality, which can stimulate awareness of the body-self and other' (2005: 107–108).

This way of working requires that what is projected into the body of analyst is represented first in the mind of the analyst, where it may need to be contained for some time before it can be presented to the patient (Ferro, 2003). Indeed, as I look back on this challenging analysis, my acceptance and containment in my mind *and* body of her need for symbiosis and its eventual working through in the transference and somatic countertransference strike me as crucial. However, as I hope I have also illustrated, Ms D.'s insistent erosion of any difference between us was experienced by me at times as intrusive and controlling, and nudged me to respond in ways that recreated aspects of her internalized relationships, such as when I defensively retreated away from her into a sleepy state, effectively abandoning her to a Mr Hyde-like object. This enactment might be understood as my reaction to the implicit seduction in the way she rhythmically twisted her own hair,[6] which I may have unconsciously experienced as suffocating and aggressive, and which led me to interpose distance between us. My haircut appeared to have been experienced by Ms D. as evidence of my separateness, and this, in turn, may have mobilized a wish in her to draw me back into her own body, Rapunzel-like, using her hair to re-establish a symbiotic link.

The recollections of abuse by the mother that ensued in this particular session could be heard as giving expression in the transference to Ms D.'s experience of me as somehow intrusive and abusive. Different analysts will understand this in different ways and it is beyond the scope of this book to engage with the richness of alternative interpretations. Suffice to say that I heard it as resulting from two processes. First, how exposure to the separation between us, as triggered by my altered appearance, was felt by her to intrude into the symbiosis, that is, as an act of aggression towards her. Second, I then became a Mr Hyde-like object abandoning her in the session as I reacted unconsciously to her wish to restore the symbiosis. These experiences in the transference, in turn, may well have mobilized these recollections or screen memories of intrusion and abuse.[7]

It was only when I could meet Ms D. *in her own setting*, in a space where the differentiation was lacking, and we were exposed to the emergence of terrifying anxieties when the fact of separateness presented itself to her via changes in my body, that we started to make progress towards creating a space where symbolization was possible. Meeting Ms D. in her own setting required understanding of the phantasies the changes in my body aroused in her mind, and using my somatic responses to edge closer to an understanding of what she was communicating non-verbally. I am not suggesting that this was the primary or only focus that enabled her to make progress, but it appeared to provide a very helpful opportunity to understand her longing for fusion with the object and the psychotic terror that separation heralded.

Most helpful to me in working with my patient was Bleger's observation that because the symbiosis resides in the setting itself it becomes a refuge for the psychotic part of the personality, which demands that nothing will change. This was painfully apparent in the way Ms D. related to the embodied aspects of the setting when these were subject to change. For example, on the occasion of my haircut most patients commented on it: it was clear that they made use of it to elaborate fantasies about me, that is, they could 'play' with my physicality (Wyre, 1997) and we could think about this transferentially. Ms D.'s reaction, along with that of another very disturbed patient, was strikingly different: I felt it was experienced by Ms D. as a deep incision into the symbiotic phantasy that my interpretations had hitherto failed to make any impression on. In her mind I had not cut my hair: I had cut the umbilical cord that linked us.

Especially in his work with psychotic patients, Bleger noted their

> exaggerated sensitivity concerning the infringement of any detail of what the patient is 'used to' (in the setting), and how the patient may become disorganized or violent … if there is a difference of a few minutes at the start or end of the session.
>
> (Bleger, 1967[2012]: 233)

With Ms D., when the body of her analyst to which she had become 'used to' as part of the setting looked or felt different to her she became disturbed as if she was being deprived of what she needed to survive. Here Bleger's observation that the setting itself can become a kind of 'addiction' is very apt: when my body changed I sensed powerfully the urgency with which Ms D. needed to restore it to how it looked in her mind.

Analysis of the transference–countertransference matrix eventually brought to light the seductions and perils of the erotized dimension to the relationship with an object felt to be seductive but also colonizing and rejecting. Whilst at first the longed-for fusion with me dominated the transference, this eventually gave way to her experience of me as the one seducing and trapping her.[8] This, in turn, proved central to understanding her difficulties with sexual intimacy, which exposed a strong homosexual orientation that she consciously resisted acknowledging for a long time.

In the transference it was possible to discern Ms D.'s longing to engage in a relationship with me without anything coming between us. This desire is well captured by Chasseguet-Smirgel (1990), who has proposed a more archaic wish than Klein (1936) describes of appropriating and destroying the insides of the mother, that is, a wish to return to a smooth maternal abdomen. This reveals a primary desire, as she put it: 'to discover a universe without obstacles, without roughness or differences, entirely smooth' (Chasseguet-Smirgel, 1990: 79). For Ms D., access to this smooth 'universe without obstacles' left in its wake developmental obstacles because no differentiation was possible on which to lay the foundation for the development of a separate sense of self.

Just as Chasseguet-Smirgel outlines a more primitive wish for merger with the mother's body, Bleger's 'glischro-caric' position also underlines the symbiotic tie to the object. Here the characteristic anxiety, he suggests, is confusional rather than persecutory (Churcher and Bleger, 2012). This was indeed my experience transferentially and countertransferentially with Ms D. when she reacted to changes in my physical state or appearance: she did not become paranoid; rather she became primarily confused. It was as if she desperately needed to cling on to the expectable qualities of my physical appearance and sensory experience with me. When she was faced with changes, a gaping hole appeared between us.

The foundations of the self as separate, as I have suggested repeatedly in previous chapters, are shaped by the more or less successful integration of bodily experience within mental representations. This developmental achievement was thwarted in Ms D.'s case by the mother's seeming appropriation of her body, giving rise to a shared phantasy of a body that was owned by the mother (Pines, 1993). Ms D. appeared to struggle at first with the essential difference between being identical to the object and being 'like it'. This suggested a deficit at the level of what French psychoanalysts describe as 'primary homosexuality', that is, the transition from primary identification to a relational modality that disrupts the primitive feeling of unity, of being identical to the object (Denis, 2010). The implications of a developmental deficit in this domain – perhaps resulting at least partly from emotional and sexual intrusiveness by her actual mother – were manifest in Ms D.'s persistence in maintaining or re-establishing an undifferentiated mode of relating that, I am suggesting, became explicit partly through the way she related to changes in my body.

In Bleger's (1967[2012]) view of early development *discrimination* is a fundamental concept that also relates to technique. Discriminatory interpretations have the purpose of initiating separation between agglutinated psychotic aspects and neurotic aspects of the patient's personality. In my work with Ms D. this was partly achieved through paying close attention to her experience of my body and slowly introducing some discrimination (i.e. an 'outside') through my gradual articulation of her affective states and her unconscious wishes, anxieties and phantasies, which at times I first needed to contain sensorially.

A focus on sensoriality concords with Bleger, who considered that the body was the locus of symbiosis. Even though Bleger does not refer to the *analyst's* body as part of the setting, he helpfully establishes the relevance of the setting to the patient's own body schema, establishing a link to the notion of undifferentiation:

> In sum, we may say that the patient's setting is his most primitive fusion with the mother's body and that the psycho-analyst's setting must serve to re-establish the original symbiosis but only in order to change it.
>
> (Bleger, 1967[2012]: 240)

If, as Bleger suggests, *'the patient's setting is his most primitive fusion with the mother's body'*, then we can expect not only that aspects of the patient's own setting may be embodied and become manifest, for example, through posture (e.g. Ms D.'s weighed-down posture), but also that the embodied features of the analytic setting may act as powerful stimuli for the patient's unconscious phantasies and become the depositories for her own idiosyncratic setting.

In the early part of the analysis, even when the setting 'stood out' for Ms D. (or as Bleger beautifully puts it, when the setting 'cries'), because of changes in my body this was not open to being reflected upon. And yet these moments created opportunities for understanding the internal world of the patient. The work of analysis lay precisely in gradually helping Ms D. to develop a capacity for thinking about the setting of her 'phantom world'.

The tension in our work lies precisely in the delicate balance required between allowing the patient's setting to emerge so that we get the direct experience of the patient's primitive symbiosis while contemporaneously maintaining the analytic setting, which is the only way to transform the setting into a process that can be analysed. Moreover, although Bleger argues that the task of analysis is fundamentally anti-symbiotic, this outcome can only be achieved by allowing the symbiosis to become established through the setting so as to help the patient to progress to more integrated levels of functioning – a position with which I find myself in agreement.

Conclusion

Although I have focused on clinical work with only one particular patient, I consider her nevertheless to be representative in certain key respects of patients who struggle to discriminate between self and object. I have suggested that the embodied aspects of the setting require careful attention with individuals who need to create a symbiotic fusion with the object in order to maintain their psychic equilibrium. These individuals are highly sensitized to the body of the analyst and relate to it as a concrete part of the frame that must remain constant. Any variance in the analyst's body is experienced as highly destabilizing and results in confusional anxiety.

However, unlike other features of the setting that we strive to keep stable, the body is always changing more or less subtly even if it remains broadly the same. Consequently, the patient's own setting (their meta-ego) is likely to be more frequently challenged by these perceived changes. By virtue of the body's reactivity and unstable nature, 'ruptures' in the patient's symbiotic tie to the analyst may bring the setting to the fore with greater force and frequency than other changes to the setting. These, in turn, impact on the analyst at many levels, not least their somatic countertransference.

Perhaps irrespective of the patient's pathology, the body of the analyst may be helpfully conceptualized as an ever-present feature of the setting, which contributes to its felt constancy and hence its containing function such that any changes may mobilize phantasies and anxieties in the patient as well as in the analyst. One clinical advantage of conceptualizing the body of the analyst as a part of the setting would be that just as we are always alert to how changing a session time, say, may impact on the patient's unconscious mind, it reminds us that we need to be equally mindful of how changes in the body of the analyst may impact on all patients to varying degrees, with some patients very significantly affected while others seem relatively unperturbed and/or can more readily make creative use of it. This is an open question, not a statement of fact, and one that merits further consideration in relation to our general theories about the setting.

Notes

1. I am using the terms setting and frame interchangeably.
2. There are many interesting strands to this analysis that I will not be able to discuss. I am of necessity being selective to illustrate a particular point. I have therefore quite deliberately selected sessions where the interpretations I gave, or my countertransference, are relevant to this thesis.
3. The highly complex relationship between unconscious motor, affective, memory and phantasy processes is beyond the scope of this book.
4. A note about technique: the distinctiveness of psychoanalytic work, in my view, lies in the analyst's *systematic use* of the transference, which involves maintaining an analytic stance rooted in the analyst's experience of the transference in order to inform her understanding of the patient's state of mind and how to intervene most productively. We should always 'use' the transference in this sense, whilst being curious about the different ways we can engage and support the patient's curiosity about his own mind, not least, *but not only*, through the verbal interpretation of the transference. From this perspective representational work or supportive work is no less 'analytic' than transference-focused work (e.g. Ogden, 1982; Lecours, 2007; Lemma, 2013) and may be essential in the early stages of an analysis with a patient like Ms D.
5. Were it not for the fact that she very regularly flew back to her country of origin on a Friday morning for the weekend, she would have come five times a week.
6. What she was doing to her own hair could be understood to be a manifestation of an embodied phantasy of an erotically charged entanglement with the maternal object. Here we can only speculate as to whether we are in the realm of what Bronstein describes as an 'embodied state of "proto-thoughts" that have the imprint of an archaic moment in the relationship to the object, in particular the maternal body' (2013: 18), which she contrasts to a projective identification into the body of more 'distinct and better organized phantasies that cannot be tolerated and integrated' (ibid: 18).
7. Whether Ms D. had been abused or not by her mother remained an open question in my mind throughout the analysis. However, the material that emerged later led me to believe that there was probably some truth in what she related.
8. One could understand the symbiotic bond as a defensive position against the confrontation with the psychic impact of the abuse that would then have to be experienced if the symbiosis were relinquished. However, I gained the impression that for Ms D. the symbiotic bond was a developmental necessity rather than a primarily defensive one, which had to be worked through in the transference first before we could begin to explore the sequelae of the abuse and how these were also relevant in understanding her need to control my body.

Chapter 8

Rapunzel revisited
Untangling the unconscious meaning of hair

Hair crosses the boundaries between inside and outside, hidden and shared. Perhaps because hair begins inside of us, its roots invisible, and then grows outside, some part of us feels exposed by its journey, as if it carries secret truths from within and broadcasts them from the tops of our heads. We can manipulate hair to make it look different to its normal, so-called 'given' state and hence 'cover up' its origins, but more or less consciously we all know the truth about our hair, which we carry inside us – one narrative amongst others that is revealed through our body's appearance.

Hair is public, political but also, always, highly personal. For all of us head hair is one of our most important physical features, so much so that both men and women in all cultures and across historical periods have been invested in its adornment and/or modification. Curled, slicked-back or straightened, tied in tight little buns or floating out in the breeze like a windsock, human beings have been cutting, styling and colouring their hair for an extraordinarily long time (Corson, 2012).

In this chapter I want to focus on the psychic roots of hair, that is, its emotional significance in our unconscious. But before turning to a specifically psychoanalytic focus I will start by briefly reviewing biological and sociocultural perspectives on hair.

Hair stories

The hair's external health and beauty, or its opposite brittleness and fragility, are felt somehow to reflect in some fundamental way our internal state – a periscopic reversal we cannot control. Indeed we all have a sense that hair contains vital information about us, that it somehow tells a story. By 'information' I am referring here to biological, social and psychological information.

Let us start with the *biological information*[1] contained in hair. This is important because it may provide a biological basis for hair's felt-to-be emotional significance in so far as hair is felt to be revealing of the self's state (somatic and psychic). Even though hair itself is not a living organism, but is merely pushed through the follicles of any part of the anatomy where hair is found, it still contains DNA, our genetic code. The general state of our physical health is reflected in hair: glossy hair denotes well-being and fertility. For example, research studies have repeatedly found that men are attracted to long hair because it signifies good health and fertility in women. Men appear to be hardwired to notice physical details in women that indicate a good partner for passing on genes, healthy enough to carry their offspring to term and beyond, and hair is one such feature.

The hair shaft also records cortisol levels through time, similar to the way tree rings reflect age. Nowadays it is therefore used in research studies because hair captures cortisol levels over a long period and it thus gives us a biological marker for chronic stress.[2] In this biological sense hair then may be said to tell the story of our psychic distress as measured in our stress levels and general physical health.

Ever since Caesar insisted on shaving the heads of the newly conquered Gauls and used their unattached blond hair to fashion wigs of triumph, hair's *social significance* as a sign of status or political affiliation can also be traced across history and cultures. As far back as the fifteenth century, in most West African societies hair functioned as a carrier of information about marital status, age, wealth and rank (Byrd and Tharps, 2011). In China, possibly more than in any other culture, hair has long had strong political and social meaning. In ancient times the Chinese people cherished their hair as a symbol of self-respect, valued as highly as the body itself. In 770–476 BC a punishment called *kun* required sinners to shave their head and beard. Compared with other physical punishments this was considered more devastating because it insulted the soul. Closer to home we need only think back to hippie hair: it was long, unkempt, 'down-to-there' hair celebrated in the eponymous musical *Hair*. Growing one's hair was a political act – a revolutionary assault on a felt-to-be corrupt regime.

Individuals and societies have always expressed themselves through hair. Ancient and contemporary cultures have invested hair with a totemic power. To avoid falling prey to contagious magic, ancient warriors buried their hair trimmings, along with their saliva and nail clippings (Simon, 2000). In the hands of unknown others, one's hair became one's weak and unprotected self. In the mythical world baldness takes on the mystique of tragic defeat: Samson, whose strength was unrivalled, was shorn while his head lay prone on Delilah's knees. Once hairless he was only able to muster the strength to kill himself as the Philistines gathered to mock him.

The anthropological literature testifies to the numerous rituals and rites of passage that include hair as their centrepiece. Its symbolic relationship to taboo, power and beauty are well recognized. Its phallic significance and the related castration anxiety mobilized by the cutting of hair has been noted in both the anthropological as well as psychoanalytic literature (Barahal, 1940; Leach, 1958).

Hair's relationship to mourning is especially well documented in various cultural rituals. For example, it was usual for Victorian mourners to wear lockets or rings containing a lock of hair from the deceased person. In several Hindu cultures shaving the scalp is associated with both mourning processes and separation (Krishnan et al., 1985). Of course such public rituals typically assert something about the social status of an individual within a wider group, whereas private rituals using hair convey something about the psychological state of the actor and are therefore of greater interest to analysts.

Because hair does not rot, it provides a gateway between the living and the dead. Hair is one of the better preserved parts of the body and, in some situations, is even better preserved than bones, which is one reason why hair is of such importance in forensics (Saferstein, 2014) and in the study of early humans and human evolution. Hair as a symbol of 'connection' with the dead can be identified across many cultures. For example, in New Caledonia, Kanak mourner-priests let their hair grow for three years to create giant domes of hair mounted upon wood-and-feather masks because they believe the hair connects them to their ancestors like a cable. This sentiment is captured well in John Donne's poem *The Relic* when he imagines his grave being broken into years after his death. In it 'A bracelet of bright hair about the bone' is found intact – a symbol of the survival of his lover's still-gleaming hair and the uniting of their souls despite the perishing of the flesh.

Notwithstanding the evident importance that hair holds for us all in everyday life, psychoanalysts have, however, been very silent on the subject of hair relative to the contributions made by sociologists and anthropologists. A Pep-Web based literature search reveals a paucity of papers on this subject: six in total and all are very dated (the most recent was published in 1983).

This strikes me as an interesting omission. After all, as analysts we spend much of our time sitting behind the couch from where we have a privileged view of the back of our patient's head and the hair that covers it or should be covering it when it is absent. Hair reveals not only biological and social information about us, as we have just seen, but it also offers a privileged entry point into our internal world of object relations. How we style our hair or the way we relate to our 'given' hair and modify it (e.g. from curly to straight or straight to curly) are psychologically determined decisions, not simply or even primarily fashion statements or expressions of vanity. This may account for why going to a hairdresser is often an emotional experience for people laden with anxiety or anticipation about a transformation of the self, not just its bodily incarnation.

Psychoanalytic formulations about the symbolic significance of hair have typically singled out how hair as a phallic symbol (Berg, 1936; Barahal, 1940) allows us to acceptably displace our exhibitionism and castration anxiety from the penis to the hair (Berg, 1936). Andresen (1980), using the tale of Rapunzel as a starting point, identified three symbolic meanings of hair, namely castration, loss of the mother and reparation. The theme of castration is also central to Sperling's (1954) understanding of hair cutting, drawing attention specifically to how cutting off or losing hair may express giving up of the feminine part of the self.

The emphasis on hair as a phallic symbol chimes with the way hair has often been associated culturally with symbols of strength, virility and sexual potency such that the act of hair cutting has been construed as a symbolic destruction of the phallus (castration) with resulting sexual impotence (loss of strength) (Barahal,

1940). Women's hair has often been connected to sexuality felt to be threatening to men: Medusa's snaky locks propelled enemies towards her eyes; Lorelei, mythical siren of the Rhine, untangled her golden tresses while she awaited unsuspecting sailors; and medieval Europeans shaved the heads of suspected witches because they believed that the evil demons nested in their hair. Perhaps this sheds some light on Judeo-Christian and later Muslim and Jewish standards of 'modesty' that require women to cover their hair or shave it off and then cover it with a wig.

Most of the psychoanalytic accounts frame hair within a more classical Freudian view of the Oedipal struggle with little attention paid to early object relations. There are two exceptions to this. Buxbaum's (1960) understanding of hair pulling is firmly rooted in an object relational understanding of hair, underlining the way hair may be used as a means of gratifying the need for tactile and skin sensations, suggesting that it may be deployed as a kind of transitional object. Likewise Galski (1983), also in a study of hair pulling, concluded that it was related to unresolved symbiotic relationships – typically with the mother – where the hair symbolized the need-gratifying object felt to be lost (when the hair is pulled out) and, importantly, regained when it is eaten or restored. Reincorporation of the need-gratifying object was understood to provide much needed reassurance that security could be re-established, thereby fuelling the compulsive need to pull out the hair reigniting the cycle in an obsessional manner.

The psychic roots of hair

I would now like to build on the sparse contributions just outlined. However, I am not concerned here primarily with the psychological meaning of cutting hair or trichotillomania, but rather with how we can understand the psychic roots of hair's *relational* significance that can be traced in everyday idioms such as 'washing someone out of one's hair'[3] or 'keep out of my hair', both of which represent hair as the locus of connection with the other and of separation from the other. Unlike other parts of the body, with the exception of nails and skin, hair can be cut and regrown, thus making it an eminently pliable medium for the expression of conflicts around union and separation.

I want to suggest that our relationship to hair in its broadest sense is intimately connected with the earliest relationship to the mother's body and how separation from the mother's body was experienced. In other words I am situating the developmental origins of the significance of hair in the unconscious pre-Oedipally.

The head and hair are the physical loci for many of the earliest tactile exchanges between mother and baby. As we know, tactile and skin sensations in the context of the relationship with the primary caregiver – typically the mother – are integral to the development of attachment. The experience of handling mother's hair and rubbing oneself against it are part of these tactile and skin sensations. Likewise the experience of the mother stroking the baby's head and hair is also very important. Everyday observations of babies illustrate the way the baby clings on to the mother's body, often tugging at her hair or clutching on to it and even sometimes eating it. During feeding we can make similar observations as the baby feeds at the breast whilst holding or gently tugging at a strand of the mother's hair. There is clearly here a complex relationship between hand and hair where the erotogenicity of the hand is most likely central to the pleasure that comes to be associated with hair – a theme that is, however, beyond the scope of this chapter.

Imre Hermann (1976) – a not often quoted yet very interesting early Hungarian psychoanalyst – has informed my understanding of hair's significance. He emphasized the role that is played in man's psychic structure by his desire to cling to the mother's body[4] and the far-reaching consequences of the early dissolution of this initial dyadic union. According to Hermann the separation from the mother's body always entails a degree of trauma.

When all is going relatively well this separation becomes the basis from which the individual develops an autonomous sense of self that is referenced back to the maternal body as its origin, allowing it to be used as its inspiration to develop, as it were, rather than to recreate a fusion with it or to triumph over it (see Lemma, 2010; and Chapters 1 and 4, this book). Where this separation has in some way been traumatic, Hermann suggests that the individual may either react by clinging desperately to the object (or its animate or inanimate substitute) or may need to violently separate from it.[5] Within this attachment framework therefore hair cutting, for example, may not simply or even primarily be understood as a form of displaced castration, but might signify detachment from the mother as the object to cling to.

Other theorists have also contributed to our understanding of defences that involve clinging to the object and that are relevant to the present discussion. Bick, for example, described 'adhesive identity'[6] to denote a state when the infant attaches himself to the surface of the object, adhering to it to maintain a sense of safety and manage anxieties about catastrophic ruptures in the coherence of the body-self that feels threatened by the possibility of spilling out into boundless space. Conceptually this is reminiscent of Balint's (1959) description of the clinging to objects characteristic of ocnophilic states.

Throughout life hair remains deeply evocative. It is a source of pleasure or pain because, I am suggesting, it reconnects us viscerally to the maternal body and our experience of separation from it. Our idiosyncratic relationship to hair, and its significance in our internal world, is fashioned out of the earliest relationship to the mother's body and her hair to which the baby clings, rubs against, is smothered by or may feel slipping away from its hand.

Our relationship to hair therefore invariably reveals an affectively toned internalized object relationship that unconsciously scripts our experience of separation and individuation. *How* the separation from the mother's body is experienced leaves its emotional residues in us all. When this separation has been traumatic in some way we may discern this in the relationship the individual has with their hair. The extent to which the individual remains in search of a (re)union with the maternal body as a permanent state, unable to achieve separation, may manifest in the use of hair to recreate the longed-for union just as in other cases it may serve to enact a felt-to-be necessary separation from it. This should not be taken literally in so far as I am not suggesting a direct relationship between growing hair or cutting it as symbolic expressions respectively of the need to fuse with or tear away from the object. I am, however, suggesting that the patient's own relationship to their hair, and the use made of hair in the analytic relationship, can provide helpful entry points for approaching very early conflicts and deficits relating to differentiation from the object.

Clearly such conflicts are not *only* to be discerned in our relationship to hair. As I suggested in Chapter 2, dermatological conditions or body modifications generally also act as vehicles for the expression of very similar dynamics. I am merely wishing here to draw attention to the way the use made of hair in the context of the analytic dyad can convey important information about internalized object relationships and therefore deserves our attention as analysts, as I hope to now illustrate through the case of Ms E.

The case of Ms E.

Ms E. came into a four-times-weekly analysis following the death of her mother. She was in her thirties at the time and herself the mother of a four-month-old baby daughter. She had not long been married. I gained the impression that the husband seemed to be somewhat peripheral, not unlike how she had felt about her father, who was said to have been 'removed' emotionally from the family. She had one younger brother with whom she was not very close. Her primary focus as she was growing up had been her mother. She said that she had always felt very close to her and that she had been her main confidante eclipsing any peer relationships when she had been at secondary school. But she also recognized that her mother had been 'unpredictable' in her moods and at times could be very rejecting of her.

Ms E. explained that she was seeking help because she felt that her mother's death had exposed her to a lot of ambivalent feelings towards her that she had not felt able to acknowledge when her mother was alive. Becoming a mother herself had also challenged her: she worried excessively that her baby might be harmed in some way or simply stop breathing. This meant she found it very hard to sleep at night because she had to repeatedly check that the baby was still alive. She was consequently becoming very tired. The sleep deprivation, in turn, fuelled paranoid anxieties about the quality of her own mothering and how others viewed her in this role.

When I invited her to tell me a bit about her anxieties and what she would do when she checked her baby, Ms E. told me that she would lift her daughter out of her cot and stroke her 'soft head of fine hair', pressing her face against the head to check that she was still breathing. When she could hear the breathing she would then hold her very tight against her chest and stroke her head.

Ms E. was an attractive woman with a striking head of very long, dark wavy hair. As she lay on the couch the very first time, my attention was immediately drawn to how she arranged her long hair. Whilst some patients with long hair twist it and tuck it under their head, behind the pillow, or simply let it fall behind their head such that the hair is mostly submerged under their back, Ms E. rather studiously lifted her hair above the nape of her neck and positioned it over the pillow such that the hair, like a wedding veil, was strewn across the couch. Some of her hair would thus invariably cascade over the end of the couch nearest to where my seat was positioned. This became a fixed ritual every time she lay on the couch.

In addition to how she positioned her hair and displayed it to me – as I was clear that she was communicating something very powerfully to me through this non-verbal gesture – Ms E. also had the habit of often looking at the pillow as she sat up on the couch at the end of sessions. Even though there would invariably be some of her hairs on it she never once picked them off the pillow or commented on this as some patients have done, for example, commenting on the mess they leave behind. Instead she looked and then got up. I had the impression that she was leaving part of herself behind *for me*, as a kind of love token. In other words, along with the beautiful hair that she displayed for me to look at, I thought that her strands of hair represented a strong homosexually charged erotic transference that spoke of a longing for an exclusive union with me bound together by her hair.

Ms E.'s anxiety about her baby was her main focus in the early months of the therapy. Even though this attenuated within the first six months, she remained very preoccupied with thoughts of death and in particular the impact of the death of her mother.

She described her mother as a very intense woman with an unpredictable temper: she could be the 'most loving mother', she said, but this could just as easily give way in her experience to a mother who insensitively pushed her out, leaving her feeling as if she was somehow in the way. When in this latter mood, one of the mother's expressions had been to yell to Ms E., 'Just keep out of my hair!' As Ms E. recounted these childhood memories she became very tearful before she would fall silent for long stretches of time, unable to communicate with me. This left me feeling shut out by her wall of silence. Curiously, on such occasions, I noticed that my attention was drawn to her hair, which looked seductive in its rather imperious display. I began to feel as though she invited me towards her via her hair and contemporaneously pushed me out with her silence, perhaps recreating something of the unpredictable emotional atmosphere she experienced with her mother as a child except this time it was I who was on the receiving end of this kind of object.

Ms E.'s relationship to her own hair and what this represented became a very strong theme in the analysis and provided helpful opportunities for approaching core dynamics around separation. I would now like to share some material from three consecutive sessions over one week when it became possible to begin to reflect with her about the meaning of hair in her mind and how she used it in our relationship.

Nine months into the analysis Ms E. brought a very interesting dream about which she said she felt very embarrassed:

She is lying on the grass in a field next to a female friend from childhood. They don't speak but she feels very close to this friend who is gently stroking her hair, running her fingers through it. Then a storm starts and the friend rises up suddenly and disappears. Ms E. feels disoriented and realizes that there is lightning but there are only trees to shelter under and she remembers that would be dangerous. She then wakes feeling very anxious.

In her associations Ms E. recalled that the friend, whom she had not seen for over 20 years, had been 'very clingy' and their friendship had been rocky as she demanded a lot of Ms E.'s attention and 'devotion'. She recalled an incident when the friend had become very upset when Ms E. refused a sleepover at her house. She then associated to the storm and recalled how as a child she had been terrified of thunderstorms and, if at home, would rush to her mother and want to snuggle up to her. She recalled that her mother had very long hair, like hers but straight, and she found it comforting to feel it against her skin. She said that her mother would always infuse her hair with perfume and Ms E. enjoyed 'rubbing my nose right into her hair'. It felt like a 'safe place', she observed.

I took up the dream as expressing her longing to be very close to me, to get right inside my hair and be embraced by it, as it were, but that this longing gave way very quickly to a sense that she was too clingy and that I might just suddenly disappear, like the friend in the dream, or tell her to 'keep out of my hair'.

Ms E. became tearful and said that she had realized that she found the ending of our sessions hard to manage. She often left and felt lost but unable to tell me about it because she was sure that I would not want to know. She worried that I had other patients who were more 'deserving' than her, and that she was lucky to have the life she had.

I said it was hard to trust that I would not switch unpredictably from being very close and attentive to her into someone who pushes her out and has no space in my mind for her.

She said she always felt that she was easily forgotten, that she did not make an impression on others.

I said that I wondered whether the long hair that she so carefully displayed in my view as she lay on the couch and the strands of her own hair, which she left on the pillow, were attempts to make an impression on me and leave a part of her behind for me.

Ms E. was silent and then said she felt embarrassed. She was not sure why she felt this way.

I said it might perhaps be because of the observation I made about how she used her hair in our relationship to secure a link with me.

She paused again. When she resumed talking she sounded thoughtful and said that when she held her daughter in her arms to check that she was still alive, she realized that she would often push her right up into the nape of her neck such that the daughter was covered under her hair – a bit like she had done with her own mother when she ran for shelter during thunderstorms. She said this made her feel like they were one and she was then reassured that her daughter would be fine after all.

The image of the daughter covered by Ms E.'s mass of hair conjured up in my mind a disturbing image of a baby suffocating – the very thing Ms E. so feared. But I also sensed that if I said that, I might be going in a bit too quickly and overwhelm Ms E. with her own ambivalence towards her daughter and to me in the transference, so I decided to approach this more obliquely.

I thus simply observed that her daughter appeared to be tucked under her hair-blanket.

Ms E. paused and then said that the closeness she had felt with her mother perhaps had been restricting in some ways. At times she felt her mother would demand so much from her, like when she was dying and she seemed unaware that Ms E. had her own needs as a pregnant woman.

I said she seemed to be asking herself whether one could be too close for comfort.

Ms E. was silent for a long time and then said that she was horrified by the realization, which had only just occurred to her, that her daughter might not be able to breathe under her hair. She then insightfully observed that her 'loving concern' perhaps covered up something more 'ugly'.

I sensed her palpable anxiety, and courage, as she approached in her mind the way that her longing for closeness, for a perfect union, could smother her daughter.

I spoke with her about her fear that I too would suffocate under the pressure of her demand for a close fit between us that left no room for separation, which felt so terrifying, and that she was aware that too much closeness also carried its own risks.

In the next session Ms E. began by saying that she had been unable to sleep and had stayed up much of the night nursing her daughter who had run a high temperature. She had been 'worried to death' about her.

I reminded her that in the previous session she had been very unsettled by her realization that her concern for her daughter might be suffocating.

Ms E. said that she had felt very anxious after the session and during the night her anxiety had escalated. Her husband, who not insignificantly figured little in her accounts as if no third existed, had taken their daughter's temperature and said it was only 37.5° Celsius – hardly a high temperature, he had remarked – but she had been unable to hear it, convinced that her daughter was seriously unwell.

I said that her daughter had become very confused in her mind with her own baby-self who felt dangerously ill and unsure she would be taken care of by me, that I might not take seriously her rising temperature after I reminded her of how close she wanted to be to me.

Ms E. nodded and then told me that in the hour that she did manage to sleep as she camped by her daughter's cot she had a very vivid dream:

> *She is very small, not quite a baby but almost, she said, and she is looking out of a window at the top of a skyscraper, feeling dizzy, vertiginous, because there was nowhere to cling on to. I suddenly appear out of nowhere and she falls into my arms, clinging to my hair, which is very long, scraping the floor.*

Ms E. then said that she often felt like a baby when she was on the couch. As she sat up she said she felt vertiginous, like in the dream.

I said that in the dream she panicked at first but then finds she can cling on to my hair so she does not fall.

She replied that as a child she had liked the story of Rapunzel and the idea that long hair could be used to bring together two people who loved each other. Her husband had told her from the start of their relationship that her hair was her best feature and he liked playing with it. She said she took a lot of care of her hair and had always hated haircuts as a child. Even as an adult she was always anxious when she went to the hairdresser and needed to make sure they cut very little off.

I observed that her hair and that of the other person was a way she felt she could stay connected with and be protected by the other. But I also added that in the story of Rapunzel, the enchantress locks Rapunzel away and deprives her of her freedom to be a woman in her own right and have her own lover.

Ms E. said she had forgotten about the enchantress and was really only thinking of the prince in the story. She then added that she felt she was 'silly' to place such significance on hair: 'People think I am vain because I am so preoccupied with my hair but it's really not about vanity.'

I said she was worried that I would not understand the emotional significance of her hair to her and yet it was clear that it had been a very important part of our relationship from the very start.

Ms E. said she had made a mental note of my hair the very first time she came to see me. She always looked at people's hair, she added. She had thought I had 'strong' hair because it looked thick. Her mother's hair had been thick too, she added.

I was struck by how Ms E. avoided elaborating on how the enchantress kept Rapunzel all to herself, and thus skirted away from the homosexual dimension of their relationship, which was live in the transference. However, it felt important to allow Ms E. to edge towards this at her own pace so I did not make any interpretations about this.

In the final session of the week Ms E. started by saying the conversation about hair had stimulated a lot of thoughts, some of which she felt rather embarrassed about. She said she had caught herself out making a point of washing her hair that morning before coming to see me as she felt she needed to look nice. A long silence ensued, which she eventually broke saying that whilst driving over she had fantasized about me stroking her hair from behind the couch. This had been very pleasurable. She had wanted to continue the daydream but made herself stop because she did not like the implication that she fancied me and that I might think she was a lesbian.

After a long silence Ms E. said she knew she had to tell me because she recognized now that her relationship with her mother was very complicated. 'And,' she added, 'my relationships with women generally are too. I know I am not a lesbian, I am not sexually drawn to women, but I know I need a lot from them.'

I said that perhaps my comments the previous day about the relationship between Rapunzel and the enchantress had led her to become more aware of a sexual dimension in her relationship to me, which was unsettling to her because she feared that this would be read by me as confirmation that she must therefore be a lesbian.

Ms E. said she was worried that was indeed how I might read it, but now that I had said what I had said she was a bit more reassured that I had an 'open mind'. When she had studied psychoanalysis at university she had come across Freud's notion of inherent bisexuality and it had made sense to her because she had felt very drawn to a female friend even though she had never wanted to have a sexual relationship with her. Yet she had longed for a closer intimacy with her. She recalled that on one occasion when they were both due to attend the college ball they had helped each other out with their hair. She remembered this as a very 'tender' moment.

As the analysis progressed my work with Ms E. focused on the regressive pull towards a tender and erotized longing for union with me, which however also exposed her to a vertiginous fall as she anticipated being cut off from me. In part this was worked through the way she presented her hair in our relationship as a kind of ladder to invite me into this kind of fusion with her.

Unsurprisingly 'hair ladder' stories have a long history. This is most likely because of the unconscious resonance of hair with the earliest relationship between mother and baby and as such it stands as an evocative symbol of union. These stories and their numerous variations play on the theme of hair as a connection and of hair as a symbol of something precious – often of a sexual nature – that is offered to or appropriated by another.

Most of us will be familiar with the Grimm brothers' version of Rapunzel, but in fact one of the earliest recorded instances of a 'hair ladder' story comes from tenth-century Persia. Ferdowsi (AD 932–1025) is the literary alias (his real name is unknown) of a poet who wrote a *Shahnameh*, or history of kings. In the 'Maiden in the Tower' sequence of Ferdowsi's *Shahnameh*, Roudabe offers to lower her hair to her true love, Zal, to use as a ladder to climb up on to the roof of the women's enclosure. Zal interestingly refuses, pointing out that it would hurt her head if he did, and throws up a rope instead.

Zal's response is in stark contrast to the way the enchantress in the Grimms' tale uses Rapunzel's hair to meet her own selfish need. We might of course speculate that when presented with Roudabe's strong phallic hair Zal's response is to reassuringly throw up his own phallic rope. But we might also read that version as representing the way that Zal's love for Roudabe means he will work to reach her and does not require her to suffer *for him*. The enchantress in the Grimms' tale, who raises Rapunzel, locks her in a tower so she can keep her all to herself and literally uses her as an extension of herself. The girl, and hence the hair, are the enchantress' possession. In a cruel twist the enchantress cuts Rapunzel's hair once she discovers the prince has also made use of this ladder to reach her.

Rapunzel and her hair are thus cherished only as long as they remain the enchantress' exclusive property – no man is allowed to come in the way of what could be understood as the homosexual dimension of this relationship. This is not the interpretation made by Andresen (1980) in the only psychoanalytic paper about hair that draws on this tale:

> The act of cutting hair has three important functions in the story. It causes loss of a beautiful part of the girl's body; it severs the link of the girl to her mother; and it enables the mother to have for herself something which had formerly been the girl's. These are the three symbolic meanings of the cutting of hair. In different language we know them as castration, loss of the mother, and reparation.
> (1980: 71)

Andresen's interpretation of the story offers one interesting perspective. However, if the tale is at least in part about loss, the loss that has to be mourned must surely be also that of the biological mother whose baby is taken away by the enchantress as part of the bargain made with the biological parents over Rapunzel's birth. The enchantress is a single adoptive mother who wages her exclusive rights over Rapunzel: there is no adoptive father in actuality or in her mind, we might say. The relationship she establishes with Rapunzel, and specifically with Rapunzel's body via her hair, may be read as reflecting a homosexually charged dimension[7] as well as her own narcissism.

In Rapunzel, of course, we are inclined to read the homosexual dimension as imposed by the enchantress on the helpless Rapunzel. In my clinical experience with female patients such as Ms E., I have, however, been struck by how the analysis of the meaning of hair invariably takes us to an experience of hair as closely tied in the unconscious with the mother's body, laden with homosexual longings and anxieties that originate in the child too.

As the work with Ms E. progressed, and as can be already discerned in the three consecutive sessions here described, Ms E. was able to reflect on the way that her relationships with women in particular were dominated by a longing for exclusivity and 'vertiginous' anxiety that she would not be enough for them. She began to understand that her hair, which she so feared cutting, stood as the symbol of a 'perfect' oneness with the object: she displayed it to me on the couch in all its glory, expecting me to admire it and want to be enveloped by it.

This perspective was helpful to her in relation to her daughter, with whom she sought to create a similarly fused relationship and yet her anxiety about the daughter's potential death signalled her own recognition at some level that what she was doing was indeed suffocating her. As she let go of this fused relationship with her daughter she was able to position herself as her husband's partner in a way that enhanced their relationship overall, including sexually.

Concluding thoughts: hair and dignity

As we have seen, hair is a very pliable, rich medium for the expression of unconscious conflicts and deficits. It both reveals a great deal about us *and* can be used to conceal, to cover up quite literally, and metaphorically, what we may wish to disown.

By way of concluding I would like to share some observations about how we might understand why hair, in many cultures, is considered to be a symbol of dignity. This has always intrigued me: why the hair over and above other parts of the body? I want to suggest that part of the answer lies in some of the psychic origins of hair as described in this chapter.

Definitions of *dignity* within philosophical discourse tend to converge on psychological notions such as an individual or group's sense of self-respect and self-worth, the sense of physical and psychological integrity and empowerment. Dignity finds a distinctively modernizing twist in the Renaissance thinker Pico della Mirandola, who regarded human dignity as rooted in a human being's capacity, in Rosen's words, 'to shape himself according to a range of possibilities not available to other creatures' (2012: 15). In a similar vein Kant understood human dignity as related to human agency: the ability of humans to choose their own actions.

The capacity to choose our own actions requires psychologically a well-established, differentiated sense of self. Psychoanalytically we would understand this capacity to be rooted in early developmental experiences that facilitate the baby's experience of his mind *and* body as separate from that of his objects. Later in development, during adolescence, differentiation from parental figures often takes the form of defining the body as separate and it is hence fashioned accordingly. Unsurprisingly perhaps, many adolescent battles are typically negotiated over how the hair is worn.

Human dignity may be especially hard to protect when people are vulnerable in some way. A moving example of dignity as human agency by proxy,[8] and the role played by hair in this respect, can be observed in Michael Haneke's film *Amour* (2012). In this film the husband of an elderly, very disabled, bed-bound woman, who prior to her illness and during her deterioration is presented as someone who is proud, takes care of her appearance and values independence, becomes her full-time carer. Even when his wife becomes unable to speak and can barely move her limbs, we notice that her hair nevertheless remains immaculate: a striking backdrop to the otherwise painful decay of her body and mind. We later learn that the husband arranges for her to be coiffed regularly by her hairdresser in a gesture, one assumes, intended to preserve her dignity.

In stark contrast, cutting or shaving of hair has been used to torture and humiliate people, that is, to undermine their sense of dignity. We need only think of the Jewish people in concentration camps whose hair was shaved prior to being sent to the gas chambers. More recent atrocities also include hair cutting or shaving as a form of humiliation and torture across many cultures.

Hair is thus one of the seats of human dignity that can either be respected or sadistically defaced. This was the experience of a victim of torture with whom I worked for several years. This patient – Ms F. – described the degradation she suffered when soldiers repeatedly raped her. However, what struck me poignantly was Ms F.'s recollection specifically of the even greater 'indignity', *as she put it*, when her torturers cut off her long hair and burnt it. When we explored this in the therapy her associations were very revealing: she described how her hair had always been her 'pride' as it was long and thick, just like her mother's had been 'strong' hair, she told me. 'When they cut it off,' she said, 'it felt like they cut off the goodness in me. I lost a sense of who I was. It was the worst moment. I lost all my dignity.'

So what did Ms F. mean when she observed that when her hair *specifically* was cut off she lost all her dignity, more so than when she was raped? She had evidently enjoyed a very close and good relationship with her mother and in her mind her hair was closely associated with a likeness to her mother's 'strong' hair. Her 'good' hair was not only a symbol of a strong identification with her mother, but it also denoted how the hair itself was experienced by her as connected to her psychological integrity: when the hair was cut off she lost a sense of *who* she was and hence her dignity. A sense of dignity and the integrity of identity were thus closely connected via hair in her experience.

Hair is a visible signal to the world, as I mentioned at the very outset, about our state of mind, such that we could say that for Ms F. it may have felt like she could conceal the fact and impact of rape, but she could not avoid being seen by everyone to have no hair and hence she felt shamed in other people's eyes.

In Ms F.'s mind, and in fact in all our minds to varying degrees, hair was an integral part of her sense of her self as separate, as individuated, because hair, as I suggested earlier, is so viscerally connected with our earliest experiences of union, of safety or its corollary, that is, a sense of being pushed out, abandoned with no one to cling on to. What was felt to be so disorienting for Ms F. was that in the moment when her hair was so brutally cut off it felt not only like she was no longer a separate being and in charge of her own body/self – she was in fact reduced to a helpless dependency that was sadistically deployed – but perhaps too she felt that by being left bald she lost the connecting (hair) piece to an experience of unity with an other who would keep her safe – there was no one in her mind, and as represented by her long hair, that she could cling on to for safety while subjected to her horrific experiences.

When all is well hair acts as an important boundary between self and other as well as a point of meeting with the other. Crucially it is the most exposed body boundary. Perhaps this qualifies it with greater emotional significance than other body parts, which are covered by clothes much of the time, and as such it is felt to be the most readily exposed site for assault by the other. For these reasons our patients' relationship to their hair and indeed to the analyst's hair (see Chapter 7) deserve our attention and analysis.

Notes

1   The phylogenetic origin of hair remains speculative. One view holds that hair arose initially as surface insulation, retaining body heat in primitive mammalian endotherms. An alternative view is that hair evolved first as tiny projecting rods in the hinges between scales and served as tactile devices. The 'protohairs' could help monitor surface sensory data when an animal was hiding from an enemy or retreating from the weather. If such a role increased in importance, it would have favoured longer shafts and perhaps the

evolution of structures resembling vibrissae. This sensory protohair might then have evolved secondarily into an insulative pelage as mammals become endothermic.
2 Cortisol, a hormone secreted in higher levels during times of stress, is traditionally measured in blood, urine or saliva. But those measurements reflect stress only at a certain period of time, not over long stretches as is the case with hair.
3 As in the song from the musical *South Pacific*, 'I'm Gonna Wash That Man Right Outta My Hair').
4 Hermann suggests that the urge to cling is a component instinct of the libido. He sees this earliest relationship rooted in a pair of drives that he refers to respectively as the 'clinging instinct' and its dialectical opposite, 'going in search of'. In Hermann's theory, the clinging instinct refers to the infant's spontaneous reaching out to hold onto the mother.
5 Hermann conceptualized two forms of identification derived from the mother–child dual union: the 'flowing over' identification derives from the desire to re-establish dual unity, and the 'introjective identification' is related to the dissolution of the dual union. Corresponding to these two types of identification are the 'fusing into' and 'tearing away from' character types.
6 Donald Meltzer (1974) later described this as 'adhesive identification'.
7 The American poet Anne Sexton (1971), in a provocative reading of the tale of Rapunzel, focuses on what she also regards as the explicitly homosexual relationship between the old woman and Rapunzel.
8 When we are ourselves incapacitated to act for ourselves in accordance with our wishes and needs.

Chapter 9

Off the couch, into the toilet
Exploring the psychic uses of the analyst's toilet

Child analysts and psychotherapists, more than their adult counterparts, are very familiar with the myriad psychic meanings and functions of human excretions and of the toilet. As Ferro and Basile aptly observe in a discussion of how work with children differs from work with adult patients: 'A child does not evacuate projective identifications or sophisticated beta elements: he actually shits!' (Ferro and Basile, 2006: 494). Scattered throughout the literature we can find papers about analytic work with adults where mention is made of the patient's use of the toilet but typically this is not the main focus of these papers (for example, Asseyer, 2002; Proner, 2005; Clark Nunes, 2006; Steiner, 2011).

Alongside the consulting room itself the toilet is an important part of the analytic setting. Clinically it is helpful to remain curious about how patients relate to and use the consulting room toilet, about why it may *not* be used and when it is used, *how* it is used and so on. Indeed, in the patient's mind, this is often not the 'consulting room toilet'; rather it is felt to be quite specifically, and very personally, the 'analyst's toilet'.

It can prove difficult to bring the patient's use of the toilet into the analytic dialogue if the patient does not make direct reference to it. This is especially so when the use made of the toilet is split off. It is much easier to analyse what the patient is doing if they get off the couch mid-session to go to the toilet. It is harder to find a helpful, non-intrusive and non-arousing way to bring up with the patient, for example, the meaning of the mess left behind in the toilet once they have used it after the session has ended.[1] In this latter scenario, if one subsequently brings this up, the potential for shaming or persecuting the patient always needs to be carefully considered.

The difficulty we may experience in bringing up the use of the toilet within the analytic dialogue most likely also reflects the fact that despite our own analyses toilets, excrement, urine and flatulence are not subjects we all feel equally at ease with. We find ourselves in the realm of the body and its relative discomforts, secretions, holes, odours: an exposed terrain for both analyst and patient. The toilet is the physical place where we let things out that we would not let out in front of others.

If we think about toilets we cannot avoid giving consideration to smell. Odours are intimately tied to the individual sensitivities associated with toilets because our distinctive body odour and that of our human waste traces the limits of who we are (Pfeffer, 2004). Moreover, because we cannot breathe without also smelling the air around us we are defenceless against the odours of others (Süskind, 1986). The sense of smell is involuntary and so we are caught unaware by the intrusion into our space by the smell of others. The olfactory envelope constitutes a private reserve whose integrity is vulnerable to offence or violation.

Flatulence in the consulting room is one form of unwelcome and out-of-place excretion that is often experienced as exposing and embarrassing. However, it is also for some patients a moment of triumph – a bodily attack on the analyst – or indeed for others it may function as a form of protection. Sidoli (1996), for example, movingly describes her work with a boy who used flatulence to create a 'defensive olfactory container' to protect himself, skunk-like, against fears of disintegration and persecution and to create a 'protective cloud of familiarity' when threatened.

Excretion figures in many kinds of clinical presentations from phobias, obsessions, compulsions and delusions through to tics, impulse-control problems and paraphilia. Intense fears surrounding public urination, called *paruresis*, are common and often disabling, limiting people's movements and causing humiliation and pain. Bladder problems can also have psychological dimensions and causes, occurring in some cases as conversion symptoms. It is well established, for example, that urinary retention is strongly associated with the experience of sexual and physical abuse, and other voiding disturbances, and incontinence also appears at elevated rates amongst abuse survivors (e.g. Link et al., 2007). In short, adversity, trauma and suffering commonly find bodily expression in disrupted excretory and urinary functions and hence the toilet is not a neutral place in the patient's mind.

In this chapter I want to distinguish two qualitatively different uses of the toilet in the context of the analytic relationship specifically. The first concerns a perverse use of the toilet to enact sexualized, hostile, intrusive dynamics in relation to the analyst. Here the patient alternates between being the voyeur, fantasizing the analyst in the toilet, and being the one in the toilet who is looked at by the analyst.

The second use denotes anxieties about phantasized damage done to the object if the patient exposes felt-to-be unacceptable, messy parts of the self. Here the patient may not even be able to use the analyst's toilet at first, displaying phobic avoidance of it because they fear exposing a messy, dirty part of themselves that could contaminate the longed for, good, 'clean' relationship with the analyst. Such patients, we might say, cannot yet use the analyst as the toilet breast. Their eventual use of the actual toilet may be a first step towards giving expression to the warded-off dangerous feelings before these can be more safely integrated into the analytic relationship.

Both these uses will now be illustrated with clinical material taken respectively from a five-times-weekly analysis and a three-times-weekly psychoanalytic psychotherapy, both using the couch.

Toilets and secret(ion)s: the case of Mr G.

Amongst children the acquisition of bowel and bladder control is a major developmental achievement. It is well recognized that the struggle for control and the aggression it generates, either expressed or inhibited, is an important dynamic during the anal phase. The young child enjoys control over his sphincter: defecation thus not infrequently becomes the battleground for struggles between parent and child.

Because both urination and defecation expose the child to an empowering experience of 'holding in', they also function as basic models of concealment: holding onto the faeces affords control not only because the child does not let go, but also because he can conceal from the other when we he might do so. This is a somatic experience of concealing what is felt to be 'inside' the self from the object. The experience of sphincter control is thus one of the earliest somatic manifestations of keeping something secret. Kulish has indeed drawn attention to how the word 'secret' is related to secretions and she suggests that 'toilet functions become the basis for the earliest communications around secrets' (2002: 153).

Secrets and lies are developmentally necessary. In normal development the child's realization that he can choose to *not* disclose a thought, fantasy or feeling heralds the birth of an awareness of inner life as distinct from the outer world and that it is possible to separate private space from public, shared space. Indeed, the child's first lie represents a momentous step into separateness and autonomy. At the other end of the spectrum secrets can be used more destructively to arouse, control or triumph over the other (Lemma, 2005). If the child's experience of their body and its secretions is one where the need for increasing autonomy and privacy is not respected but is met instead with intrusive interest by the object this may create an erotically charged relationship to faeces and urine, and to the physical space occupied by the toilet.

From an analytic point of view what is significant about the analyst's toilet specifically is that the patient imagines, or indeed knows, that the analyst also uses this physical space. It is a space within which the analyst's body can be imagined as exposed and quite literally naked. In other words this particular toilet is like no other toilet because the patient may feel that it houses the analyst's secrets. In some patients' mind the 'toilet also used by the analyst' may then become converted into a 'toilet *shared with* the analyst', fuelling sexual and sometimes specifically voyeuristic fantasies, as I will illustrate through the analysis of Mr G.

Mr G. came in to a five-times-weekly analysis in his late twenties. He was a young man who struggled with intimacy. He was troubled by his sexuality and generally by his incapacity to function as an adult: he could not sustain a sexually intimate relationship or regular employment and he had very few friends. He managed an analysis only because he paid a very reduced fee.

As a young adolescent he had a breakdown, which required admission, and this had disrupted his education and peer relationships. He felt this had 'marked' him as different to his peers and he carried within him a sense of shame that was consciously related to the experience of being sectioned and hospitalized. He was highly sensitive to being looked down on and disapproved of by others.

From the start of the analysis Mr G.'s bowel functions featured prominently. He discussed his struggle with Irritable Bowel Syndrome (IBS) and the alternation between diarrhoea and constipation. As a child he recalled being very constipated and his mother had been very worried about this. He was fully toilet trained by the age of three. His mother had told him that around that age she had discovered him several times in the bathroom defecating on the toilet floor, examining his stool. She said that she had never been angry with him about this, despite the mess he had made. His father, she had told him, had been much more troubled by this behaviour and would get cross with him about it.

Mr G. said he had no recollection of any of this, but he told me that his mother often brought it up in a way that made him feel uncomfortable, just as he had found it uncomfortable when she used to enter the toilet unannounced when he was a teenager. In the analysis we discussed in detail his experience of his mother's intrusiveness, especially into his body.

Mr G. presented with a host of somatic complaints and anxieties about his body and its functioning. I was aware, however, that he discussed his bodily functions with an attention to detail that was excessive, as if he needed to fill me with images and smells of his bodily waste, which was experienced as exciting to him. From early on in the analysis I thus had a very direct experience of how intrusive *he* could be.

As Mr G. recounted his mother's narrative about his interest in his stool (or at least, I should say, what he had made of her narrative in his mind), I was struck by the pleasure he appeared to experience despite consciously asserting that he had felt uncomfortable about her intrusiveness. He lingered on the detail of his stool and on his speculations of what his little boy self might have been searching for. His retrospective speculations about what he might have feared and/or hoped he might have found in his stool rang hollow even if they might have been correct, but between us they had a masturbatory quality. I felt I was somehow being invited into an enactment of the sexually charged relationship he had experienced with his mother. Now it was I being invited into the toilet by him, looking at his stool as he looked at it and then me looking at him masturbating over it.

As I listened to him over many months it seemed important to take note not only of his more perverse invitation to be the voyeur, but also to keep in mind how in a very fundamental sense Mr G. felt there was no private space within which he could hide from his object and develop a sense of privacy at a basic bodily level. In other words I was concerned to stay focused both on the perverse nature of his fantasies and how he related to me *and* the way that Mr G. lacked any sense that even his fantasies could be kept secret from his object: the toilet/his mind was a public space where he was always watched and now, in a perverse identification with an intrusive object, he wanted to be watched by me and look at me.

I would now like to share an excerpt from a session that took place in the second year of Mr G.'s analysis when his use of my actual toilet became explicitly the focus of our work. When Mr G. arrived for his session and I opened the door to the consulting room he announced that he needed to use 'my' toilet, as he often did. It was clear, as it had been on other occasions, that he wanted me to know that he was going into *my* toilet and, I think, wanted me to imagine him doing so.

As I waited for him I was aware of two feelings: irritation and a wish to distance myself from him. The irritation, I think, was connected with the somewhat obsessional nature of this activity and the hostility it barely disguised: this had become a ritual. My wish to distance myself was more directly connected with the perverse nature of this ritual where I felt I was being invited to be the voyeur.

When Mr G. lay on the couch he began by telling me that he had finally booked his holiday thanks to his parents agreeing to pay for it. He would be joining them for a week abroad. He had not travelled for a long time and felt a bit apprehensive about this. He disliked all the security procedures at airports and especially the body searches.

I sensed a degree of genuine discomfort as he described the anticipated body search, as if this thought had indeed mobilized anxiety about being exposed in some way – he was not, at this point, aroused by it. However, he then quickly laughed and said that perhaps some people would get a 'kick out of this' because after all, it was a way of 'getting touched up' and of 'touching up'. He said he had read about the body scanning machines that were being talked about (and that were not yet being used widely at that time) and he imagined how it might feel to know someone could see your body, naked, in such a public space like an airport. He laughed again, saying that this might make the boring routine job of being a security officer more appealing as this was a kind of publically sanctioned 'peep-show'. This train of associations eventually led to his own use of pornography (which was marked) and to 'dirty old men' from whom he wished to distinguish himself because he did not want 'to cut a pathetic figure'. He felt very self-conscious about his use of porn and of prostitutes because he felt this might lead people to see him as inadequate.

As he spoke I sensed that he had by now become quite excited and had thus successfully extinguished the twinge of anxiety I had detected right at the start of the session. The sexualization of anxiety was a primary mode of defence for him, as it is in perversions generally (Freud, 1919, 1927).

I eventually said that despite his excitement right now, he had begun the session by voicing some anxiety at the thought of being exposed in public where people might see the 'dirty old man' he feared he was, but this quickly gave way to 'getting a kick out of' being both looked at naked and being himself a spectator at this peep-show.

Mr G. said I 'couldn't take a joke', that he had been having some fun with his speculations. I always read too much into everything, he added somewhat triumphantly, I felt.

I said he was enjoying exposing me as someone who couldn't even take a joke. Now it was me who 'cut a pathetic figure'.

Mr G. eventually said that two nights previously he had a wet dream. He could not remember what the dream was about, but when he woke in the morning and noticed the wet on his bedsheet it had reminded him of when he had been enuretic between the ages of 8 and 13. His father had been 'very tough' on him about this, establishing the rule that if he wet the bed he had to change his own bedsheets. By contrast, his mother 'rescued' him from this and would help him not only to change the sheets but she would also comfort him, hold him in her arms and reassure him that he would one day no longer wet his bed. He could not recall what he really felt about the bed-wetting, but he was clear that he felt very humiliated by his father and hated him in those moments, much preferring his mother's seemingly more tolerant and supportive response.

He then said that he had also told his mother about his wet dream. She had reassured him that this was 'normal', but she had suggested that it was a sign that he was sexually frustrated. He said he felt very humiliated by his inability to have a sexual relationship, that he knew he was not attractive to women. As he spoke it was clear that this was a sore point – and in the session it was the first point of contact with his very real pain besides the fleeting anxiety right at the start.

As I listened to Mr G. I was struck by how he invited his mother to get into his wet sheets with him, as it were, and how she allegedly obliged. I was mindful by then of the traps one can so easily fall into with a patient like Mr G. because through my interventions I could readily become a version of his sexually excited mother intruding into his body and mind under the guise of so-called understanding. I thus chose to say nothing at this juncture and see where his associations led him.

Mr G. become temporarily silent, which was unusual for him at this stage of the analysis. When he resumed speaking, he said that when he had gone to the toilet before coming into the session he had noticed that there was some 'wet' on the floor. He had wondered if it was urine or water. He thought it had been me and that it was probably urine. He thought this because it also 'smelt bad' in the toilet, so he reasoned that I must have used it, and not just to wash my hands. As he spoke, Mr G. sounded smug as if he knew with absolute certainty what I got up to in the toilet, and he had also conveniently obliterated from his mind the existence of any other patient besides himself in my toilet/mind.

I said he was very certain that he knew exactly what went on in the toilet and that this made him feel very powerful.

Mr G. said that he often wondered what went on in toilets. He felt his own life revolved so much around toilets because of the IBS. He said he had felt very reassured when I had shown him where the toilet was after our very first session. He had been anxious about whether I had one because he might need to use it urgently if he had diarrhoea. He had once been to see a therapist who had no toilet. He added that this had outraged him: how could a therapist offer to see a patient and not provide a toilet! He could see that the only way that therapist could have provided one would have been to let the patients go through his house, and he considered that this was precisely what this therapist should have done.

I said he seemed outraged at the possibility of anyone closing the door on him, not letting him into their private space when he wished to enter. It was so outrageous that with me he created a toilet space in his mind where he could always see me.

Mr G. replied that he could never have seen that other therapist even once per week. The anxiety about not being able to rush to the toilet in the middle of a session should he need it would have been overwhelming. At least here he did not have to worry about that and it made the whole experience of analysis possible.

I said that the toilet was an important space for him because he could rush to it either actually or in his mind when he was anxious and needed to make himself feel better by getting excited at what he could find out about me.

Mr G. said, 'Well, it's reassuring to know that however bad I feel about myself everybody shits, including you!'

I said that perhaps what helped him with his bad feeling about himself was getting a kick out of his fantasy of me in the toilet, feeling we were both the same: made up of shit.

Mr G. laughed, nervously I thought. He hesitated and then said in a rather broken up voice, as if he wanted to cover up the words as he spoke, that he had sexual fantasies about people defecating on him. After he said this he started to twitch uncomfortably on the couch. I had the impression that he felt he had exposed himself by revealing this fantasy for the very first time and feared my judgement. This had made him anxious, not aroused like he had been earlier when he thought of me in the toilet and I shared this observation with him.

Mr G. said he had been worried about telling me for a long time because at some level he knew this was disgusting, but he couldn't help it. He did not want me, or anyone else, to see him as a 'lonely sexual freak'. He had wondered many times if he could find a prostitute who would do this to him, but had always been too shy to ask, even when he had frequented prostitutes.

I will not go further into this session. Suffice to say that what eventually emerged over subsequent sessions were his fantasies of me defecating on him and that these were aroused in particular when he used my toilet. Tracking and analysing his use of my toilet to fuel the omnipotent fantasy that there were no boundaries between us and that he could access the contents of my body whenever he wished became a focus in the analysis. Importantly this lay the groundwork for helping Mr G. to develop awareness of his need for privacy and the need for respecting other people's.

Over time, and through his use of my toilet concretely and in fantasy, we were able to approach his fantasies about me entering the toilet without asking and him entering it without asking me. This became more marked around breaks, as if separation from me could only be managed by imagining himself connected with me in a perpetual sexual orgy located in my toilet.

I have been referring here, of course, to conscious sexual fantasies that were nevertheless underpinned by unconscious phantasies related to his omnipotent takeover of the object and appropriation of the insides of the maternal body. Mr G. had managed to turn the passive experience of being intruded upon by his mother into a sexually exciting one in which he was now in control. Through the transference we came to understand how he both resented his mother's intrusiveness into his body and mind and yet also longed to be right inside her and to feel she was right inside him. However suffocating at one level, the inside of the maternal body was felt to be a better place to be because *inside* he was spared the humiliating experience of being a lonely, sexual freak. Importantly, when inside the object, he did not have to experience any separation.

The libidinal value of both faeces and urine was clearly outlined by Freud (1905) and was strikingly apparent in the content of Mr G.'s sexual fantasies. We might say that Mr G. inhabited an anal-sadistic universe 'in which all particles are equal and interchangeable' (Chasseguet-Smirgel, 1983: 295) and which abolishes the genital universe of differences – the essence of perversion.

In a very interesting paper Clark Nunes (2006) discusses patients who on the surface appear to be similar to Mr G. in so far as they too have an erotized relationship to their excretions. She describes an incident in the analysis when her patient sees used toilet paper and concludes that it must have been used by the analyst, which left the analyst feeling intruded. She argues persuasively that such individuals display a particular kind of character formation predicated on the denial of dependency on the object and with marked aggression born of the hatred of dependency. Although Clark Nunes (2006) does not ignore the likely impact of later external impingements on her patient's development, she nevertheless emphasizes his 'very early aversion to the object', but it is unclear as to whether she might consider this to have some constitutional basis.

My experience with Mr G., however, leads me to consider an alternative pathway that converges nevertheless at a symptomatic level with Clark Nunes's observations in relation to the anal and urethral erotism that does not undergo the more typical repression after the polymorphous perversity of early childhood (Freud, 1905). In Mr G.'s case his faeces and urine remained highly erotized as a defence against loss of the object, not dependency on the object. I understood this to be due to the early colonization of his body and its products by the maternal object who had seemingly used him as a narcissistic extension of herself (Glasser, 1992) and whose loss was felt by Mr G. to herald an internal catastrophe. His way of defending against this was to get right inside the object, into its faeces and urine, smell its odour as a way of penetrating right into the core of the object, as he tried to do with me through his fantasies about my toilet and my use of it. In the transference it was possible to discern how the absence of a physical and psychic boundary between him and his primary object had contributed to an excited, erotized relationship with the toilet, within which he alternated between fantasizing about me looking at him and him taking up the position of voyeur.

The analyst's toilet *as* toilet breast: the case of Ms H.

I now want to turn away from patients like Mr G. who enact their perverse fantasies and dynamics through the way they use the analyst's toilet, to consider a quite different use of the toilet. I have in mind here how the analyst's toilet may be used to enact relational dynamics that cannot yet be brought directly into the consulting room and hence into the analytic relationship. In these cases the toilet becomes quite concretely the location of the 'toilet breast' (Meltzer, 1967b) so as to preserve a more idealized relationship with the analyst, as I hope to now illustrate through my work with Ms H., whose avoidance at first of the toilet, and later her actual use of it, denoted her marked struggle with the expression of her hostility towards the object and the accompanying fear of retaliation from the object.

Meltzer understood the toilet breast to be the most primitive representation of the mother. More specifically he was referring to a part-object relationship defined by the 'quality of being valued and needed, but not loved' (1967b: 20). For some patients the analyst's toilet as a concrete physical space functions as a toilet breast where the patient *literally* dumps their split-off aggression so as to preserve a good relationship with the analyst as the feeding breast. This denotes a more paranoid-schizoid use of the toilet per se and represents a twist on what Meltzer described as the toilet breast since what he had in mind was the way that for some patients 'the analyst is in effect only a toilet' (1967b: 20) and all goodness is felt to come from other people in the patient's life.

I am suggesting here that for some patients there is an even earlier psychic step that results in the literal evacuation of the patient's shitty or dirty or leaking feelings and which is reserved for the toilet qua toilet. Here the toilet by virtue of its nature as part of the analytic setting, and yet sufficiently separated from the consulting room, provides a safe boundary protecting the 'good' relationship with the feeding analyst. Indeed although I am referring here to a concrete toilet, Meltzer's understanding of the function of the underlying primary splitting process remains very apt:

> The reason for the rigidity of this splitting is clearly to be seen when the split begins to break down and the severe anxieties of soiling, polluting and poisoning the feeding breast become so clear.
>
> (Meltzer, 1967b: 20)

Ms H. – a woman in her late thirties – was one of two sisters. Her mother was described as a caring, but emotionally needy woman, towards whom, it soon became clear in the transference, she had been anxiously attached. She described a childhood dedicated to pleasing her mother and effectively becoming her confidante as the mother had a difficult marriage and had been experienced by Ms H. as having turned away from the father. Her sister was described as 'wayward' and more defiant towards the mother and father. Ms H. had a close relationship with her but felt that her sister left it to her to take care of both parents.

By contrast Ms H. had become the model daughter, succeeding highly academically, marrying the kind of man her mother approved of and soon starting her own family to whom she was devoted. All this was inevitably achieved at some considerable cost to her own development as a separate individual with her own needs and desires. She also detailed difficulties with sexual intimacy: she said she loved her husband but found it hard to be close to him. She had friends but sometimes felt exploited by them, and yet she was careful not to be critical of them.

By the time she started three-times-weekly psychoanalytic psychotherapy with me, Ms H. was depressed. She had started a course of academic study as a mature student, which she had interrupted mid-point feeling unable to concentrate. It seemed as though she could not allow herself any kind of pleasure for very long and this was also apparent in her relationship to food. She had been bulimic as an adolescent. She would then binge but could never keep in the food she had eaten, guiltily vomiting it no sooner had she ingested it. When I met her she was not actively bingeing and purging but she was very conscious about how much she ate and carefully avoided anything that could be construed as indulgent excess.

In the transference I experienced her as very keen to please me: she invariably agreed with what I said and regularly thanked me for the help I offered her even when it was clear to me that she was not feeling any better or when I was aware that what I had said was not in fact quite right. I felt she always had to steer herself very close to where she thought I needed her to be. Attempts to take up the negative transference were met with a wall: she would concede that unconsciously she *might* feel angry, but that really she was not aware of any such feelings towards me. Aggression towards others too was similarly dismissed or played down: anger was always translated into 'mild irritation' at best. She worried a lot if ever she did betray more than irritation, concerned that the other person would withdraw their friendship or love from her. It was through my own countertransference of often feeling irritated and stifled by her accommodating surface that I gained a sense of the rage she had to desperately split off.

One of the things I only noticed after the first year of the therapy was that Ms H. had never once used the toilet. This made her stand out relative to all my other patients who at one time or another had used the toilet at least once and some, like Mr G., had intrusively appropriated it.

One day, towards the end of the second year of our work, Ms D. arrived late and flustered. She hated being late, something we had discussed on other occasions, because she feared I would read this as her being disrespectful and ungrateful. I had taken up many times on such occasions how she became very anxious whenever the possibility of any aggression towards me reared its head or indeed that I might feel irritated with her. Both these possibilities had to be strongly defended against. I sensed how imperative it was for her to protect our relationship from any conflict.

On this occasion her lateness had meant, however, that she had not been able to go into the café near my consulting room to use the toilet before the session. I was taken aback by this revelation, as I had not known about this routine.

I eventually said that I was intrigued by what had made it impossible for the past two years for her to use my toilet.

Ms H.'s response was as striking as her revelation because she said she had not known that I had a toilet she could use. She thought there was no toilet.

As I heard this I began to question whether I had in fact told her. This is what I usually do with all patients after we agree to work together when I then routinely point out where they can wait and where the toilet is located. It was, of course, possible that I had not done so with her, but I thought this was unlikely because it was a well-established routine with all new patients. It seemed more likely that I had said it and that she had not taken this in for very specific psychic reasons.

I eventually said that I thought I had mentioned it but that even assuming I had not, she might have asked me and yet even that had evidently felt impossible for her.

Ms H. remarked that it was indeed odd when I put it that way. She thought now that it was remarkable that she had never asked because it had been something of an inconvenience to have to use the café all the time as she then felt she always had to have a drink before the session in order to 'legitimize' her use of their toilet. But because of this, by the time the session ended, she experienced the need to return to the toilet again. Then she felt too embarrassed to go into the café *again* so she often ended up driving home desperate to get back so she could use her own toilet.

I said a lot of emotional and physical energy had been invested in sustaining a toilet routine that did not require using mine, as if this option was out of bounds.

It was only at this point that Ms H. told me that ever since childhood she had been very particular about which toilets she used. She could never sit down on the toilet unless it was in her own home. She hated toilets in public places because she thought they were dirty. She was a very clean person, she added, and although she was 'not obsessional' she liked all her spaces at home to be clean.

I said that despite her hatred of public toilets this had been preferable to using mine.

Ms H. acknowledged that this was indeed a paradox and that the thought of using my toilet left her feeling very anxious. Toilets were 'private' places, she added. She never liked using other people's toilets. She feared picking up germs and getting ill. She was not sure why she had found it so difficult to take in that I even had a toilet and then to use it, as she imagined my toilet would be clean. But, she added, she would need to do so today because she was desperate. She then went on to recount an incident with a friend, which had clearly upset her, but she could not allow herself to voice any criticism of the friend. The session ended on this note.

After the protracted period of phobic avoidance of my toilet, Ms H. did indeed use the toilet that day for the first time in almost two years. After she left, and before my next patient arrived, I went to use the toilet myself and I was very struck when I discovered that the toilet seat was covered in urine, the floor below the toilet was wet and the sink tap had not been turned off properly. I was thus very concretely exposed to a rather different Ms H. Here was not the very polite, grateful, contained and 'clean' Ms H. but a more messy, angry part of Ms H. that had now literally leaked out and was left for me to see and significantly, I thought, left for me to clean up. I noted that I felt somewhat 'put-upon'.

Her next session was two days later and she made no conscious reference to her use of my toilet. I tried to listen carefully to her associations to see if they might lead us back to the toilet and what she left there for me to see and clean, but I could not find an entry point in the content that would allow me to make a link. I was mindful too that I seemed to need to find the entry point as if it had become imperative in my mind that I *had* to make the interpretation as a way perhaps of ridding myself of intolerable feelings. I thus decided to stay quiet and reflect on my countertransference: a sense of being forcefully exposed to a dirty toilet that I had to clean up and which she had completely dissociated herself from and that I needed to confront her with as if its deposited contents were indeed dangerous and I had to hand them back to her. She had spent two years protecting me from her aggression, and had phobically avoided my toilet where she felt she would have exposed 'her germs' that I might then have 'picked up' and so damaged our 'good' relationship. Now she had given me a clear measure of her aggression but split it off very concretely and left it in the toilet. I understood this to denote the activation of anxieties about damage to the 'good' object and its anticipated retaliation, that could only be managed through marked splitting.

On reflection I decided that if I did bring all this into the transference too soon this might backfire given how entrenched her defences were and I risked shaming her. I considered that it might be important instead to let her use the *toilet-as-breast* to deposit her hostility and to build up confidence in the toilet as the first container before she could use me as a toilet breast. This already represented a development relative to her previous phobic avoidance of the toilet. I therefore decided to say nothing about it.

In the subsequent months Ms H. used the toilet on several other occasions. Every time she left it in the same state, and occasionally worse. I gained the impression that as time passed, and as she did not experience any retaliation on my part, the toilet functioned as an increasingly safe container for what she had not yet been able to think about with me. I thought that my role was that of ensuring this concrete container could function as such by not interpreting it prematurely. And so it was for about eight months.

Then, in the first session of the week towards the latter part of the third year of her therapy, it seemed to me that the material she brought invited an interpretation that could allow us to move towards integrating the toilet and its contents into our relationship.

Ms H. started this session by recounting a rather difficult weekend with her husband. They had decided to have a weekend away alone without the children. She had been dreading this weekend because she now recognized that the children provided an 'acceptable screen' – as she put it – for the distance that had been increasing between her husband and her. As she had feared, no sooner had they reached their hotel, the tension mounted: her husband wanted to make love but she was not keen. He became upset and started to question the marriage and whether it could continue on this basis. She described her rising panic as her husband spoke. She then 'gave in' to making love, which they did but later the husband had told her that he was fed up with her 'avoidance tactics' and that he was not sure the therapy had done much to help her to change. This had incensed her, she said, because she felt the therapy had helped her a lot.

I said that she was filled with a range of feelings that she had spent many years avoiding between us: any anger or dissatisfaction had to be covered up behind an 'acceptable screen'. She would sooner make love with her husband even if she did not feel like it, or tell me how helpful the therapy was so as to keep things nice between us, than own up to what she really felt.

Ms H. said that the therapy had helped her in this respect: she was now able to hear what her husband was saying and she had become upset in front of him like she had not done before. He had been a bit shocked, she said, because she was generally so contained. As she spoke I sensed that she was brittle and almost too insistent about how helpful therapy had been.

I said that she had been very contained with me too, but that she had indeed started to also show me what she really felt 'once removed', in my toilet, where she left traces of a more messy, uncontained part of her.

Ms H. seemed taken aback and said she was not clear what I meant.

I said that she might perhaps not be aware of this, and that she might find it hard to hear me say this, but when she used my toilet she always left the seat and the floor covered in splashes of urine and sometimes left the tap running too, which seemed to be at odds with the image of herself that it had been so important to impress on me so as to keep our relationship clean and 'nice'.

Ms H. was silent and her body on the couch stiffened. She said she felt utterly embarrassed and was not sure she could ever look me in the face again.

I said that taking down that 'acceptable screen' inevitably left her feeling exposed to my scrutiny of her less acceptable feelings that she had struggled so hard to keep out of our relationship. I acknowledged how dangerous it might now feel between us.

At first Ms H. was silent, then she got up and without looking at me left the room. I immediately felt I had made a mistake in bringing this up, that it had been too soon or that I had done it insensitively. I thought she was leaving altogether but in fact I then realized that she had left her bag and that she had gone to the toilet where she stayed for five minutes. When she returned she said I would probably want to know what she had been doing and she was going to tell me rather than me discover it: she had thrown up. She then added in a shaken up but also irritated voice: 'Maybe I left some mess but I did my best to clean up.'

I said she had felt reprimanded and exposed by me when I brought up the toilet and what she did in it. I said she appeared to be both anxious but also angry.

Ms H. replied that she was not angry; she just felt sick. She had felt sick during the night too; it must be some stomach virus. She said, uncomfortably, that she had diarrhoea during the night too and it had in fact been touch and go if she would make it to the session today.

I said that might well be so but that I couldn't help but think that the feelings I had generated in her today by bringing up the toilet and her angry feelings towards me had also been hard to keep inside her and to reflect on with me; instead she got rid of them in the toilet again.

After she left I went to the toilet and I was immediately hit by a strong odour. I wondered whether she had in fact vomited or had diarrhoea and if so why she had not felt able to say as much. Ms H. cancelled the two subsequent sessions due to the alleged stomach virus. Although I was sorry that she felt the need to do so, I was also encouraged that she felt she could do so as this was a way of communicating that things between us were not alright. She had never cancelled a session before.

When she returned the following week the tenor of the sessions for several weeks thereafter was more distant and critical. She began to question the therapy and whether we had got as far as we could go. She denied this had anything to do with the fact that I had made a link between the toilet and us. She said that she felt the therapy had helped her to complete her studies, that she got on better with her mother and was able to set clearer boundaries and that generally she felt less stressed.

All of this was true, but it was clear to me at least that her thoughts about ending were directly connected with how dangerous the therapy had become now that there was a live conflict between us and the toilet no longer provided a safe container as my interpretation had exposed what she did with it. Inevitably I questioned if I had done the right thing by taking this up and whether I had enacted a scenario where I pushed Ms H. out of my mind/toilet and she no longer had anywhere safe to hide. On balance, however, I thought that if I had not done so I would have been colluding with a defence, which whilst necessary at first, also required understanding if Ms H. was to integrate her aggression more effectively and bring it into the room, as it were.

Ms H. did manage to stay in the therapy. Over the subsequent months the work became very difficult, but more alive, as she started to use me as the toilet breast. She became more overtly critical and though this gave rise to anxiety it felt more manageable. She continued to use the toilet, but I noted that it was not left in a mess as before. Around this time she developed a new friendship with a woman she had met at a social event and this friend was now her new confidante (her feeding breast). This made it possible, I thought, to bring into our relationship her resentment and anger.

At the start of the fourth year of the therapy, she brought an anxious dream:

> *There was a tsunami and she looked on as a small woman desperately tried to cling on to some railings to avoid being washed away by the tide, but the tsunami swept her away.*

In her associations she remarked that she had been horrified by how unforgiving 'nature' could be. We were able to use this dream to approach not only how frightened she was that her 'nature', which now she knew contained some very powerful and felt-to-be dangerous feelings, might kill me, but also that I might retaliate and be unforgiving towards her for now hating me. It was of note that the dream image is of water killing the small woman and this made me think about the early use of Ms H.'s urine in the toilet and her wish to submerge me with it and the corresponding fear that it would indeed do so.

In this same session an interesting train of thought prompted by the word 'nature', which had appeared in her dream, led Ms H. to tell me that her mother had never been at ease with anything 'too natural'. She said that when her children were babies her mother never helped out with nappy changing and Ms H. thought that this was because at some level her mother felt disgusted by the smell of dirty nappies. She recalled her mother saying that she had not enjoyed nappy changing when Ms H. and her sister were babies and had delegated this 'task' to the nanny.

Ms H. added that she never had that problem with any odour produced by her children, but she was always worried about leaving a foul smell behind if she used somebody's toilet. She acknowledged that this was one reason why she still felt uncomfortable using my toilet even though she now felt she could use it. She said that many months previously she had used it when she felt unwell and she knew she had left a smell. She had been put out by the fact that I did not provide air freshener; on that day she had forgotten the perfume she always typically carried in her handbag otherwise she would have used that to cover the smell. As she related this to me I sensed that she had become agitated.

I said that she really could not trust that I could bear her 'bad' smells and that these had to be covered over. I then wondered aloud what she had made of the fact that I did *not* provide air freshener.

Ms H. was quiet at first and then said that although she had felt angry with me about the lack of air freshener at the time she had in fact also later thought that this must be because I was not bothered about this kind of stuff and she had rather envied me for being relaxed about it. There was something about body odour and smells coming from her body waste that she found especially difficult – she still did not feel she could 'let out air' in front of her mother or husband, for example.

'Or, here with me,' I added.

Ms H. agreed and said that she wanted to protect me from these 'foul' parts of herself. As she spoke I felt she was much more connected with depressive anxieties about the damage that her aggression could do to me. I also sensed her longing that I could relate to her as a whole person with both 'foul' and good parts.

The question of smell, and whether I could tolerate the smells coming from her body, provided a very important opportunity for approaching Ms H.'s early experience of an object that could not accept her as she was. It seemed as though she felt that her mother could not tolerate her smelly, less 'nice' parts and only related to her 'clean', accommodating self, which she had perfected over the years, becoming the model daughter.

For patients like Ms H. the use of the analyst's toilet may be phobically avoided at first, but its eventual use may provide the first prototype of a safe container for felt-to-be dangerous or unacceptable feelings and parts of the self. Once this can become more integrated into the analytic relationship it becomes possible to edge towards the analyst being safely used as a toilet breast before a more depressive integration of the good and the bad object can become consolidated. As Meltzer understood it:

> Only with the establishment of the toilet-breast as an object in psychic reality through the repeated experience of it externally in the transference, is the relinquishment of massive projective identification possible, since this mechanism aims at escaping from an unbearable infantile identity. Once this separate identity has thus been made bearable through the modulation of pain, the way is opened for other developmental steps.
>
> (Meltzer, 1967b: 21)

Ms H.'s experience of an object that refused to take in the smells of her body was felt to be a profound rejection of the most basic aspects of her self. In normal development the shared experience of smell, of smelling the other and of being smelt by the other, represents one of the earliest somatic prototypes of introjection and projection. An object that cannot receive the baby's bodily smells is an object that cannot function as a receptive olfactory container. This may lead to the need to split off parts of the self that are felt to be smelly or dirty so as to preserve a more idealized relationship with an object that is presented only with the clean parts of the self.

Ms H., as I came to understand it over time, had no internal model of olfactory intimacy. My work with her reminded me of the developmental necessity early on for the baby to feel that the object is prepared to enter, without intrusion, the intimate physical space between them, and is able to breathe and smell the baby and so receive its bodily projections and, we might say, transform them into alpha elements. Ms H., however, could not trust that her object would receive her smell and allow itself to be penetrated by it. This, as it turned out, helped us too to understand her difficulties around sexual intimacy with her husband, which significantly improved by the time we ended a six-year-long psychoanalytic therapy.

The analysis of Ms H.'s initial 'ignorance' of the existence of my toilet, followed by its use to split off her smelly, unacceptable self, culminating in her greater confidence that she could use me as the toilet breast, allowed her to finally re-own her split-off aggression.

We all carry within us a deep-seated sense that what emanates from our body reveals not only our physical interior, but also our psychic interior, which is why our relationship to toilets deserves psychoanalytic interest. The analyst's toilet comes to represent many things in the context of the analytic relationship, not least because it is a shared physical space where the patient 'knows' the analyst's body is on a level with his: there they are both literally and metaphorically naked. Of course not all analysts provide a toilet as part of the consulting room arrangements and that in itself raises interesting questions about how a patient might experience the absence of this provision, or how its very provision might be said to gratify the patient – a subject that is beyond the scope of this chapter.

Note

1 Here I am referring to work in a private context where there is only one toilet and the analyst is aware of the state it was left in prior to the patient's use of it. This is impossible to control in public health service settings.

Chapter 10

Entrepreneurs of the self
Some psychoanalytic reflections on the psychic and social functions of reality TV makeover shows

The body, as I have argued throughout this book, is the primary site for elaborating and representing a nascent sense of self and of the other. It is the site for carving out our individuality and for engaging with others. The body, both so idiosyncratic and ultimately the expression of our individuality, is also and *always* a social body. Through the use made of the body we can discern not only the literal enactment of our internal world but we can also gauge the emotional climate of a given sociocultural period, its malaise, if you like, and also its ethics. In my view, as analysts we should be concerned not only with the body in the consulting room but also beyond it because social processes can unhelpfully reinforce internal dynamics, providing socially sanctioned avenues for perverse solutions to psychic conflicts. In saying this I am arguing for a psychoanalysis that engages not only with other disciplines, which is implicit in how I have approached the subject matter of this book, but also one that is politically relevant and engaged – a position that was embodied with integrity by the late Hannah Segal.

In this final chapter I will therefore approach the body through the prism of the way it is represented and used (as in 'manipulated') in reality TV (RTV) makeover shows to go beyond the individual body and consider the *social body* from a psychoanalytic perspective. TV plays a role in organizing the construction of the social body through the regulation of symbolic manifestations of the individual body. My ideas are based on my experience of assessing participants for such shows, and on my personal reflections as a viewer – as one of many gazes looking at and projecting into the participants in these shows. This kind of programming – and specifically, in my view, the dubious notion of 'democratization through access to the media' that such shows promulgate – provides us with important information about our own historical and culturally bound moment, highlighting the relationship between the individual body and the social body.

I will focus on three strands of thinking. First, I suggest that TV makeover shows promote a very particular type of relationship to the self, namely that of *entrepreneur of the self*[1] via the manipulation of the surface of the body. Second, and following on from the first, I propose that such shows promulgate a corrupt notion of empowerment through subordination to a socially sanctioned superegoish structure, which can become deeply seductive in the internal world of the individual because it provides a way of managing anxiety, including the existential anxiety that has been intensified by global and virtual economies. However, this comes at a high cost not just to the individual but also to society. This is because the culture of narcissism reinforced by these shows erodes a sense of community through individualizing problems and locating them in the individual body rather than addressing the wider, and often unconscious, social processes that create pain or disenfranchisement, thereby effectively removing the obligation of the state to provide for those who need mental health and social care, not appearance on RTV. Finally, I will suggest that RTV as a genre plays into a *total surveillance psychic economy*, which corrupts the gaze as a form of 'looking after' into a form of superegoish 'watching'.

Reinventing the self

David Ely's (1964) book is the inspiration for the film *Seconds*, which charts the story of Arthur Hamilton's re-invention. Arthur Hamilton is a middle-aged man. His life has lost purpose. He feels disengaged at work, and the love between him and his wife has dwindled. One evening Hamilton receives a late night phone call from Charlie Evans, an old friend Hamilton believed had committed suicide a year before. Intrigued, he follows Charlie's directions and is approached by a secret organization, known simply as the 'Company', which offers wealthy people a second chance at life. The Company, in the person of Mr Ruby, interviews Hamilton, and resorts to blackmail to persuade him to sign on, foreshadowing the unfortunate consequences of accepting the Company's assistance.

The Company fakes Hamilton's death by staging an accident with a corpse disguised as him. Through extensive plastic surgery (and a rather dubious form of psychotherapy), Hamilton is then transformed into Tony Wilson. As Wilson, he has a new home, a new identity, new friends and a devoted butler.

Relocated to a fancy home in Malibu, California, Wilson is literally installed in a new, more romantic life, commencing with his transformed look. He starts a relationship with a young woman named Nora Marcus and for a time he is happy, but soon becomes troubled by the emotional confusion of his new identity and its consequences.

After the initial thrill at the 'second life' Wilson soon develops misgivings, which are compounded by the discovery that his new friends are not real but makeovers like himself: the world that has been given to him is entirely false. It turns out that his neighbours have been sent to keep an eye on his adjustment to his new life. Nora is actually an agent of the Company, and her attentions to Wilson are designed merely to ensure his cooperation.

With its futuristic vision of plastic surgery as literally the creator of life itself, *Seconds*, seen now through the lens of the twenty-first century's obsession with makeover shows and the staggering rise in the use of cosmetic procedures and surgery, should inspire some second thoughts at the very least.

The Company – so reminiscent of Rosenfeld's (1971) notion of an internal 'Mafia'[2] – is an apt and chilling corporate personification of the psychotic state of mind that can operate both at a group, societal level, and at an individual intrapsychic level, in relationship to the seduction of cosmetic surgery and the central fantasy of quite concretely reinventing the self.

The seduction of the path chosen by Wilson is clear enough. As Wilson, Hamilton manages to temporarily escape his own depression and mid-life crisis through a manic flight into a narcissistic, omnipotent state of mind, supported by the literal physical transformations and the new, improved life this seemingly gives him access to. But in exchange for a new customized self he has to kill off, *and to keep killing off*, the true self, ultimately leaving him feeling confused and alienated, trapped in an enslaved relationship to the superegoish Company who won't set him free. As soon as he questions his new predicament, thereby challenging the propaganda of the narcissistic self, he is violently threatened by the Company.

In violation of 'Company' policy, Wilson visits his old wife in his new persona, and learns that his marriage had failed because he was distracted by the pursuit of career and material possessions, the very things in life that others made him believe were important. He returns to the Company and announces a desire to start again with yet another identity. The Company offers to accommodate him, but asks if he would first provide the names of some past acquaintances who might like to be 'reborn'.

While awaiting his reassignment, Wilson encounters Charlie Evans again, the friend who had originally recruited him into the Company. Evans was also 'reborn', and like Wilson could not make a go of his new identity. Together, they speculate on the reason for their failure to adjust, attributing it to the fact that they allowed others, including the Company, to make their life choices for them. This realization, however, comes too late, as Hamilton learns that failed reborns are not actually provided new identities, but instead become cadavers used to fake the next clients' deaths. Only by recruiting more men, as Charlie recruited him, can Wilson avoid the fate of becoming the corpse to fake another man's death and re-invention.

I am dwelling here on this narrative twist because it captures the savagery of the superego. There is no escape from this kind of internal psychic organization: only submission or death. The notion of submission to an allegedly higher power or authority in order to empower the self, I want to suggest, lies at the heart of RTV makeover shows. This inherent contradiction exposes the fallacy that one can increase personal freedom through its very surrender.

The very popularity of makeover programming in the early part of the twenty-first century offers important information about our own moment, primarily the hope that in controlling the real physical body made legible through RTV we might better regulate and protect the vulnerable social body.

Social theorists such as Mary Douglas (1966) have long argued that the individual body is a microcosm of the larger social body so that both material and metaphorical bodies influence one another. TV plays a role in organizing the construction of the social body through the regulation of symbolic manifestations of the individual body. More specifically the makeover's implicit discourse concerns what we could regard as a climate of panic that requires the elimination of impurities that potentially contaminate the larger social body.

Makeover culture perfectly dovetails other cultural trends, in particular as identified by several sociologists (e.g. Giddens, 1991) who argue that the intensification of uncertainty in life has compelled a higher degree of self-regulation. Furedi (2004) has argued that in times of uncertainty self-improvement gurus acquire iconic status. Given the makeover's sweeping promise to bring about a 'better you' and promote healthier relations this is perhaps no surprise. Rather than critiquing the gaze, which the eye of the camera embodies, such shows glorify it, suggesting that in the cultural spectacle removal from the gaze is neither desirable nor permissible: the goal is to be looked at approvingly.

Entrepreneurs of the self: the body as project

I have suggested in earlier chapters that in our advanced technological culture the body can be subjected to extensive modification 'at will'. Weber (2009) suggests that neoliberal ideologies, which she views as underpinning makeover shows, thus position the subject as an *entrepreneur of the self*, who must engage in care of the body in order to be competitive in a larger global marketplace. The notion of *entrepreneur of the self* is a very apt one in my view. Weber does not use it with reference to psychoanalysis, but I want to suggest that it provides a helpful way of conceptualizing a particular kind of *psychic economy* where the self is both producer and consumer of the self – in other words it denotes an omnipotent state of mind in which the body is objectified, can be manipulated at will and effectively re-invented. This is an omnipotent state of mind because by bypassing the origins and limitations of the body it denies any acknowledgement of both our inevitable dependency on others (i.e. we are 'given' a body by our parents) and of our finitude.

Let us now look more closely at RTV makeover shows and how they promote such a state of mind. In *Extreme Makeover* a range of interventions are suggested to improve the participant's appearance: for example, cosmetic dentistry, rhinoplasty, breast augmentation and liposuction. The participants often cite the individual parts of celebrities (e.g. Angelina Jolie's lips) that they would like to have themselves. The programme 'makes over reality' by creating a part-object universe: we enter the domain of bits of people (e.g. someone else's lips), which can now be appropriated. By encouraging this, the makeover show promises the appearance of autonomy over one's bodily representation. Importantly, it does so within the normalizing framework of popular TV that masks the reality of the human distress that, in my experience of assessing potential participants for such shows, all too often lies behind the conscious wish to participate in these shows (Lemma, 2010).

These shows override the fact that not everyone has the psychological, and let alone the financial, capital to feel at home in their bodies. And here lies the seduction of the makeover shows: they promulgate the fantasy that despite differences, we 'are all the same really'. At the level of the internal world it is this promise of *sameness* that makes the makeover show so compelling because it bypasses any exposure to an experience of difference, and the sense of insufficiency we all have to find ways of managing in ourselves. With surgical transformation, however, the promise of sameness with an ideal is forever (Fraser, 2007). Such shows encourage an approach to difference that bypasses the normal pain that the perception of difference between self and other may give rise to and that is a fact of life, inciting instead a sense of injustice about the perceived difference. The accompanying grievance and humiliation then mobilizes an urgent need for relief, which renders the individual vulnerable to the seduction of bodily transformation.

The after-bodies, as Weber (2009) aptly refers to them, revealed by the makeover show inevitably beg the question of what the 'given' body represented for these individuals in the first place. The meaning of the body in the mind, as we have seen, will reveal inevitably idiosyncratic meanings that rest on unconscious identifications. As analysts we know the arduous task that unravelling such identifications entails, let alone changing them when they are the source of psychic distress experienced as located on or in the body and expressed through its modification. In the transformational shell of the makeover show, however, there is both the promise of cause and effect, of before and after, fuelling the illusion that an 'after-body' can sever its ties to the given body and what it represents, proposing instead a form of self-cure that can be very seductive.

RTV, particularly in the US but also increasingly in the UK, is inundating viewers with imperatives about self-appraisal, self-critique and self-improvement. Many of the participants involved in makeover shows appear to feel they have failed to approximate the gendered indicators of personhood, leaving them feeling powerless. Post-makeover, beautiful and enabled to please the gaze of the audience, such participants state that social judgements no longer matter to them. For example, participants will say that they no longer care about what others think about them as they are now 'happy' with who they are. Such newfound satisfaction with one's self appears paradoxically to have been acquired by capitulating to socially normative standards about appearance: here, rather dubiously, subordination empowers.

In these mediated transformations the body stands as the gateway to a better self. Importantly, it's not just the physical body altered through plastic surgery, weight loss or style, but also the symbolic body represented in RTV shows focusing, for example, on interior/house makeovers: a less cluttered home also offers a key that will unlock the self and give access to greater riches. Notwithstanding the different manifest contents of these shows (houses, gardens, bodies), in all of them selfhood becomes intricately linked to social locations and practices marked as normative, frequently designated through images that connote upward mobility, heterosexuality, consumer orientation, conventional attractiveness, ethnic anonymity and confidence (Wood and Skeggs, 2011). Perhaps one of the more unsettling features of such shows is how they relate to questions of class, race and ethnicity, which are either rarely explicitly mentioned, or if they are, are handled as aesthetic details that can be tweaked in the service of a desirable body.

In the makeover's heteronormative economy the participants are thus 'unreal people' (Butler, 2003) – those so far outside a normative frame that they cannot be recognized as valid subjects until they are subjected to the process of transformation, as if there is no acceptable self before the intervention of the programme. The makeover show thus fundamentally promotes an essentialized, inauthentic idea of the self that is stable, coherent and ultimately normative.

The makeover show exists in what we might regard psychoanalytically as a paranoid-schizoid universe. Makeover logic insists that feelings of sadness or depression or even injustice can be overcome – indeed can be eliminated – through manipulation of the body's surface and conformity to a 'higher power'. This 'higher power', I want to suggest, is personified by the style gurus and cosmetic surgeons who purport to 'strip off' and 'cut out' the pain. In so doing we could say that the makeover show positions itself as a potent cure for the postmodern condition, promising coherence and empowerment to a fractured self.

The savagery of the makeover show: a psychoanalytic reading of the BBC's *What Not to Wear*

Makeover TV invites us to relate to our bodies as ledger sheets: a combination of assets and debts that is offered up to the scrutiny of the style gurus who host such shows and, of course, also to the scrutiny of the audience's gaze.

The notion that one can achieve greater empowerment by fully surrendering to someone else's unquestioned authority over appearance is central to the makeover show's basic premise. Show after show plays out this theme as visibly demonstrated in the BBC's version of *What Not To Wear*, which I will focus on briefly by way of illustration. This show, hosted by the infamous Trinny and Susannah duo, involves inviting participants' bodies to be visually dissected and transformed through a wardrobe overhaul. This transformational process is invariably a humiliating one.

For example, in one episode called 'Sisters', Trinny and Susannah are musing about how 'You can choose your friends … but you can't choose your family'. What follows are not considered observations about family dynamics but incitement to rivalry and humiliation between siblings over their respective bodily appearance. We are shown a stampede of women as they come through the revolving doors of a large building whilst Trinny and Susannah strut majestically down a corridor. They then invite one of each pair of sisters to share what they refer to as a 'video nasty'. This is a video made by one of the sisters to show the so-called help their sister needs in order to look better. 'All these women have made a video nasty of their other halves at their worst,' Suzannah tells us. The notion of a 'video nasty' is a chilling reminder of the state of mind that such shows promote and appeal to. As this exchange captures, exposure to the shaming gaze of the 'other', coupled with the frenzied, manic atmosphere created by the style gurus, is all in the service of the transformation to follow, which will redeem the shamed subject. The archaic superego wags its finger whilst inviting its victim to collude with its savagery, promising redemption through submission to its stranglehold.

A total surveillance state: at the intersection of internal and external reality

There is a consensus of opinion amongst academics that RTV functions as an agent of governmentality, enacting a 'regulatory pedagogy' (Weber, 2009) that implicitly conveys to the viewer what is required in order to avert the censorious gaze that the makeover show 'victim' has been subjected to under the guise of 'taking control' of their self via the transformation of the body. The form of control on offer in these shows thus turns out to be yet another form of submission. But it is nevertheless seductive because we all want to avoid the censorious, shaming gaze.

It is at this intersection between the social and the intrapsychic that RTV gains traction. Psychoanalytic ideas can shed helpful light on how these processes can become dynamically intertwined to give rise to the enactment of individual pathology on a socially sanctioned stage.

The notion that one can achieve greater empowerment by fully surrendering to someone else's unquestioned authority is fundamentally illogical, but psychoanalysis helps us to understand that this follows to the letter the tyrannical logic of Bion's ego-destructive 'super'ego (Bion, 1962). The temporary relief from anxiety that submission to such a terrifying superego serves up as consolation, in fact, only serves to magnify anxiety, feeding into escalating cycles of cruelty and punishment. This pathological superego watches the ego from a 'higher' place and is fundamentally against the pain that comes from thinking and understanding (O'Shaughnessy, 1999). It is the rule of the tyrant.

Indeed the makeover methods often require the humiliation of their subjects. A programme such as *Ten Years Younger*, for example, concretely frames the place of ridicule in a Plexiglass box in which the makeover participant stands as passers-by give their two pennies' worth about how old they think the person looks due to her wrinkles and sunspots. The end product of heightened happiness and self-esteem makes the humiliation and shame only a means to a highly desirable end, but it is painful nonetheless. In some of these shows one can discern how the participants are invited into a kind of totalitarian state in which as long as you follow the rule of the tyrant you are made 'good'.

In some individuals this external state, as it were, neatly maps onto what I want to refer to as an internal state of *total surveillance of the self and of the other*. In this state of mind the imperative is to work at how one is looked at by the other and through this to control the other. Another way of putting this would be to say that the internal imperative is to control what the other sees and hence to create the illusion that one knows with certainty the mind of the other. The promise of total surveillance is that it might rehabilitate access to a frustratingly elusive other who could instead become totally visible to the self. If the other can be totally known to the self – and hence possessed – we can eliminate any experience of uncertainty, difference or dependency.

Let us return to the social level, however, because this kind of total surveillance state reveals another pernicious process. As disturbing and insidious in its impact on society is the way that visual monitoring in makeovers is coded as a form of social care. In other words we are here in the grip of a superegoish object that promises to take care of the self, but it is fundamentally a corrupt object.

These shows reinforce a form of individualism that opposes a sense of community. The makeover subject is self-cultivating and can provide for their own needs: the unemployed, depressed 'housewife' who has been left by her husband for a younger woman is invited to reinvent herself through cosmetic surgery so as to take control of her life, thus removing any obligation from her broader community to attend to her deprivation or depression. Almost all makeover shows reify the notion that it is important to create the beautiful and thus happy self rather than address larger social issues that have brought about pain or systemic social disenfranchisement (Weber, 2009). The transformational message, by contrast, suggests that the suffering person's misery, whether caused by protruding ears or a flat chest, is individualized and thus non-systemic.

The insistence on individual experience places the focus squarely on self-management and self-production. One important reason for taking seriously the nature of these programmes and their appeal is that it alerts us to the way we have perverted a form of 'looking after' – where you and I as citizens take care of each other – into a harsh, excluding form of watching from on high, that is a 'critical gaze'. Such a gaze represents a humiliating aspect of a primitive type of superego to be differentiated from the more mature superego of the depressive position (Steiner, 2011). We know well from our consulting room experience the savagery of this primitive type of superego – it only acquires greater savagery when the internal world finds itself reinforced through social processes.

The ethics of the gaze

We live in scopophilic times in which voyeurism and vicarious living are the order of the day. Whether we are committed fans of RTV or its arch critics, at some stage or other we have *all* at the very least stumbled over someone's trauma as we flick through our TV channels. The voyeur – which is in all of us – always participates through the gaze. The gaze can never be innocent – we can never be innocent bystanders. By definition if we 'see' something there is no looking back, as it were. This applies as much to us in our role as analysts as it does to us as citizens.

In this chapter I have suggested that RTV as a genre corrupts the social gaze as a form of 'looking after' into a form of superegoish 'watching'. Looking can never be free from the snares of unconscious projection. The best we can strive for is to commit ourselves to an ongoing analytic process within ourselves, by which I mean that we remain humble in relation to the unconscious and our more or less partial ignorance of it, so that we can strive to undo the projections through which we rid ourselves of anxiety – not least anxiety about the fact of our unavoidable lack and dependency – and the incorporations (not introjections) through which we cover up this lack over and over again.

We can only ever strive for partial success in these domains. But this is no excuse for abrogating social responsibility towards each other. We need to take responsibility for how we look at the other and the ethical necessity of renewing our commitment to this self-questioning project. The ethical moment requires us to be prepared to look again but with a different lens (Silverman, 1996). Psychoanalysis and the internal work it encourages us to do provides us with one such invaluable lens.

Notes

1 I am grateful to Weber (2009) for coining this turn of phrase.
2 This notion is central to Rosenfeld's (1971) view on destructive narcissism which emphasizes a gang-like structure in the mind (a destructive component of the personality) whose *raison d'être* is to sustain the self in the thrall of the superiority and power of destructive narcissism.

References

Ainsworth, M., Blehar, M., Waters, E. and Wall, S. (1978). *Patterns of Attachment: A Psychological Study of the Strange Situation.* Hillsdale: Lawrence Erlbaum.
Aisenstein, M. (2006). The indissociable unity of psyche and soma. *The International Journal of Psychoanalysis*, 87: 667–680.
Allison, S., von Wahide, L., Shockley, T., and Gabbard, G. (2006). The development of the self in the era of the Internet and role-playing fantasy games. *American Journal of Psychiatry*, 163: 381–385.
Almodóvar, P. (Producer) (1989). *Tie Me Up! Tie Me Down!* [Film]. USA: Miramax.
Almodóvar, P. (Director) (1991). *High Heels* [Film]. Spain: El Deseo.
Almodóvar, P. (Director) (1999). *All About My Mother*. Spain: Warner Sogefilms.
Andresen, J. J. (1980). Rapunzel: The symbolism of the cutting of hair. *Journal of the American Psychoanalytic Association*, 28: 69–88.
Anzieu, D. (1989). *The Skin Ego*. New Haven, CT: Yale University Press.
Anzieu, D. (1990). *A Skin for Thought: Interviews with Gilbert Tarrab on Psychology and Psychoanalysis.* London: Karnac.
Aouizerate, B., Pujol, H., Grabot, D., Faytout, M., Suire, K., Braud, C., Auriacombe, M., Martin, D., Baudet, J. and Tignol, J. (2003). Body dysmorphic disorder in a sample of cosmetic surgery applicants. *European Psychiatry*, 18(7): 365–368.
Argentieri, S. (2009). Transvestism, transsexualism and transgender: Identification and imitation. In G. Ambrosio (ed.), *Tranvestism and Transsexualism in the Psychoanalytic Dimension*. London: Karnac.
Arias, R., Soifer, R. and Wainer, A. (1990). Disavowal of the danger of nuclear war: Effect of cultural factors on mental attitudes. *International Review of Psychoanalysis*, 17: 89–95.
Arizmendi, T. (2008). Nonverbal communication in the context of dissociative processes. *Psychoanalytic Psychology*, 25, 443–457.
Asseyer, H. (2002). The exclusion of the other. *The International Journal of Psychoanalysis*, 83: 1291–1309.
Baker, R. (1984). Some considerations arising from the treatment of a patient with necrophilic fantasies in late adolescence and young adulthood. *The International Journal of Psychoanalysis*, 65: 283–294.
Balint, M. (1959). *Thrills and Regressions*. New York: International University Press.
Barahal, H. (1940). The psychopathology of hair-plucking (trichotillomania). *Psychoanalytic Review*, 3: 291–310.
Barale, F. and Minazzi, V. (2008). Off the beaten track: Freud, sound and music. Statement of a problem and some historico-critical notes. *The International Journal of Psychoanalysis*, 89: 937–957.

Baudrillard, J. (1986). *America* (trans. C. Turner). London: Verso.
Baudrillard, J. (1988). *The Ecstasy of Communication* (trans. B. Schutze and C. Schutze). Paris: Editions Galilee.
Becker, E. (1973). *The Denial of Death*. New York: Free Press.
Bell, D. (2006). Existence in time: Development or catastrophe. *Psychoanalytic Quarterly*, 75: 783–805.
Benjamin, J. (1998). *Shadow of the Other: Intersubjectivity and Gender in Psychoanalysis*. New York: Routledge.
Berg, C. (1936) The unconscious significance of hair. *The International Journal of Psychoanalysis*, 17: 73–88.
Bick, E. (1964). Notes on infant observation in psychoanalytic training. *The International Journal of Psychoanalysis*, 45: 558–566.
Bick, E. (1968). The experience of the skin in early object relations. *The International Journal of Psychoanalysis*, 49: 558–566.
Bick, E. (1986). Further considerations on the function of the skin in early object relations: Findings from infant observation integrated into child and adult analysis. *British Journal of Psychotherapy*, 2: 292–299.
Bion, W. (1962). *Learning from Experience*. London: Karnac.
Bion, W. R. (1967). *Second Thoughts: Selected Papers on Psychoanalysis*. New York: Basic Books.
Bion, W. (1970). *Attention and Interpretation*. London: Maresfield.
Birksted-Breen, D. (1996). Phallus, penis and mental space. *The International Journal of Psychoanalysis*, 77: 649–657.
Birksted-Breen, D. (2009). 'Reverberation time', dreaming and the capacity to dream. *International Journal of Psychoanalysis*, 90: 35–51.
Bleger, J. (1967[2012]). Psycho-analysis of the psycho-analytic setting. In J. Churcher and L. Bleger (eds), *Symbiosis and Ambiguity: A Psychoanalytic Study*. London: Routledge.
Blos, P. (1967). The second individuation process of adolescence. *Psychoanalytic Study of the Child*, 22: 162–186.
Bollas, C. (1994). Aspects of the erotic transference. *Psychoanalytic Inquiry*, 14: 572–590.
Bonaparte, M. (1949). *The Life and Works of Edgar Allan Poe: A Psycho-Analytic Interpretation*. London: Imago.
Boris, H. (1987). Tolerating nothing. *Contemporary Psychoanalysis*, 23: 351–366.
Boris, H. (1994). About time. *Contemporary Psychoanalysis*, 30: 301–322.
Briggs, S. (2002). Working with adolescents: A contemporary psychodynamic approach. London: Palgrave.
Britton, R. (1998). *Belief and Imagination*. London: Routledge.
Britton, R. and Steiner, J. (1994). Interpretation: Selected fact or overvalued idea? *The International Journal of Psychoanalysis*, 75: 1069–1078.
Bronstein, C. (2009). Negotiating development: Corporeal reality and unconscious phantasy in adolescence. *Bulletin of the British Psychoanalytical Society*, 45(1): 17–26.
Bronstein, C. (2013). Finding unconscious phantasy in the session: Recognizing form. *Bulletin of the British Psychoanalytical Society*, 49(3): 16–21.
Bucci, W. (2008). The role of bodily experience in emotional organisation: New perspectives on the multiple code theory. In S. Anderson (ed.), *Bodies in Treatment*. Hove: Analytic Press.
Burka, J. B. (2008). The therapist's body in reality and fantasy: A perspective from an overweight therapist. In B. Gerson (ed.), *The Therapist as a Person: Life Crises, Life Choices, Life Experiences and Their Effects on Treatment*. Hillsdale, NJ: The Analytic Press, pp. 255–275.

Busch, F. (1995). Beginning a psychoanalytic treatment: Establishing an analytic frame. *Journal of the American Psychoanalytic Association*, 43: 449–468.
Butler, J. (1998). *Bodies that Matter: On the Discursive Limits of Sex*. London: Routledge.
Butler, J. (2003). *Undoing Gender*. London: Routledge.
Buxbaum, E. (1960). Hair pulling and fetishism. *The Psychoanalytic Study of the Child*, 15: 243–260.
Byrd, A. and Tharps, L. (2011). *Hair Story: Untangling the Roots of Black Hair in America*. New York: St Martin's Griffin.
Calef, V. and Weinshel, E. (1972). On certain neurotic equivalents of necrophilia. *The International Journal of Psychoanalysis*, 53: 67–75.
Caper, R. (1999). *A Mind of One's Own: A Kleinian View of Self and Object*. New York: Routledge.
Celenza, A. (2005). Vis-à-vis the couch: Where is psychoanalysis? *The International Journal of Psychoanalysis*, 86: 1645–1659.
Chasseguet-Smirgel, J. (1983). Perversion and the universal law. *International Review of Psycho-Analysis*, 10: 293–301.
Chasseguet-Smirgel, J. (1990). Reflections on some thought disorders in non-psychotic patients: Certain disturbances of thinking in individuals and groups. *Scandinavian Psychoanalytic Review*, 12: 5–21.
Chung, W., De Vries, G. and Swaab, D. (2002). The sexual differentiation of the bed nucleus of the *stria terminalis* in humans may extend into adulthood. *Journal of Neuroscience*, 22: 1027–1033.
Churcher, J. and Bleger, L. (eds) (2012). Introduction. In *Symbiosis and Ambiguity: A Psychoanalytic Study*. London: Routledge.
Civitarese, G. (2008). *The Intimate Room: Theory and Technique of the Analytic Field*. London: Routledge.
Cixous, F. (1976). The laugh of Medusa. In E. Marks and I. de Courtivon (eds), *New French Feminisms*. Brighton: Harvester.
Clark Nunes, V. (2006). All holes are the same: Emerging from the confusion. *The International Journal of Psychoanalysis*, 87: 1587–1601.
Clyman, R. B. (1991). The procedural organisation of emotions: A contribution from cognitive science to the psychoanalytic theory of therapeutic action. *Journal of the American Psychoanalytic Association*, 39S: 349–382.
Cohen-Kettenis, P. T., Schagen, S. E., Steensma, T. D., De Vries, A. L. and Delemarre-van de Waal, H. A. (2011). Puberty suppression in a gender dysphoric adolescent: A 22-year follow-up. *Archives of Sexual Behavior*, 40: 843–847.
Corson, R. (2012). *Fashions in Hair*. London: Peter Owen.
Creed, B. (2005). Horror and the monstrous-feminine. In J. Donald (ed.), *An Imaginary Abjection*. London: British Film Institute.
Curtis, A. E. (2007). The claustrum: Sequestration of cyberspace. *Psychoanalytic Review*, 94: 99–139.
Damasio, A. R. (1999). *The Feeling of what Happens: Body and Emotion in the Making of Consciousness*. New York: Harcourt Brace.
Damasio, A. R. (2006). *Descartes' Error: Emotion, Reason and the Human Brain*. London: Vintage.
Davies, M. (1989). The body in child analysis. *The International Journal of Psychoanalysis*, 34: 129–141.
Dean, T. (2002). *Beyond Sexuality*. Chicago: University of Chicago Press.

Delemarre-van de Waal, H. A. and Cohen-Kettenis, P. T. (2006). Clinical management of gender identity disorder in adolescents: A protocol on psychological and paediatric endocrinology aspects. *European Journal of Endocrinology*, 155: S131–S137.

Denis, A. (1995). Temporality and modes of language. *The International Journal of Psychoanalysis*, 76: 1109–1119.

Denis, P. (2010). Primary homosexuality: The foundation of contradictions. In D. Birksted-Breen and S. Flanders (eds), *Reading French Psychoanalysis*. London: Routledge.

De Toffoli, C. (2011). The living body in psychoanalytic experience. *The Psychoanalytic Quarterly*, 80: 585–618.

Dhejne, C. Lichtenstein, P., Boman, M., Johansson, A. L., Langstrom, N. and Landen, M. (2011). Long-term follow-up of transsexual persons undergoing sex reassignment surgery: Cohort study in Sweden. *PLoS One*, 6(2): e16885.

Diamond, D. and Blatt, S. (2007). Introduction. In D. Diamond, S. Blatt and J. Lichtenberg (eds), *Attachment and Sexuality*. New York: Analytic Press.

Di Ceglie, D. with Freedman, D. (ed.) (1998). *Stranger in My Own Body: Atypical Gender Identity Development and Mental Health*. London: Karnac.

Di Ceglie, D., Skagerberg, E., Baron-Cohen, S. and Auyeung, B. (2014). Empathising and systemising in adolescents with gender dysphoria. *Opticon1826*, 6, March.

Dimen, M. (1991). Deconstructing difference: Gender, splitting and transitional space. *Psychoanalytic Dialogues*, 1: 335–352.

Dini, K. (2009). Internet interaction: The effect on patient lives and analytic process. *Journal of the American Psychoanalytic Association*, 57: 979–988.

Doel, M. and Clarke, B. (2006). Virtual worlds: Simulation, suppletion, s(ed)uction and simulacra. In M. Crang, P. Crang and J. May (eds), *Virtual Geographies*. London: Routledge.

Donnet, J. L. (2005). *La Situation Analysante*. Paris: Presses Universitaires de France.

Douglas, M. (1966). *Purity and Danger: An Analysis of Concepts of Pollution and Taboo*. London: Routledge and Kegan Paul.

Edelman, G. M. (1992). *Bright Air, Brilliant Fire: On the Matter of the Mind*. New York: Basic Books.

Edgcumbe, R. and Burgner, M. (1975). The phallic-narcissistic phase: A differentiation between preoedipal and oedipal aspects of phallic development. *The Psychoanalytic Study of the Child*, 30: 161–180.

Edgerton, M., Langmann, M. and Pruzinsky, T. (1990). Patient seeking symmetrical recontouring for perceived deformatives in the width of the face and skull. *Aesthetic Plastic Surgery*, 14: 59–73.

Elliott, P. (2001). A psychoanalytic reading of transsexual embodiment. *Studies in Gender and Sexuality*, 2: 295–325.

Ely, D. (1964). *Seconds: A Novel*. London: André Deutsch.

Ercolani, M., Baldaro, B., Rossi, N., Trombini, E. and Trombini, G. (1999). Short-term outcome of rhinoplasty for medical or cosmetic indication. *Journal of Psychosomatic Research*, 47(3): 277–281.

Erikson, E. (1968). *Identity*. London: Faber.

Ervin, B., Turk, C., Heimberg, R., Fresco, D. and Hantula, D. (2004). The Internet: Home to a severe population of individuals with social anxiety disorder? *Journal of Anxiety Disorders*, 18: 629–646.

Ewald, F. (1993). Two infinities of risk. In B. Massumi (ed.), *The Politics of Everyday Fear*. Minneapolis: University of Minnesota Press, pp. 221–228.

Fain, M. (1971). Prélude à la vie fantasmatique. *Revue Française de Psychanalyse*, 35: 291–364.

Favazza, A. (1996). *Bodies Under Siege: Self-Mutilation and Body Modification in Culture and Society*. Baltimore, MD: Johns Hopkins University Press.
Featherstone, M. (ed.) (2000). *Body Modification*. London: Sage.
Fenichel, O. (1945). *The Psychoanalytic Theory of Neurosis*. New York: Norton.
Ferenczi, S. (1938). *Thalassa: A Theory of Genitality*. New York: Psychoanalytic Quarterly.
Ferrari, B. (2004). *From the Eclipse of the Body to the Dawn of Thought*. London: Free Association Books.
Ferro, A. (2003). Marcella: The transition from explosive sensoriality to the ability to think. *The Psychoanalytic Quarterly*, 72: 183–200.
Ferro, A. and Basile, R. (2006). Unity of analysis: Similarities and differences in the analysis of children and grown-ups. *The Psychoanalytic Quarterly*, 75: 477–500.
Flanders, S. (2009). On the concept of adolescent breakdown. *Bulletin of the British Psychoanalytical Society*, 45(1): 27–34.
Fonagy, P. (2001). *Attachment Theory and Psychoanalysis*. London: Karnac.
Fonagy, P. (2006). Psychosexuality and psychoanalysis. In P. Fonagy, R. Krause and M. Leuzinger-Bohleber (eds), *Identity Gender and Sexuality*. London: IPA Publications.
Fonagy, P. (2008). A genuinely developmental theory of sexual enjoyment and its implications for psychoanalytic technique. *Journal of the American Psychoanalytic Association*, 56: 11–36.
Fonagy, P. and Target, M. (1996). Playing with reality: I. Theory of mind and the normal development of psychic reality. *The International Journal of Psychoanalysis*, 77: 217–233.
Fonagy, P. and Target, M. (2000). Playing with reality. *The International Journal of Psychoanalysis*, 81: 853–873.
Fonagy, P. and Target, M. (2007). The rooting of the mind in the body: New links between attachment theory and psychoanalytic thought. *Journal of the American Psychoanalytic Association*, 55(2): 411–456.
Fonagy, P., Gergely, G., Jurist, E., Target, M. (2002). *Affect Regulation, Mentalisation and the Development of the Self*. New York: Other Press.
Fonagy, P., Gergely, G., Jurist, E. L. and Target, M. (2004). *Affect Regulation, Mentalization, and the Development of the Self*. London: H. Karnac.
Foucault, M. (1976). *A History of Sexuality: The Will to Knowledge, Vol. 1*. London: Penguin.
Foucault, M. (1980). *Power/Knowledge: Selected Interviews and Other Writings*. New York: Pantheon.
Fraser, K. (2007). 'Now I am ready to tell how bodies are changed into different bodies …': Ovid, the metamorphoses. In D. Heller (ed.), *Makeover Television: Realities Remodelled*. London: I. B. Tauris.
Freud, S. (1905). Three Essays on the Theory of Sexuality. In *The Standard Edition of the Complete Psychological Works of Sigmund Freud*. London: Hogarth (*Standard Edition*, 7).
Freud, S. (1913). Further recommendations on the technique of psychoanalysis on beginning the treatment. *Standard Edition*, 12: 121–144.
Freud, S. (1914). On narcissism. *Standard Edition*, 14.
Freud. S. (1915). Instincts and their Vicissitudes. *Standard Edition*, 14.
Freud, S. (1917). Mourning and Melancholia. *Standard Edition*, 14: 237–258.
Freud, S. (1919). A child is being beaten. *Standard Edition*, 17: 177–243.
Freud, S. (1923). The ego and the id. *Standard Edition*, 19: 12–66.
Freud, S. (1927). Fetishism. *Standard Edition*, 21: 149–157.
Freud, S. (1930). Civilization and its discontents. *Standard Edition*, 21: 64–145.
Frosh, S. (1994). *Sexual Difference: Masculinity and Femininity in Psychoanalysis*. London: Routledge.

Furedi, F. (2004). *Therapy Culture: Cultivating Vulnerability in an Uncertain Age*. London: Routledge.
Gaddini, E. (1969). On Imitation. *The International Journal of Psychoanalysis*, 50: 475–484.
Gaddini, E. (1987). Notes on the mind–body question. *The International Journal of Psychoanalysis*, 68: 315–329.
Gallagher, S. (2005). *How the Body Shapes the Mind*. Oxford: Clarendon Press.
Gallese, V. (2006). Intentional attunement: A neurophysiological perspective on social cognition and its disruption in autism. *Brain Research*, 1079(1): 15–24.
Gallese, V., Eagle, M. N. and Migone, P. (2007). Intentional attunement: Mirror neurons and the neural underpinnings of interpersonal relations. *Journal of the American Psychoanalytic Association*, 55, 131–176.
Galski, T. (1983). Hair pulling (Trichotillomania). *Psychoanalytic Review*, 70: 331–345.
Garcia-Falgueras, A. and Swaab, D. (2008). A sex difference in the hypothalamic uncinate nucleus: Relationship to gender identity. *Brain*, 131: 3132–3146.
Garland, C. (2002). *Understanding Trauma: A Psychoanalytical Approach* (2nd enlarged edn). London: Karnac.
Gergely, G. and Unoka, Z. (2008). Attachment, affect-regulation and mentalization: The developmental origins of the representational affective self. In C. Sharp, P. Fonagy and I. Goodyer (eds), *Social Cognition and Developmental Psychopathology*. Oxford: Oxford University Press, pp. 303–340.
Gibbs, P. L. (2007). Reality in cyberspace: Analysands' use of the Internet and ordinary everyday psychosis. *Psychoanalytic Review*, 94: 11–38.
Giddens, A. (1991). *Modernity and Self Identify*. Cambridge: Polity Press.
Gillespie, W. (1940). A contribution to the study of fetishism. *The International Journal of Psychoanalysis*, 21: 401–415.
Gilman, S. (1999). *Making the Body Beautiful: A Cultural History of Aesthetic Surgery*. Princeton, NJ: Princeton University Press.
Glasser, M. (1979). Some aspects of the role of aggression in the perversions. In I. Rosen (ed.), *The Pathology and Treatment of Sexual Deviations*. Oxford: Oxford University Press.
Glasser, M. (1992). Problems in the psychoanalysis of certain narcissistic disorders. *The International Journal of Psychoanalysis*, 73(3): 493–503.
Glover, E. (1933). The relation of perversion formation to the development of the reality sense. *The International Journal of Psychoanalysis*, 14: 486–504.
Goldberg, L. (1979). Remarks on transference–countertransference in psychotic states. *The International Journal of Psychoanalysis*, 60: 347–356.
Goldberger, M. (1995). The couch as defense and as potential for enactment. *The Psychoanalytic Quarterly*, 64: 23–42.
Goldner, V. (1991). Towards a critical relational theory of gender. *Psychoanalytic Dialogues: The International Journal of Relational Perspectives*, 1: 249–272.
Goldner, V. (2011). Trans: Gender in Free Fall. *Psychoanalytic Dialogues: The International Journal of Relational Perspectives*, 21: 159–171.
Goldwyn, R. (2006). Psychological aspects of plastic surgery: A surgeon's observations and reflections. In D. Sarwer, T. Pruzinsky, T. Cash, R. Goldwyn, J. Persing and L. Whitaker (eds), *Psychological Aspects of Reconstructive and Cosmetic Plastic Surgery*. Philadelphia, PA: Lippincott, Williams and Wilkins.
Goodall, J. (2000). An order of pure decision: Un-natural selection in the work of Stelarc and Orlan. In M. Featherstone (ed.), *Body Modification*. London: Routledge.

Green, A. (1998). The primordial mind and the work of the negative. *The International Journal of Psychoanalysis*, 79 (4): 649–665.
Green, A. (2000). The intrapsychic and intersubjective in psychoanalysis. *Psychoanalytic Quarterly*, 69 (1): 1–39.
Green, A. (2004). Thirdness and psychoanalytic concepts. *Psychoanalytic Quarterly*, 73: 99–135.
Green, R. and Fleming, D. (1990). Transsexual surgery follow-up: Status in the 1990s. *Annual Review of Sex Research*, 1: 163–174.
Grinberg, L. and Grinberg, R. (1981). Modalities of object relationships in the psychoanalytic process. *Contemporary Psychoanalysis*, 17: 290–320.
Grosz, E. (1990). *Jacques Lacan: A Feminist Introduction*. London: Routledge.
Guignard, F. (2008). Envy in Western society: Today and tomorrow. In P. Roth and A. Lemma (eds), *Envy and Gratitude Revisited*. London: Karnac.
Haag, G. (1985). La mère et le bébé dans les deux moitiés du corps. *Neuropsychiatrie de l'enfance*, 33: 107–114.
Hägglund, T. and Piha, H. (1980). The inner space of the body image. *Psychoanalytic Quarterly*, 49: 256–283.
Hakeem, A. (2008). Changing sex or changing minds: Specialist psychotherapy and transsexuality. *Group Analysis*, 41(2): 182–196.
Hakeem, A. (2010). Deconstructing gender in trans-gender identities. *Group Analysis*, 43(2): 141–154.
Haneke, M. (Director) (2012). *Amour* [Film]. USA: Sony Pictures Classic.
Harris, A. (1991). Gender as Contradiction. *Psychoanalytic Dialogues*, 1: 197–224.
Harris, A. (2011). Gender as a strange attractor: Discussion of the transgender symposium. *Psychoanalytic Dialogues: The International Journal of Relational Perspectives*, 21(2): 230–238.
Hartocollis, P. (1974). Origins of time – a reconstruction of the ontogenetic development of the sense of time based on object-relations theory. *Psychoanalytic Quarterly*, 43: 243–261.
Hayles, C. (1999). *How We Became Posthuman*. Chicago: Chicago University Press.
Heartney, E. (2004). Orlan: Magnificent 'and' best. In R. Durand and E. Heartney (eds), *Orlan: Carnal Art*. Paris: Flammarion.
Hermann, I. (1976). Clinging – going-in-search – A contrasting pair of instincts and their relation to sadism and masochism. *The Psychoanalytic Quarterly*, 45: 5–36.
Hillis, K. (1999). *Digital Sensations: Space, Identity, and Embodiment in Virtual Reality*. Minneapolis: University of Minnesota Press.
Hinshelwood, R. (2013). *Research on the Couch: Single Case Studies, Subjectivity, and Psychoanalytic Knowledge*. London: Routledge.
Hoffer, W. (1949). Mouth, hand and ego integration. *Psychoanalytic Study of the Child*, 3: 49–56.
Hoffer, W. (1950). Development of the body ego. *Psychoanalytic Study of the Child*, 5: 18–24.
Hulshoff, P., Cohen-Kettenis, P., Van Haren, N., Peper, J., Brans, R., Cahn, W., Schnack, H. Gooren, L. and Kahn, R. (2006). Changing your sex changes your brain: Influences of testosterone and oestrogen on adult human brain structure. *European Journal of Endocrinology*, 155: S107–S114.
Hurst, R. (2012). Negotiating femininity with and through mother–daughter and patient–surgeon relationships in cosmetic surgery narratives. *Women's Studies International Forum*, 35(6): 447–457.
Iacoboni, M. (2008). *Mirroring People: The New Science of How We Connect with Others*. New York: Farrar, Straus & Giroux.

Isaacs, S. (1983). The nature and function of phantasy. In M. Klein, P. Heimann, S. Isaacs and J. Riviere (eds), *Developments in Psychoanalysis*. London: Hogarth Press, pp. 67–121.

Isaacs-Elmhirst, S. (1988). The Kleinian setting for child analysis. *International Review of Psycho-Analysis*, 15: 5–12.

Jacobsen, P., Hölmich, L., McLaughlin, J., Johansen, C., Olsen, J. Kjøller, K. and Friis, S. (2004). Mortality and suicide among Danish women with cosmetic breast implants. *Archives of Internal Medicine*, 164: 2450–2455.

Jones, R., Wheelwright, S., Farrell, K., Martin, M., Green, R., Di Ceglie, D. and Baron-Cohen, S. (2011). Brief report: Female-to-male transsexual people and autistic traits. *Journal of Autism Development Disorders*, DOI 10.10007/s10803-011-1227-8.

Josipovici, G. (1996). *Touch*. New Haven: Yale University Press.

Kant, I. (1787[2007]). *Critique of Pure Reason*. London: Penguin Modern Classics.

Klein, M. (1926). Infant analysis. *The International Journal of Psychoanalysis*, 7: 31–63.

Klein, M. (1936). On Weaning. In *Love, Guilt and Reparation and Other Works, 1921–1945*. London: Virago Press.

Klein, M. (1937). Love, Guilt and Reparation. In *Love, Guilt and Reparation and Other Works, 1921–1945*. London: Virago Press.

Klein, M. (1940). Mourning and its relation to manic depressive states. In *Love, Guilt and Reparation and Other Works, 1921–1945*. London: Virago Press.

Klein, M. (1957). *Envy and Gratitude and Other Works*. London: Virago Press.

Krishnan, K., Davidson, J. and Guajardo, C. (1985). Trichotillomania: a review. *Comprehensive Psychiatry*, 26: 123–128.

Kristeva, J. (1984). *Powers of Horror: An Essay on Abjection* (trans. L. S. Roudiez). New York: Columbia University Press.

Kristeva, J. (1995). *New Maladies of the Soul*. New York: Columbia University Press.

Krueger, D. (1989). *Body Self and Psychological Self*. New York: Brunner/Mazel.

Krueger, D. (2002). Psychodymanic perspectives on body image. In T. Cash and T. Pruzinsky (eds), *Body Image: Handbook of Theory, Research and Clinical Practice*. New York: The Guildford Press.

Kulish, N. (2002). Female sexuality. *The Psychoanalytic Study of the Child*, 57: 151–176.

Lacan, J. (1977). *Ecrits*. London: Tavistock.

Lakoff, G. (1987). *Women, Fire, and Dangerous Things: What Categories Reveal about the Mind*. Chicago: University of Chicago Press.

Lakoff, G. and Johnson, M. (1999). *Philosophy in the Flesh: The Embodied Mind and Its Challenge to Western Thought*. New York: Basic Books.

Langs, R. (1998). *Ground Rules in Psychotherapy and Counselling*. London: Karnac Books.

Laufer, E. (1981). The adolescent's use of the body in object relationships and in the transference. *Psychoanalytic Study of the Child*, 36: 163–180.

Laufer, M. (1968). The body image, the function of masturbation and adolescence: Problems of the ownership of the body. *Psychoanalytic Study of the Child*, 23: 114–137.

Laufer, M. and Laufer, M. E. (1984). *Adolescence and Developmental Breakdown: A Psychoanalytic View*. New Haven: Yale University Press.

Layton, L. (1997). The doer behind the deed: Tensions and intersections between Butler's vision of performativity and relational psychoanalysis. *Gender and Psychoanalysis*, 2: 131–155.

Leach, E. (1958). Magical hair. *The Journal of the Royal Anthropological Institute of Great Britain and Ireland*, 88(2): 147–164.

Lecours, S. (2007). Supportive interventions and non-symbolic mental functioning. *The International Journal of Psychoanalysis*, 88: 895–915.

Lemma, A. (2005). The many faces of lying. *The International Journal of Psychoanalysis*, 86: 737–753.
Lemma, A. (2009). Being seen or being watched? A Psychoanalytic perspective on body dysmorphia. *The International Journal of Psychoanalysis*, 90(4): 753–771.
Lemma, A. (2010). *Under the Skin: A Psychoanalytic Study of Body Modification*. London: Routledge.
Lemma, A. (2012). Research off the couch: Re-visiting the transsexual conundrum. *Psychoanalytic Psychotherapy*, 26(4).
Lemma, A. (2013). The body one has and the body one is: Understanding the transsexual's need to be seen. *The International Journal of Psychoanalysis*, 94: 277–292.
Lemma, A. and Levy, S. (2004). The impact of trauma on the psyche: Internal and external processes. In S. Levy and A. Lemma (eds), *The Perversion of Loss: Psychoanalytic Perspectives on Trauma*. London: Whurr.
Lichtenberg, J. (1978). The testing of reality from the standpoint of the body self. *Journal of the American Psychoanalytic Association*, 26: 453–484.
Limentani, A. (1979). The significance of transsexualism in relation to some basic psychoanalytic concepts. *International Review of Psychoanalysis*, 6: 139–153.
Lingiardi, V. and De Bei, F. (2011). Questioning the couch: Historical and clinical perspectives. *Psychoanalytic Psychology*, 28: 389–404.
Link, C. L., Lutfey, K. E., Steers, W. D. and McKinlay, J. B. (2007). Is abuse causally related to urologic symptoms? Results from the Boston Area Community Health (BACH) Survey. *European Urology*, 52: 397–406.
Loewald, H. (1972). The experience of time. *The Psychoanalytic Study of the Child*, 27: 401–410.
Lombardi, R. (2002). Primitive mental states and the body: A personal view of Armando B. Ferrari's concrete original object. *The International Journal of Psychoanalysis*, 83: 363–381.
Lombardi, R. (2005). On the psychoanalytic treatment of a psychotic breakdown. *The Psychoanalytic Quarterly*, 74: 1069–1099.
Lombardi, R. and Pola, M. (2010). The body, adolescence, and psychosis. *The International Journal of Psychoanalysis*, 91(6): 1419–1444.
Mahler, M. and Furer, M. (1968). *On Human Symbiosis and the Vicissitudes of Individuation*. New York: International Universities Press.
Main, M. (1990). Parental aversion to infant contact. In K. Barnard and T. Brazelton (eds), *Touch: The Foundation of Experience*. Madison, CT: International Universities Press.
Mancia, M. (1994). *L'Eclissi del corpo: una ipotesi psicoanalytica* by Armando B. Ferrari. Roma: Borla. *The International Journal of Psychoanalysis*, 75: 1283–1286.
Marty, P. and De M'Uzan, M. (1963). La 'pensee operatoire'. *Revue française de psychoanalyse*, 27: 345–356.
McDougall, J. (1989). *Theatres of the Body*. London: Free Association Books.
Meadows, M. S. (2008). *I, Avatar: The Culture and Consequences of having a Second Life*. Berkeley, CA: New Riders.
Meltzer, D. (1967a). Identification and socialization in adolescents. *Contemporary Psychoanalysis*, 3: 96–103.
Meltzer, D. (1967b). *The Psychoanalytic Process*. London: Heinemann.
Mendelsohn, D. (2010). The wizard. *New York Review of Books,* 25 March.
Merleau-Ponty, M. (1962). *Phenomenology of Perception*. New York: Humanities Press.
Mifflin, M. (1997). *Bodies of Subversion*. New York: Juno.

Mintel, (2010). Non-surgical cosmetic procedures top the million mark for first time. Available online at www.mintel.com/press-centre/press-releases/577/non-surgical-cosmetic-procedures-top-the-million-mark-for-first-time (accessed September 2011).

Mitchell, J. (2004). The difference between gender and sexual difference. In I. Matthis (ed.), *Dialogues on Sexuality, Gender and Psychoanalysis*. London: Karnac.

Morahan-Martin, J. (2008). Internet abuse: Emerging trends and lingering questions. In A. Barak (ed.), *Psychological Aspects of Cyberspace: Theory, Research, Applications*. Cambridge: Cambridge University Press, pp. 32–69.

Nieder, T. and Richter-Appelt, H. (2009). Parallels and differences between gender identity disorders and body integrity identity disorder and implications for research and treatment of BIID. In A. Stirn, A. Thiel and S. Oddo (eds), *Body Integrity Identity Disorder: Psychological, Neurobiological, Ethical and Legal Aspects*. Berlin: Science Publishers.

Ogden, T. (1982). *Projective Identification and the Psychotherapeutic Technique*. New York: Jason Aronson.

Ogden, T. (1989). *The Primitive Edge of Experience*. Northvale, NJ: Jason Aronson.

Ogden, T. (1992). Comments on transference and countertransference in the initial analytic meeting. *Psychoanalytic Inquiry*, 12: 225–247.

Ogden, T. (1997). Reverie and interpretation. *The Psychoanalytic Quarterly*, 66: 567–595.

Olivier, C. (1989). *Jocasta's Children: The Imprint of the Mother*. London: Routledge.

Orbach, S. (2009). *Bodies*. London: Profile.

O'Shaughnessy, E. (1997). Enclaves and excursions. In D. Bell (ed.), *Reason and Passion*. London: Karnac.

O'Shaughnessy, E. (1999). Relating to the superego. *The International Journal of Psychoanalysis*, 80: 861–870.

Ovesey, L. and Person, E. (1973). Gender identity and sexual psychopathology. *Journal of the American Academy of Psychoanalysis and Dynamic Psychiatry*, 1: 53–72.

Parsons, M. (2007). Raiding the inarticulate: The internal analytic setting and listening beyond countertransference. *The International Journal of Psychoanalysis*, 88: 1441–1456.

Peringer, J. (2006). The wish to look and the hatred of seeing. *Bulletin of the British Psychoanalytical Society*, 42(1): 18–27.

Person, E. S. (2005). A new look at core gender and gender role identity in women. *Journal of the American Psychoanalytic Association*, 53: 1045–1058.

Pfeffer, L. (2004). L'imaginaire olfcatif: les fantasmes d'une odeur pénétrante. In C. Mechin, L. Bianquis and D. Le Breton (eds), *Le Corps et ses orifices*. Paris: L'Harmattan.

Phillips, K., Dufresne, R., Wilkel, C. and Vittorio, C. (2000). Rate of body dysmorphic disorder in dermatology patients. *Journal of the American Academy of Dermatology*, 42(3): 436–441.

Pine, F. (2000). Preface. In M. Mahler, F. Pine and A. Bergman (eds), *The Psychological Birth of the Human Infant*. New York: Basic Books.

Pines, D. (1993). *A Woman's Unconscious Use of Her Body*. London: Virago Press.

Pitts-Taylor, V. (2003). *In the Flesh: The Cultural Politics of Body Modification*. New York: Palgrave Macmillan.

Pitts-Taylor, V. (2007). *Surgery Junkies: Wellness and Pathology in Cosmetic Culture*. New Brunswick, NJ: Rutgers University Press.

Pratarelli, M. (2005). Sex, shyness, and social Internet use. Paper presented to the American Psychological Association, Washington, DC.

Proner, B. (2005). Bodily states of anxiety. *Journal of Analytical Psychology*, 50: 311–331.

Quinodoz, D. (1998). A fe/male transsexual patient in psychoanalysis. *The International Journal of Psychoanalysis*, 79: 95–111.

Quinodoz, D. (2002). Termination of a Fe/Male Transsexual Patient's Analysis. *The International Journal of Psychoanalysis*, 83: 783–798.
Raphael-Leff, J. (in press). *Aliens and Alienation: Mind Invaders and Body Snatchers*.
Raulet, G. (1991). The new utopia: Communication technologies. *Telos*, 87: 39–58.
Resnik, S. (2005). *Glacial Times: A Journey through the World of Madness*. London Routledge.
Rey, H. (1994). *Universals of Psychoanalysis and the Treatment of Psychotic and Borderline States*. London: Free Association Books.
Rhode, M. (2005). Mirroring, imitation, identification: The sense of self in relation to the mother's internal world. *Journal of Child Psychotherapy*, 31(1): 52–71.
Robins, K. (2001). Seeing the world from a safe distance. *Science as Culture*, 10(4): 531–539.
Robins, K. and Webster, S. (1999). *Times of Techno-Culture: From the Information Society to the Virtual Life*. London: Routledge.
Rosch, E. (1992). *Cognition and Categorization*. Hillsdale, NJ: Erlbaum.
Rosen, M. (2012). *Dignity: Its History and Meaning*. Cambridge, MA: Harvard University Press.
Rosenfeld, H. (1971). A clinical approach to the psychoanalytic therapy of the life and death instincts: An investigation into the aggressive aspects of narcissism. *The International Journal of Psychoanalysis*, 52: 169–178.
Rosenfeld, H. (1987). *Listening and Interpretation: Therapeutic and Anti-Therapeutic Factors in the Psychoanalytic Treatment of Psychotic, Borderline, and Neurotic Patients*. London: Tavistock.
Ross, J. M. (1999). Once more onto the couch. *Journal of the American Psychoanalytic Association*, 47: 91–111.
Ryan, R. (2007). *This Is for You*. London: Sceptre.
Saferstein, R. (2014). *Criminalistics: An Introduction to Forensic Science*. London: Pearson Education.
Sandler, J. (1994). Phantasy, defence and the representational world. *Infant Mental Health*, 15: 26–35.
Sartre, J.-P. (1943). *Being and Nothingness*. London: Methuen.
Sarwer, D. (2006). Psychological assessment of cosmetic surgery patients. In D. Sarwer, T. Pruzinsky, T. Cash, R. Goldwyn, J. Persing and L. Whitaker (eds), *Psychological Aspects of Reconstructive and Cosmetic Plastic Surgery*. Philadelphia, PA: Lippincott, Williams and Wilkins.
Sarwer, D., Wadden, T., Pertschuk, M. and Whitaker, L. (1998). Body image dissatisfaction and body dysmorphic disorder in 100 cosmetic surgery patients. *Plastic and Reconstructive Surgery*, 101(6): 1644–1649.
Sarwer, D., Zanville, H., LaRossa, D., Bartlett, S., Change, B., Low, D. and Whitaker, L. (2004). Mental health histories and psychiatric medication usage among persons who sought cosmetic surgery. *Plastic and Reconstructive Surgery*, 114: 1927–1933.
Scarfone, D. (2002). Sexual and actual. In Widlocher, D. (ed.), *Infantile Sexuality and Attachment*. New York: Other Press.
Schacter, D. L. (1995). *Memory Systems 1994*. Cambridge, MA: MIT Press.
Schachter, J. and Kächele, H. (2010). The couch in psychoanalysis. *Contemporary Psychoanalysis*, 46: 439–459.
Schilder, P. (1950). *The Image and Appearance of the Human Body*. New York: International University's Press.
Segal, H. (1953). A necrophilic phantasy. *The International Journal of Psychoanalysis*, 34: 98–101.

Segal, H. (1964). Symposium on fantasy: Fantasy and other mental processes. *The International Journal of Psychoanalysis*, 45: 191–194.
Segal, H. (1986). Notes on symbol formation. In *The Work of Hanna Segal: A Kleinian Approach to Clinical Practice: Delusion and Artistic Creativity and Other Psychoanalytic Essays*. London: Free Association Books.
Sexton, A. (1971). *Transformations*. Boston: Houghton Mifflin.
Shai, D. and Fonagy, P. (2013). Beyond words: Parental embodied mentalizing and the parent–infant dance. *Nature and Formation of Social Connections: From Brain to Group, IDC, Herzliya*. Washington, DC: American Psychological Association.
Shelley, M. (1818). *Frankenstein*. London: Penguin Classics.
Sidoli, M. (1996). Farting as a defence against unspeakable dread. *Journal of Analytical Psychology*, 41: 165–178.
Silverman, K. (1996). *The Threshold of the Visible World*. New York: Routledge.
Simon, D. (2000). *Hair*. New York: St Martin's Press.
Socarides, C. (1970). A psychoanalytic study of the desire for sexual transformation (transsexualism): The plaster of Paris man. *The International Journal of Psychoanalysis*, 51: 341–349.
Sodré, I. (2002). Certainty and doubt: transparency and opacity of the object. *Bulletin of the British Psychoanalytical Society*, 38: 1–8.
Sperling, M. (1954). The use of the hair as a bi-sexual symbol. *Psychoanalytic Review*, 41: 363–365.
Steensma, T. D., Biemond, R., Boer, F. D. and Cohen-Kettenis, P. T. (2011). Desisting and persisting gender dysphoria after childhood: A qualitative follow-up study. *Clinical Child Psychology and Psychiatry*, 16: 499–516.
Steiner, J. (1993). *Psychic Retreats*. London: Routledge.
Steiner, J. (2004). Gaze, dominance and humiliation in the Schreber case. *The International Journal of Psychoanalysis*, 85: 269–284.
Steiner, J. (2011). *Seeing and Being Seen*. London: Routledge.
Suchet, M. (2011). Crossing over. *Psychoanalytic Dialogues*, 21: 172–191.
Suler, J. (2002). Identity management in cyberspace. *Journal of Applied Psychoanalytic Studies*, 4: 455–460.
Suler, J. (2004). Computer and cyberspace 'addiction'. *International Journal of Applied Psychoanalytic Studies*, 1: 359–362.
Suler, J. (2008). Cybertherapeutic theory and techniques. In A. Barak (ed.), *Psychological Aspects of Cyberspace: Theory, Research, Applications*. Cambridge: Cambridge University Press, pp. 102–128.
Süskind, P. (1986). *Perfume: The Story of a Murderer*. New York: A. A. Knopf.
Swami, V. and Mammadova, A. (2012). Associations between consideration of cosmetic surgery, perfectionism dimensions, appearance schemas, relationship satisfaction, excessive reassurance-seeking, and love styles. *Individual Differences Research*, 10(2): 81–94.
Thomson, J. (1995). *The Media and Modernity: A Social Theory of the Media*. Cambridge: Polity Press.
Tintner, J. (2007). Bypassing barriers to change? *Contemporary Psychoanalysis*, 43: 121–134.
Toronto, E. (2009). Time out of mind: Dissociation in the virtual world. *Psychoanalytic Psychology*, 2: 117–133.
Tranströmer, T. (2006). *The Great Enigma: New Collected Poems* (trans. R. Fulton). New York: New Directions Books.

Tuckett, D. (2011). Inside and outside the window: Some fundamental elements in the theory of psychoanalytic technique. *The International Journal of Psychoanalysis*, 92(6): 1367–1390.
Turkle, S. (1995). *Life on the Screen: Identity in the Age of the Internet*. New York: Touchstone.
Turkle, S. (2005). *The Second Self: Computers and the Human Spirit*. Cambridge, MA: MIT Press.
Tustin, F. (1981). *Autistic States in Children*. London: Routledge.
Weber, B. (2009). *Makeover TV: Selfhood, Citizenship, and Celebrity*. Durham, NC: Duke University Press.
Weinstein, L. (2007). When sexuality reaches beyond the pleasure principle: Attachment repetition and infantile sexuality. In D. Diamond, S. Blatt and J. Lichtenberg (eds), *Attachment and Sexuality*. New York: Analytic Press.
Whang, L., Lee, F. and Chang, G. (2003). Internet overusers' psychological profile: A behavior sampling analysis of Internet addiction. *Cyberpsychology and Behavior*, 6: 143–150.
Winnicott, D. W. (1945). Primitive emotional development. *The International Journal of Psychoanalysis*, 26: 137–143.
Winnicott, D. W. (1956). On transference. *The International Journal of Psychoanalysis*, 37: 386–388.
Winnicott, D. W. (1966). Psycho-somatic illness in its positive and negative aspects. *The International Journal of Psychoanalysis*, 47: 510–516.
Winnicott, D. W. (1970). On the basis for self in body. In D.W. Winnicott, C. Winnicott, R. Shepherd and M. Davis (eds), *Psycho-Analytic Explorations*. London: Karnac, pp. 261–283.
Winnicott, D. W. (1972). Basis for self in the body. *International Journal of Child Psychotherapy*, 1: 7–16.
Winnicott, D. W. (1988). *Human Nature*. London: Karnac.
Wood, H. (2006). Compulsive use of Internet pornography. In J. Hillier, H. Wood and W. Bolton (eds), *Sex, Mind and Emotion*. London: Karnac.
Wood, H. (2007). Compulsive use of virtual sex: Addiction or perversion? In D. Morgan and S. Ruszczynski (eds), *Lectures on Violence, Perversion and Delinquency*. London: Karnac, pp. 157–178.
Wood, H. and Skeggs, B. (eds) (2011). *Reality Television and Class*. London: Palgrave.
Wright, K. (1991). *Vision and Separation*. London: Free Association Books.
Wyre, H. K. (1997). The body/mind dialectic within the psychoanalytic subject: Finding the analyst's voice. *The American Journal of Psychoanalysis*, 57: 360–369.
Yang, S. C. and Tung, C. J. (2007). Comparison of Internet addicts and non-addicts in Taiwanese high school. *Computers in Human Behavior*, 23: 79–96.
Ybarra, M. L., Alexander, C. and Mitchell, K. J. (2005). Depressive symptomatology, youth Internet use, and online interactions: A national survey. *Journal of Adolescent Health*, 36: 9–18.
Zanardi, C. (1995). The maternal in psychoanalysis. *Psychoanalysis and Contemporary Thought*, 18: 419–454.
Zhou, J., Hofmann, M., Gooren, L. and Swaab, D. (1995). A sex difference in the human brain and its relation to transsexuality. *Nature*, 378(6552): 68–70.
Žižek, S. L. (2004). What can psychoanalysis tell us about cyberspace? *Psychoanalytic Review*, 91: 801–830.

Index

bisexuality xv–xviii
body; ego 3; maternal 20, 25–28, 41; in virtual reality 57; and adolescence 61–63; of the analyst 122–126
Body Dysmorphic Disorder 27, 63; and cosmetic surgery 24
body image 4–6
body schema 5, 8, 11
body self 6–7, 14
breast augmentation surgery 23; and suicide 29

core complex 30, 52
cosmetic surgery 23–25, 37–39
couch, use of 14–19, 43
countertransference, somatic 1, 13–16, 115

embodiment 2, 11, 90–91
envy; of maternal body 25–28; and cosmetic surgery 29

hair; and dignity 139–140; and mother's body 131–133; and mourning 129–130; as phallic symbol 130–131; and Rapunzel 138–139

identification 27–28

mentalisation, embodied 12

mirror neurons 11, 14

narcissism 26–27
necrophilia 41, 53–56

olfactory, relationship 20, 158

perfect match phantasy 31–32

reality television 21, 160, 165–168
reclaiming phantasy 30–31

self-made phantasy 28–30
self-mutilation; by proxy xviii–xxi
setting; embodied 111–114
sex reassignment surgery xix–xxi, 19, 74, 75, 89
skin 53–55, 102
symbiosis 122–126

temporal link 3, 75; and the parental couple 75–76
toilet breast 144, 151
toilet; and secrets 145; perverse use of 145–150; phobic avoidance of 145–158
transsexuality 88–90; in adolescence 75–76; in adults 88–91
trauma; and the body 103–108; and body modification by proxy 8

virtual reality 2; and the body 58–60

Lightning Source UK Ltd.
Milton Keynes UK
UKHW022114140319
339181UK00005B/61/P